FREE SCHOOL TEACHING

To my muse, Ann Mary!
I aspire to be like
you!

Kristan A. Morrison
June 20, 2007

FREE SCHOOL

TEACHING

A Journey into
Radical Progressive Education

KRISTAN ACCLES MORRISON

STATE UNIVERSITY OF NEW YORK PRESS

Cover photograph by Bhawin Suchak, used by permission

Published by
STATE UNIVERSITY OF NEW YORK PRESS,
Albany

For information, contact State University of New York Press, Albany, NY
www.sunypress.edu

Production, Laurie Searl
Marketing, Michael Campochiaro

Library of Congress Cataloging-in-Publication Data

Morrison, Kristan Accles, 1969–
   Free school teaching : a journey into radical progressive education / Kristan Accles Morrison.
      p. cm.
   Includes bibliographical references and index.
   ISBN 978-0-7914-7147-0 (hardcover : alk. paper)
   ISBN 978-0-7914-7148-7 (pbk. : alk. paper)
   1. Free schools—United States. 2. Free School (Albany, N.Y.) 3. Education—Aims and objectives—United States. 4. School management and organization—United States. I. Title.

LB1029.F7M67 2007
371.04—dc22   2006032528

10 9 8 7 6 5 4 3 2 1

CONTENTS

PREFACE

"But, traditional school worked for you! You turned out okay!" I often get this response from people when I propose the idea that perhaps school in America is doing more harm than good for children and for our society. This declaration has given me pause a number of times, but I've finally come up with a question in rejoinder—"Am I, or other 'successful students,' really okay? Or would I be a different, better, person had it not been for how school shaped me?" Very few people, most particularly those who were the "winners" in the school game, ever take the time to contemplate if our schooling experiences may have molded us in negative ways, ways that run counter to our society's highest intellectual, political, and moral ideals. "Success" in school can leave one uncritical toward this institution, which in turn tends to make one a supporter of traditional schooling, arguing that "I turned out okay, so something must be right." The winners in the schooling game rarely take into consideration those who are the losers; to the winners they are invisible or are collateral to the winners' success. When a winner in the school game does get a glimpse or an idea of something not being quite right with schools, she can be thrown into a turmoil of sorts, for there is no widely understood language in the mainstream for understanding the deep, underlying paradoxes of American education. With no language and little substantive public discussion on these issues, any problems one has with our education system become personalized—one feels that she or some other individual is to blame. For example, the individual student believes that he is at fault for not working hard enough or being smart enough, or that his teachers are out to get him; the individual teacher feels that he is not gifted enough, can't understand all of his students' issues, doesn't have the "right" methods, or didn't get "good" students; the individual parent feels that she doesn't understand what the teacher wants, or that she is at fault for her child's failure because she doesn't have the time to work with the child on schoolwork; the individual voter believes that if schools are "failing," then it is the fault of the school board or principal for lack of effective leadership. By personalizing problems with schools, we fail to see the entirety of the system that exists and thus fail to understand that the interconnections between the different components of this system are inevitably what lead to the problems that arise. And by not seeing the systemic context, we only conceive solutions that merely "tweak" the system in an attempt to "fix" the individuals or individual factors within that system. We need to understand that the traditional system of American schools is one choice among many possible approaches to education; once we grasp that idea, we can begin to see that other choices, other possible structurings of the system, exist. At that point, we can question whether our educational system is taking us, as a society, where we want to go. And if our response to that question is no, then we must move beyond merely "tweaking" the system; we need to begin exploring fundamental reconceptualizations and alternative visions of education— different ways of conceiving what schools are for, how they should be structured and run, who should be involved, what sort of individuals we should be helping to nurture, and so on. Without such a systemic and vision-oriented approach, we will remain locked in a personalized blame game about American schooling and will fail to progress in any substantive way.

I speak from experience on this issue—I have traveled this road and made a journey from success in school, to problems with it, to individual blame for these problems, to individual answers, to systemic examination, to exploring alternative visions. This journey is in no way complete, nor should everyone travel the same path as I have, but I do believe that we, as a society, need at least to embark on this road if we want to see significant change in how we educate and in the results of that education.

This book is the story of my journey: it is a critical examination of my own life in schools, my successes as a student, my challenges and frustrations as a teacher, and my attempts to find answers at both an individual and a systemic level. My quest for answers led me to alternative visions of education and to a school in which one such vision was enacted. I am now back in traditional schools trying to help others begin a similar journey. While I do not argue that there is only one school or one vision with *the* answer, I do believe that beginning a journey to explore alternative conceptualizations of schools will aid us all in creating a better education system and working toward a better world.

CHAPTER ONE

SUCCESSFUL STUDENT,

STRUGGLING TEACHER

For twenty-four of my thirty-six years, I was a student, and I was good at it. I generally did what I was asked, showed interest, put in a good amount of effort, and was rewarded by excellent grades and mostly positive regard from my teachers, peers, and family for my success. I felt good when I was in school—praised, validated, made much of, and so on. My success in school defined me—I was "smart" and a "good student," and I reveled in that identity. This aspect of who I was became my focus; I always wanted people to know this about me and I would try to evidence it however I could (casually mentioning my number of college degrees, using erudite vocabulary in conversation, etc.).

I thought school was a good place. I was one of those anomalous students who actually did not dread the end of summer vacation, for to me school held mostly positive connections. Because I felt so positively about school, it seemed almost natural that I would ultimately decide to become a teacher. I reasoned that if school could be so positive for me as a student, then it would surely be a positive and rewarding place for a career. I was in for some surprises.

I got my teaching license and Master of Arts in Education at the same time. My prior higher education had included a B.A. in history and sociology, and an M.A. in history, and so I was twenty-seven when I began my teaching career as a middle school social studies and language arts teacher in North Carolina.

In my first year I was assigned to teach the "middle of the road" students—those who had not been identified as either academically gifted or learning disabled. I was on a two-teacher team in which I taught language arts and social studies and my teacher partner (a second-year teacher) taught math and science. The students would also have a number of elective-course teachers, but their core teachers would be my teammate and me.

My first year of teaching was a doozy, filled with many frustrating days and jaw-clenching, troubled–dream–filled nights. My main problem was that I felt I could not be the teacher I wanted to be. I wanted to be that idealized educator who inspired all her students to be engaged, work hard, and succeed. I wanted my students to have a role in decision making in the classroom, and to develop concern and kindness toward their peers. I wanted my classes to be filled with well-mannered and well-behaved students, all of whom saw me as a friendly guide, not a dictatorial enemy. I wanted to have the autonomy to plan classes and design assessments as I saw fit. I achieved few of these goals, and felt a failure—something totally unknown to me within the realm of school.

I constantly sensed that I was in a battle with many of my students, trying to compel them to study subjects and perform activities they didn't seem interested in, forcing them to be "on task" and behave when all they seemed to want to do was socialize with one another and torment fellow students or me. I don't want to leave readers with the impression that my classes were reminiscent of early scenes of classroom life from the films *Dangerous Minds* or *To Sir, with Love*—that was definitely not the case. What I had on my hands was more flat, under-the-surface malaise, only occasionally spiked with student outbursts or blatant misbehavior. I saw a great deal of glazed eyes, surreptitious note writing and passing, lackadaisical effort, and so on. To counter this, I tried to involve the students in making decisions about what work we should do or how we would go about some tasks, but I was often met by arguments instead of reasonable discussion. Thus, my hopes for democratic classroom governance and true engagement were dashed.

I also frequently felt hypocritical. I had known, to some degree from my own experience, that being a good student was like a game—figure out what the teacher wanted and do it, determine how to appear to do the most work and get the most credit for the least effort, appear to be one type of person to teachers and other authority figures yet be someone else to one's peers, and so on. I knew these things, yet I still expected my students to be truly and personally engaged by my teaching and positively shaped by the classroom environment I had created. The hypocrisy here is that I had somewhat playacted my way through school, yet I expected my students to not play this game with me. Another hypocrisy occurred in the advisor–advisee homeroom period at the end of each day. During this time, teachers were expected to conduct "character education" lessons based on the school district's defined character traits, which included respect, responsibility, honesty, self-discipline, and so on. In teaching many of these lessons, which were planned across the whole grade and in conjunction with the guidance counselor, I truly felt like a fraud. For example, I taught about the value of honesty and never cheating, even though in my past schooling I had occasionally cheated to get a good grade.

My first year of teaching also showed me that I could not be autonomous in my planning. I was stuck with a statewide curriculum filled with quite specific goals and objectives, all of which would be tested in May in the standardized, criterion-referenced, end of grade (EOG) tests. Thus, in social studies I had to rush to cover all of Africa and Asia—including geography, sociology, history, economic and political systems, and culture. I could not often slow down for in-depth discussion or analysis of subjects the students seemed genuinely interested in for I had to expose them to the breadth of information that might appear on the test. In language arts, I had a bit more leeway, except when it came to writing. I was a seventh-grade teacher and the seventh grade had a major, statewide writing assessment that occurred in March and I had to prep my students to write a timed, fifty-minute expository essay. I went to training sessions that strongly implied I should teach students to write a formulaic five-paragraph essay to achieve a passing score. So, for much of the year up to March, I was highly focused on teaching writing in a way that I (and, I suspect, my students) found dull and lifeless.

I also discovered in my first year that I despised grading. As a student I loved to have my work evaluated because it usually meant positive praise and regard, yet as a teacher I found that grading couldn't be more awful. I had no problem with giving students tips and suggestions for improving a piece of work or rephrasing questions or comments to help them get a deeper understanding of some question or concept. All of these things helped me to assess how well students were doing and thereby plan for future instruction, and thus were authentic and formative assessments. But what I disliked so intensely was having to distill all that I seemed to know about the student's understanding into a single letter or number grade. I hated the potential impact of these evaluations and assessments. If I gave a bad grade, would the student shut down and give up? Would I receive an irate parental phone call? Would the student openly challenge me in front of the whole class? Or if I assigned a good grade to a piece of work, would the student then expect all good grades thereafter and get upset if this didn't occur? Or would the student become dependent on me to say exactly how to do something so he or she would be assured of getting another good grade? Or, worse yet, would the student develop an inflated sense of self-esteem based on these grades (or a deflated sense, if the grades were low), much as I had as a student?

I was uncomfortable, too, with the effects of my grades in the school's incentive system. During my first years of teaching, the school used a pyramid level system, an incentive program designed to motivate kids to get good grades and behave according to school rules. Students with all As and Bs and no disciplinary action on their records were placed in level one. Students with all As and Bs and one C and no disciplinary action were on level two, and so on until level five, which was made up of students with low grades (multiple Ds or one F) and disciplinary action on their record (out of school suspension, in-school suspension, detention, etc.). The students' levels changed each marking period according to report card grades and any discipline incurred during the marking period. Different benefits were associated with being on the different, higher levels (levels one–three) and punishments for being on the lowest levels (levels four–five). The most prominent benefit was a field trip for the level-one students to places like the bowling alley, roller rink, or movies, and the worst of the punishments for the level-five students was a ban on their attending school functions (plays, award ceremonies, concerts, etc.). I hated that a grade I gave could make the difference between the student's being on level one or two, thus potentially causing the student to miss out on prime benefits, or between level four and five, resulting in punitive consequences. Mainly what I didn't like about grades was that they turned the students' focus away from learning and seeing school as a place in which ability could be developed and improved on, to one involving performance and just trying to look good on the surface so one could avoid negatives and reap positives.

These discomforts about teaching, about being hypocritical, about evaluations and assessments, about the compulsory curriculum, and about students' disengaged attitudes led me to think that perhaps I was doing something wrong and that I needed to find the "right" way to teach. Hadn't many of my education courses, along with the high-sounding, motivational, beginning-of-year speeches and conference keynotes I had ever attended all promised certain guaranteed ways to be a "good" teacher? I just had to discover the "right" methods. I began signing up for as many staff development workshops and conferences as I could. I attended many during my first year of teaching; in the summer after that year, I even went to a weeklong, residential Teacher Academy devoted to creating a balanced literacy program. These programs provided a lot of great methodological ideas and my reflections on my first year of teaching also gave me some ideas on things I wanted to do differently. So, I approached my second year of teaching with a positive attitude. I thought, "Okay, now I've got it. These are the things I should have done, the methods I should have employed. I'll be all right now for the most part. This year will be better."

To some extent, this was true—the second year *was* better. I was again on a two-person team, and again teaching two language arts/social studies blocks. Of those two blocks, one consisted of higher ability and academically gifted students and the other consisted of those deemed to be average or lower ability students and some with learning disabilities. With one year of experience behind me, along with some new methodological tips gleaned from my many staff development programs, I had a better sense of how to be with my students. I had fewer behavior problems, partly because they were different people, partly because I had more techniques at my disposal for interacting with them, and partly because I had a stronger sense of confidence in front of the class. I also had some more successful lesson plans due to a combination of experience, reflection on the previous year's lessons, and new methodological techniques. Although things were better in this second year, I was still disturbed by many of the same issues I had faced the year before, and I started to get troubled by some new things.

I was still extremely uncomfortable with grading, especially with what grading really meant, particularly when one factors in students' "natural" abilities. For example, I taught generally similar content to my higher ability class as I did to my lower/average ability class. Most of the students in the higher ability class evidenced mastery over the concepts and skills and thus received high grades. My lower/average ability class struggled with the material and sometimes received lower grades because of it. I was plagued by the question: what were grades supposed to mean? Did they indicate concept attainment or effort? Many students in the high ability class mastered concepts with little effort as opposed to some students in my lower/average ability class who struggled and worked hard, yet still did not attain mastery. Who should get an A, who a B? I began planning different lessons for the two classes in an attempt to challenge all the students, but also to try to make success attainable for each student. This was no easy trick, particularly with a standardized state curriculum and end of grade (EOG) tests looming at the end of the year implying that I should teach all students the same, or when the students began to inquire why they were doing things differently from the other class, or when I got a report at the end of each grading period from the principal reviewing how many As, Bs, Cs, Ds, and Fs I had assigned—somewhat suggesting that I should be giving a mix and not aiming for all successes.

In addition to my unease about grading and planning, I also became uncomfortable with the power relationships between my students and myself. Although I had learned in my first year some new ways of dealing with students' "off task" and inappropriate behavior, all these new ways tended to make me more authoritarian than I really wanted to be. I now would disallow arguments and discussion on misbehaviors between the students and myself in order to maintain a more structured classroom, but this had the effect of silencing students more than I had anticipated. Even in employing teaching techniques that traditionally have been conceived as "successful," I was still moving away from my ideal vision of a good teacher.

In my second year, I was also confronted with a student who was placed in my lower/average ability class midyear after he had attended a wilderness camp for adjudicated and behaviorally oppositional youth. Although the student was very bright, he seemed to have absolutely no interest in doing schoolwork, no matter how I tried to interest or compel him. He was frequently disruptive in class and sorely tried my patience and compassion. I found myself wishing that his behavior both in and out of my class would warrant his removal from the school altogether. Such thoughts caused me to wonder about myself as a teacher—did I only want to teach the "good" kids, the ones "easy" to teach? If so, what did that say about me?

But even the "good" students worried me. For example, I tried out the method of curriculum compacting with the students in my higher ability class. This method involves pretesting the students before beginning a unit of instruction to see if any of them already has mastery of the concepts or skills. If such students exist, then they would be allowed to do an independent study project during the time the rest of class did the lessons instead of subjecting them to lessons on content they had already mastered. Prior to teaching a unit on some aspect of the seventh-grade writing test, I assigned students an in-class essay. Three students gave evidence in their writing that they had already mastered the skills I was about to teach, so I set them up to do independent study projects in the library during the days I would be teaching these skills to the rest of the class. At first they seemed excited by this novelty, but their enthusiasm soon waned. The independent nature of the project left many of them rootless—they seemed more content to do as I asked (even if they already knew how) rather than map out a course of action and pursue a topic on their own. Granted, these students had experienced past success in their schooling history doing as teachers asked, but it still troubled me that they appeared so reluctant to pursue studies on their own.

So, although some things felt better in my second year, I was discovering new points of dis-ease with school. I continued my quest for the "one best way" of teaching, attending staff development workshops and training programs for particular methods, and I again took part in a summertime, week-long, residential Teacher Academy—this one involving teaching to learning styles. I entered my third year of teaching with another new set of methodologies and continued to hope that I would soon be attaining my goal of being an ideal teacher.

Again, my third year of teaching was better—I was becoming more adept at handling classroom organization and management and thus was encountering fewer problems that typically plague novice teachers. Yet, I was still experiencing some old problems and uncovering new ones that I didn't quite know how to handle.

One situation arose from my new sense of confidence and use of more authoritarian management styles. Lunchtime was a prime example of how my discomfort from such management styles would surface. At the middle school where I taught, teachers escorted their classes to the cafeteria for lunch and then helped to monitor all the students in the cafeteria while eating their own lunches. After lunch, the teachers then monitored the students during a brief ten-minute break out in the commons/lobby area of the school. When walking with my students to the cafeteria, I enforced a strict straight- line policy—they walked quickly and quietly in a straight line along the right-hand wall toward the cafeteria. I asked the lead student to stop at each hallway corner before proceeding until I was sure the class was orderly and ready to go on. The class was fairly compliant with my requests and I often got a strange thrill of satisfaction as administrators or other teachers passed us on our procession toward the cafeteria. I experienced a sense of power and prestige connected to how well my students walked to lunch, of all things! This feeling was repeated when the cafeteria volume got too high and I used my whistle to gain student attention to bring the volume back down, and when, during lunch break, I would walk among the students maintaining order here and there. Sometimes, although (I'm chagrined to confess) not often, I had occasion to wonder at this feeling of power and why I enjoyed it. At the time, I merely concluded that the good feeling came because I felt effective at those moments, that the kids respected me and my rules. In the back of my mind, however, I wondered—what did it really matter whether the kids were walking down the hall in a straight line? As long as they kept the volume down, what was the problem? We weren't even passing any rooms with classes going on to disrupt. And in the cafeteria, which was located away from any classrooms, what difference did it make if the kids got a bit loud? Was it really necessary to maintain such tight control? Don't seventh graders need some degree of freedom during the school day? I never raised these questions for fear that the other teachers might see me as lax or permissive, but the doubts within me did not disappear just because I never expressed them to others.

Another discomfort revolved around feeling isolated in my teaching. While I was still ostensibly on a two-person team, my team teacher and I really didn't function as a team in any real way (nor had I with my previous years' team partners). For the most part this didn't bother me, yet I did start to sense the lack when I planned an integrated unit on the foodways of African nations that was to culminate in the preparation and eating of a variety of African dishes. Without another teacher to help with organization and implementation, I soon found myself in over my head. I was, ultimately, able to carry things off with a modicum of success, but was completely drained when it was all done. I knew I could never undertake such a project again without damaging my physical or emotional health. I wondered, after the fact, about my unwillingness to seek help from others, especially my team teacher. In many ways, school structure does not encourage collaboration, but there was also something internal, I think, that prevented me from requesting assistance when I needed it, and this realization made me question my fitness for teaching.

My apprehension about grading still persisted in my third year. I continued trying to determine if grades were more to signify effort or mastery, particularly because I had a student who, although mostly high functioning, had a medical history that included minor brain trauma. Although he was not formally identified as in need of special services and accommodations, his work quality, particularly his presentation of written or project work, was exceptionally low. Without guidance, I was frequently torn between grading him for effort, which at times was extremely difficult to gauge, versus grading for mastery and final product quality.

Student disengagement and low motivation for planned tasks were, again, nothing new—but I was still troubled by them, especially since I had obtained two grants to buy supplies to create a "learning styles-ready" class-room. The Teacher Academy staff developments I had attended the past two summers had taught me ways of engaging and motivating students by creat-ing a classroom in which students could take part in activities according to their cognitive preferences or learning styles. I used the money from the grants to purchase supplies such as headphones and classical CD tapes for kids who preferred to have music playing as they worked independently; I bought cushions, lamps, and low-wattage bulbs to create informal workspaces for students who worked most effectively in such conditions; I found mate-rials that would appeal more to those with strong tactile learning prefer-ences; planned more active learning tasks for the more kinesthetically inclined, and so on. I believe all these resources and techniques helped my students to engage somewhat, but some sort of invisible barrier still existed—the stu-dents did not seem completely *into* the tasks and activities I had planned. I realize it would be unrealistic to think I could engage all the students all the time, especially given the existence of the strict, standardized curriculum around which neither the students nor I had any substantive control, but I was still dismayed that even with all these techniques, I rarely saw instances when my students seemed truly and deeply connected or engaged in learning.

Toward the end of my third year of teaching, I was pretty discouraged. Although in many ways I had achieved more successes than in my earlier teaching, I still was aware of the lag between my performance and my ideal vision. I began to think about when I had felt most successful in my teaching and recognized that it was in working with students identified as very high ability or academically gifted. Was this because these students were easy to teach or because I was more cut out for working with this population? I ultimately concluded (perhaps self-servingly) that it was the latter, and so when a position opened up in a neighboring school district to work with this academically gifted population in two separate schools, I jumped at the chance, applied, and got the job. At the time I believed this move was the right thing for me and for the students. Perhaps all my issues concerning grading, the curriculum, engagement, unequal power dynamics, and isolation would dis-sipate in this new position.

In this job as gifted support specialist, one I held for the next two years, I was split between two middle schools, with two days at the smaller school, three days at the larger. I worked with language arts and math teachers (thus forcing me out of isolation) who had clusters (small groups of at least eight) of identified academically gifted students embedded in their average/high ability classes. I aided these teachers in making sure the curriculum was challenging and engaging enough for the high level, academically gifted learners. This meant researching and providing these teachers with addi-tional planning and classroom resources, or coming into the class to present enrichment lessons, or pulling out small groups from the class if some students compacted out (already had mastery) of the lessons and working with them on independent study projects, and so on. In this position, because I was essentially an inclusion teacher for academically gifted students, I did not have primary grading or assessment responsibilities (although for individual lessons and independent study projects I did). I thought that being free of most grading responsibilities would ease my anxiety about this aspect of teaching. And by not being one of the students' core teachers, I believed I could develop more convivial, less authoritarian, relationships with the students, thus removing some of my unease with power dynamics. I also believed that because my job involved individualizing the curriculum for the advanced ability learners, many of my misgivings surrounding the standardized curriculum would dissipate. And since these academically gifted students, for the most part, tended to be highly motivated learners, I further believed that my worries about compelling students to do things against their wishes would disappear. In some ways, these discomforts did recede, but some still nagged at me and some new ones, not surprisingly, emerged.

Because I would be working closely with twenty-six teachers at two separate schools, I approached the job of gifted support specialist with high hopes that I would move out of the isolation I had experienced in my first three years of teaching. To some extent, these hopes came true, but a flip side emerged that I had not anticipated—some of the teachers did not want to work with me. In the first weeks of my new job, I set about arranging meetings at the two schools to introduce myself, explain what services and resources I could offer the teachers, and ask what they would like to see me do for them. I thought that many of them would jump at the chance to have extra assistance in differentiating their instruction for their academically gifted students, but what I found was that most teachers were resistant to what, I believe, they saw as my intrusion into their responsibilities. At one of the meetings, I recall some passive hostility, evidenced when some of the teachers busied themselves with paperwork and grading as I was trying to speak with them about how I could serve them and their students. I was taken aback by this reception, but could understand it. Here I was, an unknown, making promises that I would help make their planning a bit easier, but also making demands on their time to meet with me, to explain their planning, to allow me to come into their classes to take over a lesson or observe their teaching. Could they rely on me? Would I judge them or their teaching harshly? Would my teaching of enrichment lessons show them up somehow or, worse, waste class time? Understanding their wariness about my involvement, I redoubled my efforts. I made sure to follow through on any commitments; I was diligent in seeking out additional resources for them; I tried to plan excellent enrichment lessons so they could feel comfortable turning over class time to me; I was supportive and positive about what I saw in their classrooms, even if I didn't always truly feel it, and so on. Although my efforts resulted in acceptance from several teachers over time, I still felt a sense of distance and isolation. Because I was itinerant between two schools, the teachers whom I worked with did not see me for all five days and if they needed something from me on a day I was at the other school, then perhaps this led them to think I was not available, reliable, and so on. They knew I did not have the same responsibilities and duties, and thus it seemed I was not one of them, not "in the trenches" in the same way. This gifted support specialist position was supposed to have removed me from my lonely class-room isolation, but instead I actually experienced a more peculiar isolation in this job than in my first three years of teaching. I felt unaccepted and unvalued by some of my colleagues and was clueless as to how to break through this.

One area in which I did find significant relief involved my relation-ships with the students, but this, too, had a darker side. Because I was not a main classroom teacher, my interactions with students could take on a more relaxed air. When I worked with students, it was generally in conjunc-tion with their core subject teacher; if any misbehavior occurred, the teacher tended to step in to assist in the smooth functioning of the class. This is not to say that I never took a role in classroom management when teaching my enrichment lessons; there was just a different feel to my role as disciplinarian in these classes. I could thus develop different relationships with students—I could be more amiable, serve more as their ally than their opponent on behavior issues, and so on. Obviously, I did not undermine the classroom teacher's role or rules, but I was more like a favorite aunt come to visit when I taught, someone who would support and help enforce the classroom rules of conduct, but was not seen as the primary "heavy" or focus of student animosity about these rules. This new role pleased me a great deal, for I felt I could get to know the students better and be more able to see what their interests were. The other side of this different relationship, though, emerged when the core teacher briefly stepped out of the room or turned the class entirely over to me. I certainly had experience with being in charge, but since it wasn't my main classroom and I wasn't a regular presence, the stu-dents sometimes saw opportunities to try to challenge or test me and our more relaxed relationship. At these times I most keenly felt the difficulty of having a more egalitarian relationship with students within the very non-egalitarian greater school environment. The students seemed to regard any letup of strict control (i.e., the core classroom teacher leaving the room) as an opportunity to push for full release and could become highly oppositional if anyone tried to reassert control, benign as it might attempt to appear. This odd situation made me wonder if it was better never to give students a sense of equality or freedom for fear they'd take it too far or whether they should regularly experience some sense of power, control, freedom, and equality so that when a core teacher left the scene, they would know how to handle it. Most teachers I asked about this seemed to favor the first scenario, but this left me cold. I questioned if, by strictly controlling the kids at all times, we weren't contributing to their lack of self-regulation and failure to see adults as human beings and not their enemies.

Another area of previous discomfort in which I experienced some relief was in the area of grading, though this, too, involved new dimensions. My job as an inclusion teacher freed me from many of the primary grading and assessment requirements; with a few minor exceptions, I did not collect homework, or administer quizzes, unit tests, or assign projects, and thus was not responsible for grading students in these tasks. This was the job of the classroom teachers with whom I worked. I was, however, responsible for evaluation and assessment on a different level. Part of my job was to determine if any students were newly eligible for identification as academically gifted. This was primarily judged by the students' grades in their math and language arts classes and their scores on the end of grade (EOG) tests in these subjects. According to the county's eligibility criteria, students needed both an A in the course and a score of four (the highest score) on the EOG test to be identified as academically gifted and thus eligible for extra services. Classroom teachers could also bring to my attention students who they sensed were gifted in math or language arts, even if the student did not meet the two criteria. At that point, I was to administer an IQ test to each student to see if the result was high enough to warrant the child's placement in the academically gifted program. I was extremely torn about this process. In some ways, I believed it was the only way to pinpoint those students in need of additional services, but I also recognized that some students who had made it through these criterion in the past and were now formally identified as academically gifted were really just good students, good teacher pleasers and test takers, and not truly gifted in the traditional conception of the word. They thus did not require a great deal of extra differentiation to make the content more challenging. I believed that in some ways the eligibility criteria were flawed because they did not truly identify exceptionality, but rather highlighted past student success in playing the school game. Another flaw of the eligibility criteria emerged after the federal Office of Civil Rights reviewed our school district's gifted education program. They indicated that our number of students of color identified as academically gifted was proportionately too low. Because approximately thirty percent of our middle school student population was identified as academically gifted (an outrageously inflated number in the first place if one considers research arguing that exceptionality doesn't occur at this high a rate), then within that thirty percent there should have been a percentage of students of color proportional to the percentage of students of color in the district as a whole (e.g., if the district has twenty-five percent students of color, then twenty-five percent of the students identified as academically gifted should have been students of color). We had nowhere near this number, thus revealing an apparent bias toward white students of European descent in our eligibility criteria. This information gave me pause—did we have the deck stacked in favor of some students? I thought about who the academically gifted students were that I served at the two schools. Although the district as a whole was rural and by no means wealthy, the students on the academically gifted rolls were, for the most part, white students from middle-class, white-collar families. So, not only did ethnicity and race come to play a role in our eligibility criteria, so, too, did social class. I was somewhat troubled by this realization at the time, but not enough to do anything about it. Was this because I didn't care? Or because nothing could be done? Or did I see it as no more than an individual effort problem? I tended to favor the last explanation, and thus was starting to confuse giftedness with effort, but my course work for my academically gifted licensing had indicated that the two were largely separate, that giftedness often exists apart from effort. I was back to the same old grading dilemma of effort and natural ability versus mastery and true understanding and learning. And this time even more was at stake. If one was identified as academically gifted, one received extra benefits not only at the middle school level (in terms of enrichment lessons, teachers who received extra help in differentiating instruction, extra before-school programs, occasional trips, and so on) but also at the high school level in terms of placement into the upper, more accelerated, college-bound tracks. My discomfort around grading and evaluation was thus still alive and kicking, just in a slightly modified form.

The final area in which I hoped for relief by taking the gifted support specialist position involved the standardized curriculum. The public schools in which I had worked always made a big deal (at least at the lip-service level) about individualization of instruction. At faculty meetings, staff development programs, and other communications from the local or state level, the presenters or senders frequently made an argument in favor of teachers individualizing their lessons. We were to modify lessons for faster learners, for students with special needs, for students' learning styles, and so on. All this talk of individualizing centered around modifying the *presentation* of the content, but rarely ventured into the idea of actually *individualizing the content itself*. The existence of the state mandated standardized curriculum largely prevented any implementation of this sort of individualization. This often struck me as odd, for if we really believe that each child is different, has different interests and motivations, learns differently and at different paces, then wouldn't it be logical to allow students to pursue whatever subjects interested them, whenever and however they saw fit? I realize that this suggestion has troubling implications for how schools are set up as a whole (what teacher can effectively help twenty-five students, each pursuing some different topic at the same time?), but I also felt really uncomfortable with trying to simultaneously individualize instruction for my students using a mandated, standardized curriculum. The whole idea struck me as somewhat oxymoronic. When I got the job as gifted support specialist I knew one of my main responsibilities would be to individualize instruction on this standardized curriculum to make it more challenging to high ability learners. But there was also the implied promise that because students were so quick to master that curriculum, we could also then move beyond it to areas in which the students had interests and thus individualize the content of what they learned. This promise was one of the biggest draws of my new position. To a very limited extent, I *was* able to help students pursue subjects of interest connected to or beyond the standardized curriculum and I did see some students genuinely engage in learning. This pleased me inordinately, but it wasn't enough, because there still were limitations. My ability to help teachers individualize the content of instruction was hampered by having to be split among twenty-six teachers at two separate schools. For example, one sixth-grade math teacher gave a pretest prior to teaching a unit on fractions; the results indicated that six students already had mastery of that content. So we set up an independent study project for those students in which I would pull them out of the class in the three days I was at the school to help them with their projects. This meant that I was unavailable to meet with other teachers who had planning time that period to aid them in differentiating instruction and that I couldn't do in-class lessons with any other classes. On my two days at the other school, I was not available to the independent study students at this school. So, although I was helping some students obtain an individualized curriculum, I was unable to help all of them due to time constraints and the structure of my job.

My ability to individualize content was also limited by many of the students' institutional histories. Because they had been successful with almost always doing what the teacher requested, many academically gifted students seemed uncomfortable with stepping away from this. Much as I had experienced in my second year of teaching with curriculum compacting, many of the students I worked with while serving as gifted support specialist were reluctant to pursue studies on their own. At times, they seemed unable to identify personal interest areas or appeared incapable of planning out any kind of individual study. To a large extent, I understood this problem—they had had no prior experience in doing any of this and they had to be shown how to pursue an interest. Even though I could understand their hesitance, I was also somewhat flabbergasted that students would not jump at the chance to study what they wanted. This set me to wondering if schools were really doing what many of their mission statements indicated—creating lifelong learners. How could schools truly achieve this mission if kids were rarely, if ever, given the opportunity to map out their own course of study and action? As I saw with the academically gifted students, few of even the brightest kids knew how to chart their own course in terms of learning on their own.

By the midpoint of my fifth year of teaching, I knew I couldn't continue with all these misgivings about teaching and schooling eating away at me. My previous attempts to solve my problems by attending staff development, summer training sessions, and so on were not getting at the roots of the problem. I started to view these methodological approaches as bandages laid over a dirty wound. The bandage wouldn't deter a potential infection or cure one already there—it just covered up the problem a bit and maybe stopped the immediate bleeding, but nothing more. The methodological solutions I had encountered made things somewhat better in my teaching, but I still wasn't satisfied. I was also still stuck in thinking that perhaps there was something wrong with me—somehow I wasn't doing something right, and if I could just figure it out, then all would be well. I was approaching problems on an individual blame level mainly because no other approach presented itself. I decided that maybe I needed to step away from teaching and go back to school myself to find out what I was doing wrong. I applied and was accepted into a doctoral program in the cultural foundations of education at a local university, and also got a job as a part-time eighth-grade history teacher at a private school in the same town.

I took the job at the private school in part to subsidize my graduate study, but mainly to see if I would experience the same discomforts there as I had in public school. I thought that the private school environment, by virtue of its affluent clientele, small class and school size, and relative freedom from statewide educational mandates, would allow me to meet my goals of being the ideal teacher. I guess I wanted to know if my problems came from within or from some aspect of how public schools were structured. Unfortunately, I encountered the same issues I faced in public schools— isolation, dissatisfaction with grading, uncomfortable power dynamics with students, student disengagement caused by a standardized curriculum that required me to try to compel students to do work, hypocrisy, and so on. While the private school environment did mute some discomforts (e.g., I had very low class sizes and the students were all pretty amiable, compliant, and motivated and thus I didn't have to come off as too terribly authoritarian), my unease still existed. Although students seemed motivated, it was mainly a motivation for good grades, which in turn made me fearful of giving out low grades, even if well deserved, for fear of student and parent responses; I still felt isolated from my colleagues; I still was asked to teach all the same content and though I did try individual projects, the students again balked, and so on. I naively believed that the problems I encountered in public school would not exist in a privileged environment such as this private school, but this was not the case.

The answers I had sought were all about isolating variables—did I cause the problem? Was it the size of my classes? Was it the state mandates? Was it the students? I had personalized my dissatisfactions with education— believing that I or some other individual factor was the main source of my discomfort. I persisted in this belief and in my quest to find a personalized, individualized solution because I had never encountered any other way to approach teaching problems. None of the staff development programs or faculty meetings I attended or readings I did ever indicated that the problems I was encountering were in need of anything beyond individualized solutions. To my knowledge, no other way of conceptualizing the discomforts existed other than "You (individual teacher, individual school) are just not doing the right things."

Through the course work in my first year of graduate school (simultaneous with my year of teaching at the private school), I began to be exposed to thinkers who suggested that the problems I was experiencing with American education were not caused by individual factors, but by the confluence of several different factors at once, and by a misguided conception of the purpose of schools. These educational thinkers, people who have been identified in the field as critical social theorists, critical pedagogues, existentialist or humanistic educators, and progressive educators, offered a new view of what I had been going through—a systemic view. Until this point, I never thought about schools in this way. I had always viewed schools on an individualistic level; the system that lay beneath had been invisible. But now I was reading authors and having teachers who laid bare the system that existed and how it gave rise to many of the discomforts I had experienced in my teaching and some that I had felt as a student. These authors and teachers offered me a *language* for understanding what I had experienced. Their words resonated with my experiences and caused me to rethink much of what I thought I knew about schools, about what it means to be a teacher, and about who I was as a person. This was powerful stuff and I was transformed by it.

CHAPTER TWO

A LANGUAGE FOR SELF-UNDERSTANDING

Prior to beginning my course work for my doctoral program, I believed that the way schools were set up in the United States was pretty much the only way they could be run. I had been exposed to plenty of critiques of certain individual aspects of schools, but never to any *systemic* critique. What I mean by a systemic critique is an interpretation of current American schools that calls into question their very function, structures, and practices. My doctoral program was largely centered on such systemic critiques, and at first I was taken aback by these ideas that challenged the institution to which I had invested so much of my life, yet the more I thought about my experiences with schools through the lens of these critiques, the more those ideas made sense. In essence, my readings and teachers in my doctoral program opened my eyes to a whole new interpretation of my life in schools.

I read authors including Henry Giroux, Maxine Greene, Paulo Freire, bell hooks, John Dewey, Ira Shor, Ivan Illich, Svi Shapiro, David Purpel, Nel Noddings, John Holt, and many, many others who all questioned the fundamental purpose of American schools. They argued that conventional schools (i.e., normative or traditional schools), schools as almost all Americans know them, are set up to serve purposes that run counter to our country's highest political, moral, and intellectual ideals.

These authors' main argument centers on the idea that schools mirror, or emulate, some of the worst aspects of American culture—hyperindividualism, alienation, competition, consumerism, social inequality, patriarchy, and so on and that through this mirroring, schools serve to validate, preserve, and perpetuate those characteristics. In other words, schools are deliberately designed to perpetuate the inequitable political, social, and economic systems in our society by molding students to accept, without question, the status quo ways of viewing and interacting with the world.

These authors argue that the primary way in which this is done is through the teaching of the "hidden curriculum" in schools. Henry Giroux,

17

in an article in *Clearing House*, defined the hidden curriculum as those "un-stated norms, values, and beliefs transmitted to students through the under-lying structure of schooling."[1] His definition is similar to ElizabethVallance's found in her article, "Hiding the Hidden Curriculum," and both authors argue that these lessons or consequences of schooling occur systematically, but are never formally recognized or made explicit in the current rationales for education. Different authors have enumerated the many lessons or func-tions of the hidden curriculum. Elizabeth Vallance listed the functions of the hidden curriculum as being "the inculcation of values, political socialization, training in obedience and docility, [and] the perpetuation of traditional class structure."[2] Philip Jackson, in "The Daily Grind," argued that the hidden curriculum teaches students to deal with three major facts of life—"crowds, praise, and power."[3] Ivan Illich, in *Deschooling Society*, argues that the hidden curriculum of schools teaches the perpetuation of class differences, and en-courages kids to be consumers of grades, classes, and degrees in order to have a "better life" and thus become good consumers as adults. He also argues that the hidden curriculum teaches that "true" and valuable learning only occurs inside a school or some other licensing arena, that what cannot be measured becomes secondary, and that students should give up individual interests and have others determine what and when they should learn.[4] John Taylor Gatto, in *Dumbing Us Down: The Hidden Curriculum of Compulsory Schooling*, out-lined seven specific lessons of the hidden curriculum. He argued that schools teach children to accept *confusion* by presenting information in a superficial manner and out of context from everything else, particularly students' lives. The hidden curriculum also teaches *class position*, that students are meant to stay in the class (social class) to which they were "assigned." The hidden curriculum teaches *indifference*, that the constant shifting from one subject to another shows kids that nothing is worth truly focusing on. Gatto also de-tailed the lessons of *emotional dependency, provisional self-esteem*, and that *one can't hide*, arguing that children are taught to identify their self-worth in accordance with how others view them, and that they cannot escape this constant evaluation. And lastly, Gatto identified the lesson of *intellectual dependency* that teaches children to wait for someone to tell them what to do and to suppress any of their own natural desires or inclinations.[5] Other authors have focused on a particular lesson. For example, Sarah McCarthy in "Why Johnny Can't Disobey," looks at the lesson of hyperobedience.[6] And Jean Anyon in "Social Class and the Hidden Curriculum of Work" examines how schools aid in the perpetuation of social class divisions by teaching the children in different economic-level schools (working class, middle class, wealthy) in different ways, ways that mirror the relationship to power and capital that each of the social classes has.[7] Through all the lessons of the hidden curriculum, the status quo political, economic, and social systems of our society are strengthened and continued. These lessons prevent any substantive questioning of the way things are and they also quell any major efforts to change them.

The concept of the hidden curriculum was a true awakening for me. I have reexamined my experiences as both a student and a teacher and realized that I was a stellar pupil in learning some specific hidden curriculum lessons. I then, in turn, naively passed these lessons on to my students. The lessons to which I refer are combinations of those outlined by the authors and educators I read in my doctoral program—insensibility, class standing, constant outside evaluation, and cognitive and behavioral dependence. Some illustrations of how I learned and then taught these lessons are in order here.

LESSON 1—INSENSIBILITY

I am sitting in my second-grade classroom. Four horizontal rows of six desks each parallel the front chalkboard. We're doing a round-robin reading activity in which each student reads one paragraph from the reading textbook. My turn was early on, and so I am not anxious about having to read aloud. Instead I'm just reading along silently what another student is reading aloud. One student ends and the next student begins his paragraph. The current reader is a notoriously poor reader, stumbling over words, laboriously sounding out syllables, and so on. I'm frustrated. I want to read on in the story, but know I'm supposed to stay with the rest of the class in case my turn comes again or if the teacher wants to ask us something specific from the paragraph. To cope with my boredom over hearing my classmate slog through his paragraph, I decide to see how many times I can read his paragraph to myself in the time it takes him to finish it.

It is the first day of school and I am in fourth-grade math class. This is a new school for me and I'm somewhat uncomfortable because I do not know anyone. I'm sitting at a grouping of four desks and the girl next to me starts talking a little bit as the teacher passes out our textbooks. The teacher, once done, goes over class rules and then introduces our assigned activity for the day. We get to work. After about forty-five minutes, the teacher informs us that it is time to change classes. This is new to me as I've always been in classes where the students stay with the same teacher for the majority of the day (with the exception of "specials," classes like physical education, art, and music). The teacher explains our schedule, and that some of us will now go to social studies and others to language arts. I'm dismayed to discover that my newfound companion and I will separate. I next go to social studies where we sit in vertical rows facing front and I have no one with whom to talk or break the ice.

It is a Friday during my sixth-grade year, which means that I and six or seven of my classmates file onto a school bus after homeroom and take a thirty-minute ride across town to another elementary school. We're been identified as "cognitively gifted" and thus attend a pull-out program across town. Once there, we go to the gifted teacher's classroom where we join other kids from various area schools. What we do during this day are critical thinking games, independent projects, and so forth. At the end of the day we get back on the bus, return to school, and arrive in time to go home. There's no time for discussing with peers or with teachers what we did at the gifted program that day and because it is Friday, most of us do not remember to bring up the subject on Monday. We're not asked on Monday to make up the work we missed on Friday, and we just pick up with wherever the rest of the class is.

I am in seventh-grade social studies. The teacher has a routine for us to follow when we come into class. We are to take our notebooks from the stack on the table and begin laboriously copying the notes the teacher has written on the multiple chalkboards in the room. She grades us on whether we copy the information exactly as written and we're not to talk while doing this. The girl sitting directly in front of me, Annie, is sort of a friend and I comment that I like her perfume, that it smells like baby powder. This gets us talking and giggling over a variety of things, but we try to be discreet, with me leaning forward and whispering and her leaning back, and both of us still copying the notes at the same time. We do not face each other since that would give the game away, but do manage to carry on a full-fledged conversation. Apparently, the teacher has her eye on us, for she reprimands us on at least two occasions to cease our talking. We try to be even more discreet in continuing our conversation. Finally, the teacher has had enough and moves me into the front right corner of the room where I will have no one to distract me.

I am a junior in college in an Appreciation of Western Art class. My majors are history and sociology, but I'm required to take one art class for my degree. The teacher is talking about a particular piece of art and the background to its creation. To my surprise, I clearly understand how the background influenced the artwork, for in one of my history classes we discussed that time period in depth. I am energized to see this connection and thrilled that two classes could link in such a way.

I am in my second year of teaching and taking a class that will allow me to get certified to teach academically gifted students. The teacher has assigned a group project and I groan inwardly, for I dislike group work intensely. I never seem to be able to connect with the others in my group and feel I can accomplish the task so much easier and faster by myself.

These experiences and countless others that I don't even recall all taught me the lesson of insensibility. This lesson is, in essence, a combination of Gatto's indifference and confusion lessons and Jackson's crowds lesson. I believe that I was taught to be insensible to those things and people around me and of the feelings, experiences, and desires within me. I was taught to disconnect from others and myself and was rewarded when successful and punished when not.

Both the fourth-grade and seventh-grade experiences taught me that I should be indifferent to those around me, that connecting with them would ultimately be no good as I would either be forcefully or perfunctorily separated from them or punished for my attempts to make connections. After twenty-one years of schooling, kindergarten through graduate school, when I found myself in the academically gifted certification course, I had thoroughly learned this lesson and so it is little surprise that I groaned at the prospect of a group project and preferred to work on my own.

The fourth-grade experience taught me to be indifferent to subject matter as well as to people and this lesson was repeated every year as I was never again in a class where I stayed with one teacher all day. John Gatto wrote in *Dumbing Us Down* that "the lesson of bells/class changes is that no work is worth finishing, so why care too deeply about anything?"[8] I found that by high school I could easily turn myself off and on at the end and start of each of my seven classes. In fact, I remember feeling somewhat relieved at the end of each class, ready to move on to something different and novel, not particularly caring if I left a subject I liked for one I found less palatable.

My sixth-grade experience with the gifted program also taught me this indifference and added in a good dose of confusion as well. What was the point of going to this separate school for one day a week? What was the connection between what I was doing Monday through Thursday and what I did on Fridays? I experienced school as a series of disconnected facts to be memorized and regurgitated. Nothing was put into any greater context, and so I saw all the things, facts, and events I studied as these isolated bubbles, separate and distinct from one another. Perhaps this was why I was so surprised and thrilled by that Appreciation of Western Art class in college when I recognized a connection between two fields. This was so novel and intellectually exciting. Sadly, it was not an experience oft repeated in the remainder of my time in schools.

The lesson of insensibility not only taught me to disconnect from and be insensible of my peers and the subject matter, it also taught me to disconnect my very being and desires and experiences while in school. The second-grade example perfectly illustrates this point. I so wanted to read on, but the class rules told me to suppress that desire, even though there was really nothing intrinsically wrong or harmful about it. The same occurred with the seventh-grade experience—I wanted to express myself to Annie, but that desire had to be repressed, in this case forcefully by having the teacher move me to a new location. I can also remember wanting to occasionally discuss what went on during my Fridays in the gifted program. I generally felt this need when I saw a connection between what I did on Fridays with what the classwork or class discussion was on Mondays through Thursdays. But my regular teachers discouraged expressing these connections for I believe they felt them to be, on some level, digressions.

The hidden curriculum lesson of insensibility feeds on itself and is self-perpetuating, for when one is discouraged from making connections, then meaning is not made. This, in turn, leads to confusion, which causes disengagement, which is simply another way of saying disconnection.

LESSON 2—CLASS STANDING

I am in tenth grade and working in the kitchen at a local nursing home. A number of other high school students are employed here as well. Today is the first day of work for John, who has been hired as a dishwasher. When I bring some dirty dishes into the dish room, I am introduced to him. John and I engage in brief small talk and I ask where he goes to school. He replies, "Sherwood High School," which is also where I go. He, too, is in the tenth grade and attended the same middle school as I did. Although the tenth-grade class is not small (it has around 350 students), I can't understand how I had never seen John before. In the course of subsequent conversations, I find out that John is in the vo-tech program this year, taking a specialized course in automotive repair for half the school day. He, too, has to take English and social studies, but he is not in any of my classes.

This experience as well as my experience in sixth grade of attending the cognitively gifted program, taught me the hidden curriculum lesson of class standing. This lesson is a combination of John Gatto's class position lesson and Anyon's hidden curriculum of work lesson. I believe that students are taught in schools how to successfully navigate in the social class to which they were born, but not in others. I also believe that they are taught to feel that the class they are in is the one they were meant to be in (due to their abilities or whatever), and that the way they are taught is thus the "normal" or "right" way for them.

I was tracked in high school, clearly in elementary school in the cognitively gifted class, and perhaps also in middle school, but it was not until I was in graduate school working on a Master's in education that I was even aware that tracking existed. I simply assumed that other students were all taking the same basic classes as I was, and that they simply had the class at a different period. Prior to meeting John, I was completely oblivious that there was a vocational-technical program offered at my high school, as I had never been introduced to it by school officials in any meaningful way. My guidance counselor who, I suppose, was the one responsible for explaining course options, had never told me about a vocational-technical course of study; instead he just informed me which courses and how many years of each I had to take to get into college.

In retrospect, I realize that I was tracked, even though I didn't know it at the time. Nor was I consciously aware that in my track were mainly students of my ethnicity and social class. The high school I attended had a minority population, but in my classes I rarely saw students who looked different from me; mainly I encountered them at lunchtime in the cafeteria. I also don't even recall seeing a diversity of faces in the hallways, for all my classes were on the second floor and all the vo-tech classes were either downstairs on the first floor or at a different location. This sameness simply did not register in my consciousness when I attended school. It is just another example of the invisibility of hegemony (for those benefiting from it).

When I read Jean Anyon's "Social Class and the Hidden Curriculum of Work," an article in which the author argues that teachers at different socioeconomic-level schools teach their students in very different ways (e.g., working-class schoolteachers teach by rote, with a heavy emphasis on not questioning, teachers in middle-class schools focus on following directions, teachers in affluent professional schools emphasize a great deal of creativity, and teachers in executive elite schools teach in a way that encourages problem-solving), I was stunned to see that most of my schooling followed the middle-class school methods with a bit of the affluent professional school methods thrown in. I had not had any substantial number of lessons that resembled those offered to executive elite students or to working-class students. I was unaware of how tracks or classes above or below me were taught. This may be the result of complete ignorance on my part, since the literature, such as the article "Ollie Taylor's Story," indicates that children in lower tracks, such as Ollie, are aware of how the upper tracks are taught.[9] But perhaps my lack of knowledge of upper tracks was due to the fact that I was in the highest track offered in my school. If Ollie Taylor had attended a school in which the top track was a working-class track, the track he was in, would he then have been aware of a higher track? Without a point of comparison, or without knowledge of those different from oneself, the lesson of class standing, through its near invisibility, ensures that students do not question their place in the social hierarchy.

LESSON 3—CONSTANT OUTSIDE EVALUATION

I am in the third grade. It is a Sunday evening in early spring. I've been playing outside nearly all day when I realize right after supper that I have a diorama project due the next day. I was supposed to make some sort of prehistoric display and arrange it inside a shoebox. I had forgotten about it completely and now I was in a fix. I ask my mother to help me, but she refuses, saying that this is too last minute and she has other things to attend to in running our family of six. In a mad rush I scribble a background with magic markers, tear out some grass from our yard and glue it into the box, snatch a dinosaur toy figure from our toy box and glue it to the box as well. I hastily write a description on an index card and attach it to the diorama. The next day I take the object to school and turn it into my teacher. A few days later the diorama is returned with a grade of D. I am disgusted with it and myself and so crumple up the diorama and dump it in the trash can.

Mitosis, meiosis: I can't keep them straight, so I write up a "cheat sheet" the night before my ninth-grade biology test. The next day, as the class settles down in preparation for taking the test, I slip the cheat sheet into the drawer of the black-topped lab table. There's no face to the drawer, so during the test I have just to reach in and pull out the sheet and it won't make a sound. The teacher passes out the test and then returns to the front of the room to watch us. I am toward the back and consider myself safe, so I pull out my cheat sheet once I get to the questions on mitosis and meiosis. I am concentrating to the point that I'm unaware that the teacher has moved. The next thing I know she has grabbed the cheat sheet and taken my test away.

I'm in eleventh-grade philosophy class. The teacher, a young, cool man who in general expresses approval of me, reprimanded me for speaking out of turn. I'm devastated and fight back tears of self-pity. I succeed in not crying, but am withdrawn the rest of the class.

I'm in eleventh grade and running for class vice president. I win. I'm in twelfth grade and running for student government secretary. I win. Do I have a genuine interest in student politics or leadership? Not really. I just want something that will look good on my college application and make me seem well rounded.

I am in Advanced Placement history class in twelfth grade. We have a weekly quiz on the text readings and the teacher has just returned our grades. I got ninety-five percent correct. Other students ask to see my grade, which I gladly show. They show me theirs, and they all scored lower than me, but still got As and Bs. I feel smug, satisfied with myself.

I am clueless and frustrated. My college geology professor has asked the class to sketch the road cut we are looking at. I've never excelled at art and generally opt out rather than trying and not succeeding. But we must submit this sketch as part of our lab report. Tears of frustration spring up and blur my vision as I try to make the sketch. When done, I'm disgusted with how it looks and go into the van and cry.

I have struggled mightily with the lesson of constant outside evaluation, one that is a combination of Gatto's emotional dependency, provisional self-esteem, and one can't hide lessons and Jackson's praise lesson. I believe, especially because of some of my own experiences as described earlier, that children are taught by the hidden curriculum that their self-worth and identity are defined by those other than themselves and that because they cannot escape the constancy of this evaluation, they develop adaptive strategies. This constant outside evaluation lesson is particularly insidious, I believe, since it tends to render children unable to fairly and honestly evaluate themselves because they internalize the evaluative views of others. It is also an insidious lesson in that the adaptive strategies it encourages are ones that are hardly morally admirable.

From as early on as I can remember in my schooling, I was hyperaware of other people, particularly teachers, evaluating me. I believe that I came into schools with cultural capital that enabled me to behave in a manner considered acceptable in school and provided me with basic background information and skills that made it appear as if I were a fast, good learner. I garnered praise from my teachers for such behavior and apparent learning, and from that point on I was addicted. To me, outside evaluation was a positive thing; it made me feel good about myself and superior to those others who did not receive the same or comparable praise. My adaptive strategy to this outside evaluation was to do everything I could to keep the praise and positive feedback coming.

From the second-grade example that I detailed in the insensibility lesson section, I can see that even on minor things, like keeping my place in reading, I was keen to do what it took to avoid the teacher's negative opinion, even if it meant suppressing my urge to learn more and be stimulated. On the rare occasion that I was the object of less-than-glowing feedback (such as when I got a D on the diorama or when the teacher mildly reprimanded me for speaking out of turn) I was generally devastated. I felt as if I were worthless, unworthy of the good opinion of others. I *know* that in both cases the negative feedback was warranted, but at the time I didn't think about that—I was incapable of such self-reflection. All I could think about was others' opinions of me; I had internalized their views to the point that I could not critically evaluate the situation myself.

This hyperawareness led me to develop a couple of other adaptive strategies to keep the stream of positive feedback flowing: (1) I would balk at doing tasks I knew would be difficult, and (2) I would do things that would create a false appearance of myself, one that would garner positive evaluation.

As illustrated by the example of my college geology class, whenever I was faced with an assignment or task for which I had not achieved past success, I balked. I either tried to avoid doing the task or did it, but experienced extreme frustration throughout. I don't know how and when I ever got the impression that I could not draw, for in the past five years I have taken up watercolor painting, which requires that one do sketching prior to painting. I'm not implying that I'm ready to be inducted into the American Watercolor Society, but my paintings are not too bad. Perhaps now it does not matter what people think of my artwork; there is no grade connected to it. It could be that I was not so much concerned with being unable to "do" art as I was with the attendant evaluation that would come if I turned in a poorly drawn lab report.

The second adaptive strategy I mentioned was that of creating a false appearance of myself to get the rewards connected to positive evaluation. In the case of running for student government office in eleventh and twelfth grades, I was almost solely motivated by a desire to have something to put on my college applications that would indicate I was more than just a person with good grades. I was creating a persona, one that did not truly reflect who I was, but would cause others to view me as admirable—a leader, a go-getter, and so on. Creating that persona was, in essence, creating a "ticket" to move on in the game of education.

My attempts at creating such a persona were not always as successful as my forays into student government, as evidenced by my getting caught cheating in ninth-grade biology. I was so intent on receiving a good grade/ good evaluation that I chose to be dishonest about the level of understanding I had of biological concepts. Though lacking in conventional conceptions of morality, this adaptive strategy is one I felt almost compelled to develop because I wanted to keep positive regard flowing my way.

Another aspect of the hidden curriculum lesson of constant outside evaluation is that evaluation comes not just from school officials, but also from one's peers; in turn, one evaluates one's peers constantly as well.[10] Sharing grades, as I did not only in twelfth-grade AP history but throughout my time as a student at all levels of schooling, is one way that peers evaluate one another. I got my positive feedback "fix" satisfied by both directions of peer evaluation—I received praise and high regard from my peers envying my high grades, and by my evaluations of others I saw that few could compare or compete with me. From both receiving and giving peer evaluation, I experienced smugness and superiority, and this fed into my already present desires to continue to appear a certain way to those around me.

I learned the lesson of constant outside evaluation well—almost too well. Although this outside evaluation was mostly rewarding to me throughout my schooling, it has also had a negative effect in my quest to become a whole and healthy person. I have noticed my obsessive need to continue to have the positive regard of others. I struggle with trying not to flaunt my schooling successes, and am constantly battling the desire to have every utterance or piece of work of mine "graded" by others. Learning to self-evaluate in an honest and fair way is exceedingly difficult after so many years of others evaluating you. Recognition of how I learned this lesson is certainly half the battle in overcoming my entrenched patterns of how I view myself and others, and though I am certainly not freed of my addiction to outside evaluation, I am aware of it and its detrimental impact.

LESSON 4—COGNITIVE AND BEHAVIORAL DEPENDENCE

I am in sixth grade; again it is a Friday and I am at the cognitively gifted program at a different school. The teacher has told us that she is allowing us to do a research project on whatever topic interests us. Some of my fellow classmates immediately become animated and start discussing what their topic will be. I, however, am stumped. Do I have an interest of my own? I listen in to the others; many are selecting different animals. I finally decide to do a project on blue whales. The teacher has given us leeway to present our gathered information in any way we choose. Again I am stymied. I ultimately decide to present in the form of a written paper, as that is what I have the most experience with.

I am in eleventh-grade German class. I do not like this teacher because he rambles, is disorganized, and has never gained the respect of the class even after two years. He is setting up a screen at the front of the room and steps behind it to lock it in place. My friend Jeremy and I glance at each other, take our gum out of our mouths, and pelt the screen with it. The teacher steps out from behind, glowering, and asks, "Who threw that?" Jeremy and I look at the teacher with composed expressions on our faces, feigning innocence. The teacher does not pursue the issue.

I am in a twelfth-grade constitutional law class. The teacher, I have found, likes to sit and discuss with the class anything but the subject matter. Today he regales us with stories of his family's vacation to Disney World. I do not like this teacher and zone out as he goes on and on, something I often do in this class. A week ago, when he was digressing on some other boring story, I muttered partly to myself and partly to the girl sitting next to me, "What an asshole." Unfortunately, he heard me and took me out in the hall to reprimand me. I told him I was just bored and frustrated, but that I was sorry for my rudeness. I was permitted to return to class without any disciplinary consequences. Today, fearing to repeat my open resistance to his "teaching" style, I simply sit, zoning out, bored.

I am a senior in college about to depart to the Virgin Islands and Puerto Rico for a month-long class on tropical and marine ecology. The teacher has assigned a project on a topic of our own choosing (with some relation to the course topic), which we will present to our classmates in the next month. Again, I am stumped and have a great deal of trouble conjuring up areas of interest so that I can settle on a topic.

The hidden curriculum lesson of cognitive and behavioral dependence is one that is a combination of Gatto's intellectual dependency lesson, Jackson's power division lesson, McCarthy's hyperobedience lesson, and Illich's consumer and giving up individual interests lessons. Although traditional schools do tend to pay a lot of lip service to the concept of individualized instruction, their structures and practices nullify that idea. Children are taught to deny any assertions of individuality by always being told what to learn, when to learn it, how to behave, and so on. To do otherwise would be to invite unfavorable consequences, for, as a student, one is in a very weak power position vis-à-vis school officials and school structures. Children are thus taught that obedience is paramount, that it often comes through suppressing one's true feelings, desires, and interests, and that if one chooses to disobey, it is best to do so in a surreptitious manner.

The lesson of cognitive and behavioral dependence goes hand in hand with the constant outside evaluation lesson. John Taylor Gatto, in his somewhat tongue-in-cheek writing about how he taught intellectual dependency when he was a teacher, illustrates this link quite effectively.

> Good students wait for a teacher to tell them what to do. It is the most important lesson, that we must wait for other people, better trained than ourselves, to make the meanings of our lives. . . . This power to control what children will think lets me separate successful students from failures very easily. Successful children do the thinking I assign them with a minimum of resistance and a decent show of enthusiasm. . . . Bad kids fight this, of course, even though they lack the concepts to know what they are fighting, struggling to make decisions for themselves about what they will learn and when they will learn it.[11]

I learned early on that I would be considered good or successful if I behaved as the teacher instructed. My second-grade reading class example, detailed earlier, in which I did not read ahead because the teacher instructed us not to illustrates my submission to the power of the teacher and her evaluation. I submitted to her power and obeyed, thus suppressing my desire to read on.

Learning to be intellectually dependent on my teachers may have garnered me their good opinion, but it also crippled me when the times came to be somewhat intellectually independent, such as when I was asked to choose my own topics for projects. I had gotten so used to people making meaning for me and so accustomed to the idea that to try to make meaning for myself was frowned on that I faced a struggle when allowed some modicum of independence.

Obviously, as my German class and constitutional law class examples illustrate, I did not and could not completely suppress my desires, interests, and needs. Sometimes my self-control was not so iron-clad, and disobedience squeaked out. But these incidents were not overtly challenging to the powers that be in the schools. I was always somewhat sneaky about any displays of insubordination and usually did not get caught. Thus, my challenges barely caused a ripple in the behavioral and cognitive control of the school and in my psyche. In some ways, these isolated incidents were like a safety valve lessening pressure, but still doing nothing to combat the cause of the pressure buildup. I remained psychologically bound and dependent on outside control of my behavior and my learning.

I was partly conscious of my mental and behavioral dependence and went along with it willingly for, as I mentioned, outside evaluators praised me for my acquiescence. I also recognized that allowing myself to be dependent in these ways would offer me further rewards. I knew that if I jumped through the assigned "hoops" that I would graduate with the tickets to the next hoop arena and would ultimately be rewarded in terms of better career and salary opportunities. I thus became a consumer of classes, degrees, and so on for the reasons fed to me by the greater society. Again, I was cognitively and behaviorally dependent not just on others, but also on the core reason for being cognitively and behaviorally dependent on those others.

I was a stellar pupil in these four lessons of the hidden curriculum and, in many ways, I was rewarded handsomely for my proficiency. I received countless awards, several college scholarships (both undergraduate and graduate), and was held in high regard by my teachers (as evidenced through grades, references, referrals, etc.). This all led me to believe that school had done right by me, that by playing by the rules of the system I had gotten nearly all I had been promised. And so, when I began a career in teaching, I never consciously questioned whether I would teach in the manner I was taught. Sure, I wanted to avoid being the disorganized teacher who never gained the respect of her class or the one who always went off on digressions, but I never considered such issues as disconnection or insensibility, ranking of individuals, obedience, or evaluations. I never questioned these things because, to me, they were unquestionable; this was the way school was run and if they could offer me rewards if I followed them, as they did, then they could offer my students rewards as well. And so with that uncritical mindset I embarked on a teaching career.

During my first five years of traditional public school teaching, I passed on to my students the four lessons of the hidden curriculum that I had learned so well. As I discussed in the previous chapter, during those years I felt some doubts and discomfort over my role as a teacher, but was unclear how to handle that frustration beyond seeking individual solutions that would just tweak the system. I was not aware that many of those discomforts were actually the result of my teaching the hidden curriculum lessons of insensibility, class standing, constant outside evaluation, and cognitive and behavioral dependence.

LESSON 1—TEACHING INSENSIBILITY

It is a Friday evening in my second year of teaching. I am sitting on my bed with papers and books arrayed around me. I am preparing lesson plans for three weeks in the future. This is my usual Friday evening activity, done while my husband is attending a high school football game or in another room. I enjoy this aspect of teaching quite a lot because it is an intellectual challenge to synthesize bits and pieces of information and prepare lesson plans that the students will find interesting and motivating. I want the kids to do a multipart social studies project, but think it may be too much and consider having them do it in cooperative groups. I'm not crazy about this idea because cooperative groups are problematic. Sometimes certain kids complain that they do all the work and someone gets a free ride. Sometimes groups end up with all low ability kids due to the homogeneous grouping of the class as a whole. And cooperative groups are certainly a pain to monitor. While I am talking with or advising one group, another will likely be off task and just socializing and not getting anything done. In the end, I reluctantly decide to do to cooperative grouping, knowing that it can be worthwhile for the students, but at the same time dreading the prospect. I set about organizing who will be in what group, making sure to have at least one "good," motivated student in each group, along with one semi-artistic student who could tackle any visual aid components.

It is the first session of teacher work days at the beginning of my third year of teaching. I have spent the summer contemplating a variety of aspects of how I will teach this year. I'm determined to have a set routine for the kids to follow in the first five minutes. In this time period, they must check their mailbox, sharpen pencils, get out notebook and textbook, and begin to solve the "puzzler" on the board. They will not be allowed to sharpen pencils or check mailboxes after these first five minutes in order to cut down on disruptions. This year I will not permit kids to go to the bathroom during class except in an emergency and they will get only one emergency each nine-week period. I want them to get used to going to the bathroom between classes, not during them. I will also arrange desks in straight rows, rather than in pairs as I did for part of last year. The pairing setup became problematic as kids were socializing too much and getting off task.

I am in my fifth year of teaching and I am the gifted support specialist. Today I am scheduled to do an enrichment lesson with Mrs. M.'s sixth-grade language arts class. I will be reading a Junior Great Books story with them and conducting a seminar-like discussion about it. I arrive before the bell rings and the students seem happy to see me, knowing that when I'm here they get a break from the ordinary. The teacher settles down behind her desk to do some paperwork as I start the class. Things go well, and at the end of the ninety-minute period I bid them all farewell. The students clamor around, asking when I'll be back, to which I reply with uncertainty and the explanation that it's up to Mrs. M.

I am at the private school and today I am handing back a test that the kids recently took on the Great Depression. Most did very well; they are good regurgitators of material. I think they were well helped by the study guide I had given them earlier that listed important terms and names to know. I overhear a student laughingly saying that in another day he won't remember half of the stuff. I am somewhat dismayed by that, but also know that he's right, for I had experienced the same thing myself.

Today's schedule is all messed up. I am in my sixth year of teaching. Here at the private school I teach two classes, each with only fourteen students—a luxury since I am used to public school loads of twenty-five to thirty students per class. The schedule is off because it is a visitation day and in my second-period class eight of my fourteen students are tour guides for potential new students and their parents. If I teach my planned lesson, then eight students will be behind. So I declare it a free day or study hall wherein the kids can work on homework or assignments from this and other classes. It is an interesting class. I converse casually with the students as we each make some stabs at getting work done. Mainly we are socializing, talking about a variety of topics that center on the kids' personal lives, what activities they're involved in, likes and dislikes, and so on. I find this an incredibly enjoyable class and lament that the other eight can't be here so I can also talk with them. But if they were here, we would not be doing this—I would be teaching a lesson.

These examples amply illustrate that I effectively taught the hidden curriculum lesson of insensibility. I taught disconnection between subjects, between student and subject, between student and student, and between student and self. In essence, I helped perpetuate the idea that it was "normal" to be insensible of others and one's own feelings and desires. By teaching the lesson of insensibility, I taught the opposite of meaning making.

In my occasional visits into classrooms while I was a gifted support specialist and by my teaching and testing superficial jargon and disconnected facts, I was communicating to my students that they should accept confusion and that what goes on in schools is not about making sense of a whole. By rarely, if ever, taking into consideration who my students were when planning lessons (aside from knowing who is "good" and who is "artistic"), I was teaching that what goes on in schools has very little meaningful connection to who they are. By strictly setting up the physical layout of my classrooms, tightly controlling student movement and student-to-student contact within that classroom and outside it, and reluctantly and rarely planning cooperative lessons, I was teaching the "culture of separated desks"—that in order to succeed, they must pretend that others are not around and thus recognize that school is an individual experience.[12] I was also teaching them to discon-nect from even themselves, to ignore their bodies and any normal human needs for stretching, going to the bathroom, and so on.

I caught a glimpse of something different, though, on that tour day at the private school. I had had briefer, somewhat similar, experiences during "down times" at my previous schools as well. These occurred while waiting for morning announcements, during after-school detention when just one child was in attendance, or in my planning period when a child would stop by my room for something and a brief conversation would ensue. What I glimpsed was the fulfilling feeling one could get in actually recognizing one's students as whole people, individuals with interests, desires, and distinct personalities who could interact with you outside an uneven power dynamic. Such glimpses and my worries that the kids were unmotivated no matter how I set up the room or planned activities all factored into the development of my unease while teaching. Again, prior to enrolling in my doctoral program, I had no names for these feelings, but I sensed something. Perhaps on some visceral level I was aware that this hidden curriculum lesson of insensibility was not what was best for children.

LESSON 2—TEACHING CLASS STANDING

I am in my second year of teaching. In the morning I have a language arts class that is a homogeneous group of middle to low readers, with some stu-dents identified as exceptional children who have some reading-related learn-ing disabilities. In the afternoon I have a language arts class that is a homogeneous group of middle to high readers. It contains some students identified as academically gifted in the area of reading. Today I am introduc-ing a new unit to both classes, but it is not the same unit. My lower ability class will get a novel to read and discuss and do projects on, while my higher ability class will be assigned a research project on a topic of their choosing. After a couple of weeks, some students in my morning class ask why they don't get to do a research project. I am momentarily stumped for a response.

It was the end of the school year. EOG (end of grade) tests were over, scores were in, and it was time for one of my least favorite tasks as gifted support specialist—time to see who was now eligible to be identified as academically gifted. I look through the list of students who scored level four (the highest level) on math and reading EOGs and who, in addition, had earned As in their math and reading classes. No surprise that the kids on the list were, by and large, white and from professional families. Earlier this year the gifted support specialists held a meeting concerning the lack of minority presence on our academically gifted rolls, but we couldn't get beyond how to label minority kids as academically gifted if they do not meet the EOG and grades criteria.

"Good morning, students and staff. Math Superstars Club is meeting in the cafeteria during homeroom today. Come one, come all, and challenge your brains!" This is the announcement I make at the two middle schools where I serve as gifted support specialist to encourage students to take part in the Math Superstars Club. We work challenging, but not impossible, math-related problems that also involve a critical thinking/puzzle component. I am always dismayed that my turnout consistently is of kids identified as academically gifted. Occasionally, a nonacademically gifted student attends, only to get frustrated and not return. There is one exception: a sixth-grade African American girl begins to attend and work the problems extremely well and with much gusto. I praise her mightily and inquire after her math grades and EOG scores, thinking that perhaps she should be considered for inclusion in the academically gifted program. I find that she is frequently absent and does not make up work, so her grades are low. Her EOG scores are respectable, but to be identified as academically gifted in this county, one must have both high grades and high EOG scores.

I am planning a lesson for my eighth graders at the private school in my sixth year of teaching. I consider teaching about U.S. environmental history by having the kids each do some research on some aspect of that history and then teach it to the class. I introduce the assignments and encourage them to be as creative as possible. I think to myself, "I could never have done this sort of project with my students in my first school or even with the gifted kids in my second job. They couldn't have handled it, nor would I have been able to juggle monitoring twenty-eight kids at one time. Here I just have fourteen per class, which is much more manageable."

Both consciously and unconsciously, I helped perpetuate class structure through my teaching. I taught different kids different ways, and while on the surface this seems desirable, I often essentialized students and taught them according to some image I had of their abilities that was developed without regard to who they really were and what they were capable of. Part of this results from homogeneous grouping and large class size, but I am still responsible for the decisions to teach different class periods in different ways. And the ways in which I taught those different classes corresponded to the different ways outlined by Anyon in "Social Class and the Hidden Curriculum of Work."[13] I tended to assign the lower ability kids the more rote, mechanical tasks, while I assigned the higher ability kids the more creative and independent-work–oriented tasks.

When I taught at the private school, a school comprised mostly of children of affluent parents, I came to have much higher expectations of what the kids could do and thus of what activities and assignments I could plan. I remember being floored on the third day of school when I found that *all* the students had done their homework. From that point on, my expectations rose, whereas in my first three years of teaching at a school with a mixture of semiaffluent kids, working-class kids, and children in poverty, I often lowered those expectations, especially in my lower ability classes (which tended to be filled with children of lower SES). By allowing my expectations to fluctuate, I was helping to perpetuate existing class divisions. The structures of the different schools (public and private) also encouraged class divisions. At the private school I only had fourteen students per class, which allowed me to plan more creative assignments, ones that were time consuming to grade. The private school students benefited from a class position that allowed them to be in a school with an extremely low student-to-teacher ratio.

In my job as the gifted support specialist during my fourth and fifth years of teaching I was exceedingly aware of class divisions between academically gifted and nonacademically gifted students, but resigned myself to the idea that this is just the way things are. Although I sometimes raised questions about the identification criteria, arguing that they unduly recognized kids who were good test takers and who knew the behaviors required to please the teacher (behaviors that I have since come to recognize as cultural capital), I alone did not have the power to change the criteria and so I just labored on.

My discomfort about the hidden curriculum lesson of class standing began in earnest over the nonacademically gifted student who joined the Math Superstars Club. Here was a minority student, one from a poor background, who was clearly, in my mind, gifted in math, but was not formally identified as such. She was often absent because she missed the bus and her family had no car, which led in part to her low math grades. I don't know much more about her home life, but Ruby Payne's research on low income students has indicated that poor children often do not have a quiet place in their homes to do homework (or, in this instance, makeup work), which can then lead to low grades.[14] This girl's social class was having a direct effect on her schoolwork and though she appeared to be gifted in math, my hands were tied and I was unable to officially identify her as such and thus provide her with additional enrichment services.

LESSON 3—TEACHING CONSTANT OUTSIDE EVALUATION

It is my first year of teaching and I am being observed by the assistant principal. This is her announced observation, and I will get an unannounced one at a later date. But today I am very ready—I have a good, interactive lesson planned and the class she is observing tends to be fairly well behaved. As the class proceeds, I am ever alert to correcting any off-task behavior on the part of the students. If I see a student zoning out while I am giving instructions, I say his or her name and touch the student lightly on the shoulder, all the while continuing to talk to the class. When the class is over, I think, "That went pretty well." Two days later, during my planning period, I meet with the assistant principal to discuss this observation. She, too, agrees that things went pretty well, but she also notes that some kids had been whispering and passing notes in the back of the room when they should have been listening to my instructions, and that one kept bouncing a ball during the independent work section of the lesson. I had missed all that!

"Ooh, Ms. Morrison, I am so psyched! Today is the level-one field trip to the roller skating rink. We'll be gone all afternoon!"

"Attention, teachers and students, we will begin seating for the play now. All seventh-grade classes, please report to the auditorium. Level five students are to report to Mrs. Morrison's room."

I am in my first year of teaching. The pyramid level system had been thoroughly explained to me at the beginning of the school year. It is an incentive program designed to motivate kids to get good grades and to behave. The students' levels change each marking period and there are different benefits from being on higher levels and further punishments for being on the lowest. Today is my day to monitor the level-five students in my room during the play. There are about fifteen of them in the seventh grade and they will stay with me for the ninety minutes that the play lasts. They are expected to remain quiet and do schoolwork. By the end of the ninety minutes I am exhausted from trying to keep a tight grip on some very rambunctious, troubled kids, and I am more than ready for the end of the day.

It is my second year of teaching and I have just handed out the weekly vocabulary test to my lower ability language arts class. I walk around the room, monitoring them, when I catch a glimpse of Brenda studying her hand. Shocked, I observe her a bit more closely and see that she is cheating by looking at something written on her hand. I go up to her and take her test away.

It is my third year of teaching and I have devised a new system for determining grades. For each class, teachers assign students an academic grade (A, B, C, D, or F) and a conduct grade (satisfactory—S, needs improvement—N, unsatisfactory—U). I have created a chart listing each child's name along the left-hand side. Across the top is each day's date. In each cell, the letters M and P appear: M for materials, P for participation. If, in the course of the class period, I notice that a student has come to class unprepared with the appropriate materials (textbook, pencil, etc.), I cross off the M for that student on that day. Should he or she disrupt class or participate in a way that is not productive, I will cross off the P. More than five letters crossed off in a grading period will result in a conduct grade of N. More than eight crossed off will result in a U.

As evidenced by these vignettes, I was constantly monitoring my students' behavior and evaluating them on so many levels. I was helping to teach them that they can rarely, if ever, hide, and that teachers' perceptions of them control the flow of rewards or punishments.

By the use of and participation in such things as the pyramid level system and conduct and academic grades, I was placing differential values on each of my students—in essence, labeling some "good" and others "bad." I believe that students often internalized these outside opinions. When I was monitoring the level-five students not permitted to attend the play, I remember asking whether they minded not attending, and what could they do to get off level five. Their responses were almost unanimous: they "didn't care" and there was no point in trying because they'd always get in trouble and receive bad grades. They had a hopelessness that indicated they had given up on forming their own identity and had just taken on the view of others, of school officials. Seeing such a hopelessness in children only twelve years old triggered misgivings about allowing the pyramid level system to continue. But, I had no language for openly opposing it. I didn't even recognize, at the time, the significance of the program's name—the *pyramid* level system.

Other feelings of unease arose when I occasionally noticed or was made aware of the students' adaptive strategies to this constant outside evaluation. When students cheated (as Brenda did) or when they hid noncompliant behavior (like whispering, passing notes, or surreptitiously balancing a ball), I was directly confronted with the fact that kids will be sneaky in order to give me a certain impression of themselves. On one level, I was righteously indignant with them for their affronts to my classroom dignity and rules, but, on a deeper level, I understood and empathized for I had done all those things myself when I was a student. Holding those conflicting viewpoints at one time was very disconcerting and started me wondering, "Was this the best way to teach kids?"

LESSON 4—TEACHING COGNITIVE AND BEHAVIORAL DEPENDENCE

It is my first year of teaching. I have a student who is lacking in the social graces. He speaks awkwardly, stands extremely close when conversing, and so on. The other kids seem not to like him at all and torment him until he explodes, hollering for them to stop or calling them "stupid." I try to control the kids' behavior, separating them from Evan whenever I can. I also talk to Evan privately to urge him to control his outbursts, for they are exceedingly disruptive. He visibly struggles with his self-control.

It is my second year of teaching. After lunch, the kids get a lunch break—a time when they can go into the commons area and socialize while the cafeteria is cleaned up for the next group. These twelve year olds run around, but sometimes we teachers think it gets out of hand. The kids are going up and touching each other (nothing major—taps, light shoves, all in a playful manner) and then running away. Finally, Mrs. H., a very controlling teacher, convinces the rest of us that this behavior is unacceptable and we should make them sit down during lunch break. They can sit with whom they choose, but they must remain seated on the floor.

I am in my third year of teaching. It is lunchtime and I am walking my kids to the cafeteria. We are required to walk quietly and in a straight line along the right-hand side of the hallway. Two of the girls in my class, I notice, are walking side-by-side, talking and laughing. I instruct them to stop talking and get in a straight line. They obey. I feel powerful.

In between my fourth and fifth years of teaching, I attend a weeklong workshop in Chicago on Brain Compatible Learning (BCL). We are taught the science of the brain and how learning occurs. Then the presenter offers ideas on how to use that scientific information in creating learning strategies and methods. For example, we are taught that energizing music raises interest and excitement and so we should start each class with a piece of fast music. We learn that repetition is a good way that knowledge is taken in and remembered. We are taught that on test days we should spray certain relaxing aromas in the air. We learn that hydration is vital to brain functioning, so we should encourage kids to drink water in class, and so on. I am excited about these ideas and eager to implement them, thinking that these methods will solve some of the motivation and boredom issues I've been observing in my students ever since my first year of teaching.

I am in my fifth year of teaching and doing curriculum compacting with some sixth graders. These students are identified as academically gifted in math and they catch on to math concepts very quickly, so the teacher and I arranged for them to compact one math unit. This means that they took the test on the unit prior to its being taught in class, passed it, and do not have to sit through the teaching of the content they already know. Instead, I set up an assignment in which they are permitted to study whatever interests them. I notice a lot of confusion at the beginning; they don't seem to know what interests them, but ultimately they select some topics.

In retrospect, I believe that I was very effective at teaching my students to be dependent on me for how they should behave and think at any given time. By virtue of my position, I had power over them inside the school and used it to train my students out of expressing their individuality, their desires, their needs.

My fellow teachers and I trained our students to deny their bodies' needs to run around, make physical contact, or socialize when we demanded obedience, under threat of disciplinary action, to our rule of staying seated during lunch break. By telling Evan to control his response when being tormented by other students, I taught him to suppress his feelings of outrage and despair—perfectly justifiable feelings—so that he wouldn't get himself in trouble.

By constantly planning out daily lessons in isolation and according to the mandated state curriculum, I helped train the kids to be dependent on teachers to tell them what to think about and be interested in. As I had experienced as a student myself, the academically gifted students I did curriculum compacting with did not know at first how to handle the intellectual independence I was offering them during our sessions. They were so used to being told what to do that they were momentarily at a loss when given choice of their own. Here was evidence that the training in cognitive dependence was working. But it wasn't always in evidence, as when the kids showed a lack of enthusiasm for what we were studying. So we teachers sought out and found ways to make the material more enticing and palatable. We would use ideas, like those of Brain Compatible Learning (BCL), to ease the transfer of information and skills. These BCL techniques, although lauded by some educational researchers for their success in increasing levels of learning, troubled me; they seemed like "tricks" to get the students to remember and were not really ways of making the learning personally meaningful.

What I was doing in teaching the hidden curriculum lesson of cognitive and behavioral dependence gave me pause. When walking down the hallway to the cafeteria with my students in a crisp, straight row, I gloried in my power, but then thought, "Have I turned into a megalomaniac?" Or when I was teaching using Brain Compatible Learning methods I noticed that the kids still weren't overly motivated and wondered, "Why is this so? Could it be simply that because they didn't get to choose the content of what they learned or when they learned it that they lacked any passion for the material I was presenting?"

With no language to understand what I was doing in teaching this lesson, I could also not see its far-reaching implications. I did not realize that I was helping to create a generation of people who would be compliant, unquestioning, and docile. I felt that teaching in the way that I did was simply the best way to deal with a difficult situation (i.e., the structure of school).

As I have mentioned, I was completely ignorant of the fact that I was teaching the four hidden curriculum lessons I had learned so well in my own schooling. I now recognize that many of the discomforts I experienced in my teaching were the result of those lessons. Perhaps unconsciously, I realized that in some profound way my teaching and the setup of schools violated my students' humanity as well as my own.

The authors I read and the professors who taught me in my doctoral program argue that through teaching the hidden curriculum, schools mold their students in extremely powerful and negative ways. They contend that the purpose of schools seems to be that of helping to perpetuate aspects of our political, social, and economic systems that are supremely inhumane, antigrowth, antichange, anti-egalitarian, and antidemocratic.

These authors question the moral rightness of serving this purpose of perpetuating such status quo systems in a society with very different intellectual, political, and moral ideals. David Purpel in his book, *The Moral and Spiritual Crisis in Education*, has defined our political ideals, or "heritage," as involving a commitment to the preservation of democratic civil rights and "the principle of government requiring the consent of the governed."[15] He depicted our moral ideals as commitments to "the dignity and autonomy of individuals [and to] an intense concern for justice, equality, forgiveness, mercy, and, most important, an aspiration for a community infused with love."[16] Finally, he defined our intellectual ideals as commitments to the following: the free pursuit of truth/knowledge (inquiry) along many different paths resulting in creative, original, eloquent, evocative, and provocative expressions; tolerance and openness to different and conflicting ideas; and the development of strong critical capacities. Purpel went on to show how these three ideals or "heritages" intertwined. He wrote, "We are a culture that has as part of its heritage a commitment to the development of a life of justice, freedom, and equality which can be built and sustained through love and compassion, utilizing human potential unlocked by the free and rigorous pursuit of truth."[17]

Traditional schooling, these critics argued, is not working to pursue these ideals and is instead acting to suppress them by supporting status quo systems that violate these ideals. These educators believe that education means change, development and growth and thus that the purpose of education is to aid in the growth and development of each individual in the direction of meeting those political, moral, and intellectual ideals. These critics, these nontraditional educators, seek to make the system of schooling in our society not a mirror to that society, but a lamp, one that lights the way and leads us to our ideals.

The nontraditional educators and educational critics and theorists I read and was taught by in my doctoral program helped me to understand my life in schools—they gave me the words to describe my discomforts with teaching and made me aware of alternative purposes to education. I was now able to see that education doesn't have to be conceived of in just one way— that, in fact, other visions existed. I had always said, when asked, that I entered teaching because I wanted to "make a difference," but I don't think I completely understood what I had been saying. Now, with the words of nontraditional educators to guide me, I can understand that what I meant was that I wanted to make things different—I did not want to help re-create an alienating, unjust, uncaring, competitive, and antidemocratic society. Rather, I wanted to make the world a better place, one filled with people who are both independent and interdependent, capable of empathy, and competent and critical. I wanted to help create schools that said and meant, in the words of Nel Noddings, that their prime directive is the promoting of "the growth of students as healthy, competent, moral people," people who are concerned for and can take care of themselves as well as those people and things around them.[18]

I had an inkling of a solution to my unease with teaching that went beyond merely tweaking individual factors within schools. What I now had was an understanding that the whole system needed to be attended to before any substantive, meaningful change could emerge. What I next needed was an idea of how to get from where we were with schools to where the educational critics wanted us to be. To aid in that process, the educational critics and other nontraditional educators offered up an entirely new way of conceptualizing schools—different ideas about learning and knowledge, about the roles of students and teachers, about what the curriculum should include and what material should be used to teach that curriculum, and about schools' learning settings and timings. The following chapter outlines this alternative vision.

CHAPTER THREE

A NEW VISION

The nontraditional educators and educational critics I read not only offer a critique of how traditional schools are set up, but they also provide an alternative vision of how things should, or could, be if done differently and more in accordance with our society's highest ideals. Not every nontraditional educator argues for the exact same ideas, and this fact poses a difficulty in naming this movement or alternative vision of education. In some respects, the authors and educators who came to guide me can be defined as progressive educators; in other respects, they fall more along the lines of existentialist or humanistic educators; in still others, they are critical social theorists. My purpose here is not to delve into the deep theoretical divisions between various educational philosophies, but it is to show how my readings of various authors within the student-centered and social reconstructionist educational philosophies impacted my view of American education and led me to explore different ways of educating. While the differences between these groups are many and can be either subtle or quite obvious, I found running through these educators' visions and writings a series of similarities that led me to believe that a fairly unified underlying vision exists. Although I have never encountered a term that would satisfy me as an umbrella name for this movement, I choose to refer to them as progressive educators. I do not use the capital "P" progressive because I am not arguing that these authors are all loyal followers of Dewey's Progressivism; instead I use the lowercase progressive because these authors are rejecting the traditional and seeking a new vision for education, one that helps us to transcend and *progress* beyond the status quo.

As mentioned, I found in these authors' writings a series of common threads about education; they offer different assumptions about learning and knowledge, assumptions that then influence the curriculum, materials, roles of teachers and students, and school settings and timings. What follows is a

41

summation of these commonalities. These are the ideas that fired my imagination and ignited a desire to see these conceptions of education played out
in a real school.

ASSUMPTIONS ABOUT LEARNING AND KNOWLEDGE

Progressive educators argue that traditional schooling is organized and structured around the inaccurate assumption that knowledge is objective, that it
exists outside of and distant from human consciousness. Learning, according
to this assumption, is the memorization of those objective facts by breaking
them down into discrete, fragmented chunks. The end product (i.e., the
successful transmission of existing knowledge) is what is of most value to
traditional educators. The purpose of this knowledge absorption is to socialize and acculturate the individual into society. In other words, absorbing this
body of knowledge allows the individual to function in society (socialization)
and, by "learning" this knowledge, the individual becomes a member of a
specific society or culture (acculturation). Zvi Lamm, in "The Status of
Knowledge and The Radical Concept of Education," wrote that in traditional schools, "the imparting of knowledge whether as a means of socialization or as a means of acculturation is a process designed to make people alike
(or at least to mold them according to patterns of given social roles or
cultural groups). . . . The difference between people is something which has
to be overcome in order to include everyone in the common denominator
which is given in society . . . or in culture."[1] Thus, the main tenets or assumptions of traditional education concerning knowledge and learning are:

1. Knowledge exists outside of human consciousness; thus it is hard
   and given vis-à-vis the students.[2]

2. "Learning" is the absorption and memorization of this knowledge by
   students who are considered soft and malleable in relation to the
   hard-and-given knowledge. Students, in order to be made to learn,
   are often manipulated so that they fit the existing knowledge.[3]

3. Knowledge is learned for the purpose of making people alike so that
   the society/culture can continue to exist as it is.

In the opinions of the progressive educators, on the other hand, the
more accurate assumption about knowledge is that it is not fixed or static—
it is, instead, individually and socially structured and created. Learning, according to this assumption, is the construction of knowledge and meaning
done through the interaction of self with others and experiences (hence the
term "constructivism" for this educational belief).

Knowledge construction is meaning making, the process of giving
meaning to the world in which we live. In making meaning, we are expand-

ing our understanding of ourselves and the people, creatures, and world around us. By constructing knowledge, we are also constructing or growing ourselves, a process called individuation.[4] Progressive educators value this process of individuation, arguing that it serves the greater society by helping to create diverse individuals who, when all put together, form a whole community that is greater than the sum of its parts.[5] Progressive educators argue that traditional assumptions about knowledge and the purpose of "learning" it interfere with the natural equilibrium of human community systems by trying to make nearly every person uniform and in keeping with the society or culture's status quo systems. To progressive educators, this conception of learning is antigrowth and excessively manipulative. In their minds, individuation would not only allow individuals to grow, but also the whole of society to grow as well. If people are not being molded to fit the current unjust, unequal, and inhumane political, social, and economic systems, then the possibilities are opened for these same people to create new and different and, ideally, more just, equal, and humane systems.

Thus, the main tenets or assumptions of progressive educators regarding learning and knowledge are:

1. Knowledge is individually structured and created.

2. Learning is the process in which knowledge is constructed and whereby individuals are concomitantly constructed or grown.

3. Knowledge construction/individual construction is for the purpose of creating a different, ideally better, society than currently exists.

These three assumptions, about knowledge, learning, and their purposes, determine how schools (both traditional and progressive) are structured in terms of the teacher's role, the student's role, the content of the curriculum and materials used to teach that content, and the coordination of the learning settings and timings.[6]

CURRICULUM AND MATERIALS

The assumption by traditional schools that knowledge exists outside of and distant from human consciousness has far-reaching repercussions for what is studied and what resources are used to aid in that study. Most traditional schools teach a canon—an authoritative list of knowledge bits and skills that is largely the same for everyone, regardless of life experiences or particular sensibilities. This canon is what makes up the curricular content and students are all expected to master the same body of content materials with its attendant underlying values and assumptions about the world. The items within this canon are quite often atomized and fragmented one from the other, along the traditional discipline lines (math, reading, literature, science, history, etc.) and rarely are the connections between disciplines explicitly, or even implicitly, discussed.[7] If there is a standardized list of what is to be learned, then it logically follows that traditional educators would believe that standardized materials are what are most useful and efficient in aiding this knowledge consumption. Hence, standard textbooks and workbooks in which knowledge is broken down into these discrete subjects, fragments, or units are the norm in traditional classrooms.[8] Any nonstandard materials must, generally, be adaptable for use inside the school building and inside the individual classroom. So, for example, if a teacher gets the idea that the American Revolution is best learned or memorized by the students following the movements of Washington's troops, then she had better make up some sort of simulation of these movements, for to truly follow them in body as a whole class would be, to say the least, a difficult task.

The content of curriculum and the materials used in traditional schools are, in the minds of progressive educators, stumbling blocks put in the way of students becoming critical and creative thinkers who recognize connections and make meanings, and who understand that there are many ways of knowing and thus value those who come into their lives who are different from them.

Because they view knowledge as individually constructed and thus not something that can or should be standardized across all students, progressive educators argue for learning materials and curricular content that are very different from those of traditional schools. In the progressive conception of education there is no *one* set of subjects for students to learn; rather they learn or spend time on those subjects or issues that hold the most meaning for them. When there isn't a teacher lecturing on a fixed body of knowledge, using standardized materials (such as textbooks), and expecting students to regurgitate that information on a performance evaluation, the door is opened wide for all sorts of activities and materials to pour in. The world, and specifically the local community, becomes the curricular content and reality-centered projects become the activities that foster knowledge development. Progressive educators advocate using "real-world" and "real-life" experiences of students to help educate. This means that the problems of the world as well as its resources should be brought into the school or the students should be taken out into this world to interact with these resources. Progressive educators believe in a vital wholeness or connection between the school world and the world "outside."[9] To achieve this wholeness also requires that subjects or disciplines not be artificially fragmented as they are in traditional schools, that students should instead experience things in a holistic or interdisciplinary fashion. A holistic approach also implies a challenge to the mind–body–heart split. In progressive educators' vision for schools, students are allowed and encouraged to bring their bodies and their emotions into school, rather than just being told that schooling is only about one's rational mind, the brain, the intellect.[10]

Progressive educators do not reject the traditional subjects and academic skills out of hand. They believe in their value, but just not in the way
and for what broad purposes that they have been taught in traditional schools.
As mentioned previously, progressive educators seek an education that allows students to openly pursue and construct meaning, one that helps to
create individuals critically aware of the world in which they live, who are
creative and approach acting and knowing from many different sides, and
who see connections between themselves and those people and things around
them. They seek an education that develops students' critical consciousness
and embodies and teaches democratic ideals.

THE ROLE OF THE TEACHER

Progressive educators point out that in traditional schools, the schools that
dominate our society at this time, the role of the teacher can be very limited
and fixed. The teacher is charged with the responsibility of exposing students
to the objective knowledge of the world, knowledge that has been organized
and categorized, most often not by the teacher, but by curriculum specialists
at the state or national level. The teacher's job is to slowly feed this pre-
organized and pre-categorized knowledge to the students, bit by fragmented
bit. Teachers accomplish this distribution of structured knowledge through
such activities as lecturing and demonstrating, and they check to see if the
knowledge has been successfully transmitted by the use of tests and other
forms of assessment.

This definition of the teacher role is, again, the traditional, or normative, one. Of course, there are many teachers who have moved well beyond
this definition of what it means to be a teacher and have worked steadfastly
to help nurture critical, caring, and active citizens. I do not mean to mini-
mize their contributions by lumping all teachers into one monolithic carica-
ture. These teachers *do* exist, as publishers such as *Rethinking Schools* prove
over and over in their magazine and books. But until my doctoral program,
I never encountered any such teachers in all of my twenty-four years of being
intimately involved with education as both a student and teacher, and so I
believe it would be folly to argue that *most* teachers have the courage and
knowledge about the systemic nature of schools to step outside the norm, for
that simply does not seem to be the case. I also want to make clear that the
progressive educators' critiques of the role of the teacher (a discussion that
immediately follows) are not concerned so much with vilifying individual
teachers' actions as with excoriating the role that teachers are made to play
in traditional schooling. This is not to say that individual teachers have no
agency in affecting that role, but progressive educators recognize the power
that the assumptions and surrounding structures and practices have on shaping that role, especially among teachers well schooled in the traditional
system themselves.

Progressive educators, in their critiques of the traditional conception of the teacher role, argue that teachers, by their actions in feeding students a set, mandated body of knowledge, are encouraging overdependence, that the students get so used to being told what, when, and how to do something that when given the opportunity to make independent choices or actions they are at a loss. And this force feeding of the standardized body of knowledge serves to mold children into cookie-cutter replicas of one another, thereby violating the cultural ideal of having unique individuals who are all valued equally. Teachers, in this traditional conception, disallow students from substantively questioning why they are "learning" certain knowledge at a certain time, actions that, progressive educators argue, lead to a lack of critical thinking or awareness in students. By denying the emergence of individuality and criticality, traditional teachers, wittingly or unwittingly, prevent growth and thus support the status quo.[11]

Progressive educators envision the role of the teacher as something quite different from the traditional conception. Because progressive educators view knowledge as individually structured and created, they choose to honor the dignity and autonomy of each individual by allowing her to discover and make her own personal meanings, rather than "pouring in" or "making a deposit" of a set body of knowledge with attendant meanings premanufactured.[12] Progressive educators, by and large, do not believe that teachers should feed students a preset, standardized curriculum composed of fragmented bits of knowledge; instead, teachers should contribute to providing an environment in which children can find and pursue ideas and activities that interest them, thereby allowing the children to create their own knowledge and grow as human beings.[13]

This doesn't mean that in the progressive conception of education teachers are obsolete; rather they are just not the sole repositories of information who then distribute that knowledge to their charges with no thought as to who their students are, what their interests and needs are, and so on. Teachers, in the progressive conception, teach the student in whatever way is best for each individual learner; the teacher's starting point is always with who the students are.[14]

Finding this out is done by teachers and students deeply interacting with one another, almost to the point that the student and teacher roles meld into one, or as Paulo Freire wrote in The Pedagogy of the Oppressed, "the teacher-of-the-students and the students-of-the-teacher cease to exist and a new term emerges: teacher–students with student–teachers. The teacher is no longer merely the-one-who-teaches, but one who is himself taught in dialogue with the students, who in turn while being taught also teach."[15] Dependence is thus symmetrical between teacher and students, rather than weighted to the teacher.[16]

This symmetrical interaction takes the form of the teachers spending a great deal of time getting to know their students as one-of-a-kind individuals—listening to them, observing them, trying to "walk in their shoes," or, in the words of Maxine Greene, "look through [their] eyes," in order that they might then be able to serve as better resources to the students.[17] Sylvia Ashton-Warner, in her book *Teacher*, phrased the teacher's role thusly: "The teacher must be there . . . solely for the purpose of calling on the child's own resources, which in practice means that she must have the patience and wisdom to listen, to watch and wait, until the individual child's 'line of thought' becomes apparent."[18] She further wrote that "the teacher [considers it her] duty to assist the children in their search for knowledge by adjusting [her] method of approach to the individual child and by finding the best way of proffering assistance in each case."[19]

In the progressive educational conception of the teacher's role, the teacher must live in the moment with the child; she cannot prepare set lesson plans far ahead of time that she will impose onto the student.[20] But she can gently guide and provide information and tools that will help the child in the process of learning, which, again, is the process of knowledge creation and individual growth. In this guidance, the teachers would point out connections between interest areas and other ideas and concepts, assist the students in developing the necessary tools and skills to move forward with their pursuit of some interest area, help the students uncover interest areas by offering (*not* mandating) exposure to certain ideas and topics, encourage students to persevere if they were to hit a stumbling block, offer themselves as sounding boards for students' ideas, provide materials that would connect to the students' interests, and so on. The teachers would also sometimes simply offer support and trust by staying away and not interfering if that was what the child seemed to need.

In all this, the progressive teacher is mostly unconcerned with assessing the level of information transmission and assigning grades that will then be used as a sifting and sorting mechanism in the greater society. The sort of assessment that a progressive teacher is most interested in is the kind that will help the teacher figure out how to help students progress, develop, and reach their fullest potentials. The progressive teacher is also much more interested in the students developing skills of self-evaluation since this is so much more crucial to true knowledge construction and meaning making.

THE ROLE OF THE STUDENT

The flip side of the teacher's role is, of course, the student's role. If, in the traditional conception of education, the role of the teacher is to feed, then the role of the students is to be fed. In traditional education, students are expected to pay attention to the teacher's lectures on and demonstrations of pre-organized and pre-categorized bits and pieces of "objective" knowledge and skills; they are expected to learn these bits and then provide evidence, through some sort of evaluated performance (tests, projects) that the knowledge and skills have been successfully transmitted. Their performance is then ranked with the performances of the other students in the group, leading the children to understand that they are in competition with others to, among other things, see who is considered the best able to swallow and keep down the knowledge and skills fed to them. And in all this, the student is passive and dependent on the teacher for not only what to do and when and how to do it, but also for information on his or her worth or value vis-à-vis the other students.

Progressive educators critique this traditional conception of the student, arguing again that it discourages any development of critical consciousness on the part of students. They also argue that this conception of the student's role dehumanizes or objectifies the students. Paulo Freire wrote, in *The Pedagogy of the Oppressed,* that this banking model, this narrating to students, "turns [students] into 'containers,' into 'receptacles' to be 'filled' by the teacher," and that "the scope of action allowed to the students extend only as far as receiving, filing, and storing the deposits."[21] When one is objectified, one tends to objectify those around one. Thus, it is no surprise that under the banking model of education, in which children are invidiously compared to one another in terms of how well one receives and stores the "deposits," children begin to view others as competitors with whom they are to compare and rank themselves. The traditional conception of the role of the student thus violates our society's highest ideals, as outlined by Purpel, in that it discourages any commitments to justice and equality, compassion, or the free and rigorous pursuit of truth.

The traditional ideas of what it means to be a student are completely turned on their heads by the progressive conceptualization of education. In progressive education, students take an active role in learning; they are far from being passive or dependent receivers because they are the ones choosing what they study, when, and how. And although students may receive assistance from teachers in terms of locating resources, seeing connections, and modeling certain techniques or skills, they are not controlled by those teachers in anything close to the same way that children in traditional schools are. The emphasis is not on control and predictability of outcomes and end products, but on the process of discovery and individual meaning making.[22] When the focus of education becomes the process, not the product, cooperation rather than competition becomes the rule. Students do not need to compete with one another for the teacher's scarce resources (praise, grades, etc.) since many of those resources are either no longer scarce or are moot. So, instead of competing, the students cooperate with one another and with teachers in creating knowledge.

Part of that created knowledge is an understanding of oneself. Students in progressive education, because they are not pelted with constant outside evaluation that controls the flow of rewards to them and thus influences their view of themselves, have the space to honestly self-evaluate, to think about what interests or compels them, to think about who they are and what obstacles they face, and to determine if they're mastering something and are ready to move onto something new.

Another part of that created knowledge is an understanding of the world in which one lives and an ability to overcome obstacles that one faces. Many progressive educators, particularly those who write about critical peda-gogy, believe that students should develop a critical consciousness—that they should become able to analyze, deconstruct, and question dominant ideas in society—and use this analysis to formulate possible courses of action that are commensurate with their values and beliefs, and then act on those values and beliefs in order to overcome limit situations that they encounter.

In the progressive educators' conception of both student and teacher roles, our society would get much closer to fulfilling our cultural ideals than it ever has under the traditional assumptions and practices. Perhaps if schools were to adopt progressive assumptions and proposed practices, our society would be well on its way to becoming more humane, more egalitarian, and more compassionate.

COORDINATION OF LEARNING SETTINGS AND TIMINGS

Progressive educators, in their critiques of traditional education, equate tra-ditional schools with factories. As repeatedly mentioned, these traditional schools are places in which all students are expected to learn the same objective body of knowledge and skills; in other words, these factory schools are turning out one product: a person who has absorbed a set body of infor-mation, skills, and values. This factory metaphor also carries over into how the progressive educators view the school's settings and timings. Efficiency is the watchword in most factories and so it is in traditional schools. The common wisdom in traditional schools is that although students are all to learn the same body of knowledge, some knowledge needs to be taught before other types, and some knowledge requires a higher level of cognitive development than others. Thus, the proponents of modern schooling designed learning setting in which there is age grading (first grade, second grade, third, and so on) so that the knowledge that is appropriate for a six year old's brain is taught to an entire group of six year olds at one time, and abstract concepts, like those found in the field of chemistry or physics, are taught when a person is older and has reached the appropriate stage of cognitive development. This focus on efficiency has also led to setting up classes of multiple students (averaging twenty-five to thirty students per class these days) with one teacher. These classes are all grouped into specific, age-organized buildings, called elementary schools, middle schools, or high schools. Sometimes the children travel from classroom to classroom within a certain building and so certain classes are placed physically closer. Just as there is a work shift in factories, so, too, in schools do the "workers" (teachers and students) work a shift, often lasting seven to eight hours and generally occurring between the hours of 8 A.M. and 4 P.M. Within that school shift, there is a further breakdown of time units—with one hour or so devoted to one task, the next to another task, and so on.[23] This whole scheduling and physical organization is decided on or coordinated following an authoritarian governance model. At the top of the local level is the school board, who work in conjunction with the top administrator, the superintendent. The superintendent and board set policies that principals hand down to teachers who then hand them down to students.

Progressive educators critique this metaphor of school as factory, arguing that such coordination of settings and timings is just as dehumanizing and damaging to students as it is for actual factory workers. Repetitive routines desensitize people and atrophy their critical thinking capacities. Being treated as a dehumanized "cog" in a machine leads to devaluing the humanity in others. Authoritarian rule causes hyperobedience, which in turn involves the further crippling of a person's critical thinking capabilities. Such hierarchical rule also leads to placing different values on different people (some are more important than others), rather than on seeing others as equal.

According to the progressive conceptualization of education, the coordination of the learning settings and timings should be done entirely differently. First, progressive educators reject the factory metaphor for schools because they do not seek to create one uniform end product. When students are each pursuing their own interests either independently or in community with others, the traditional walls of classrooms must dissolve. In the progressive vision of education, age grading and class timetables become largely irrelevant because different children have different learning paces, rhythms, and cycles, and different interests at different times in their lives. This is not to say that there are no classes or groupings of students, or that progressive educators ignore the findings of developmental psychology; rather, if there are classes or groupings in a progressive school, then they are very different. In the vision of progressive educators, different ages mix when appropriate, and lessons or activities are scheduled according to when it is best for the parties involved.[24] The physical setting for learning, according to progressive educators, should have less to do with efficiency and more with connection to the learner. If that means that learning requires spilling out into the community or going somewhere where resources are or where interests lie, then so be it.[25] And unlike traditional schools that are coordinated and ruled in an authoritarian manner, progressive schools are run by any means that the direct community (the learners and teachers) sees fit. This often takes the form of democratic governance in which each individual has an equal say not only in the running of their own lives through freedom of choice in activities and subjects, but also in the day-to-day running and coordinating of the school.[26] The students learn to negotiate physical settings and synchronize timings with other members of the school community; they are not asked to unquestioningly accept settings and timings imposed by others.

Clearly, the progressive conception of the coordination of learning set-tings and timings allows for the development of commitments to democratic civil rights, to the idea that any government must need the consent of the governed, to the dignity and autonomy of each individual, to justice and equality, and to tolerance and openness to different ideas and different people. In schools run under these progressive educators' proposals, students would have the opportunity to think critically about and play a role in decisions that shape their days and their lives, thus developing their critical capacities.

The progressive educators' vision, encompassing ideas about learning and knowledge, curriculum materials, roles of teacher and student, and school settings and timings, is centered on creating a world in which people are critical, just, compassionate, unique, and democratic individuals. While many might argue that today's traditional schools are also set up to seek these ends, examination of what really goes on shows that these ends are often not met, even by the most "successful" students. My life examples, both as student and teacher, show this to be the case and have caused me to pose a series of questions about how our highest cultural ideals are more likely to emerge: Will a child be more inquisitive and critical in an environment in which he is free to ask whatever questions come to mind, or in one in which he is told what questions to ask and how to think, regardless of life experiences and interests? Will a child become open to a wide variety of viewpoints if, for the sake of coverage and time issues (so much more in evidence in traditional schools than in the progressive vision), she is only exposed to the narrow and homogenized selection of views that appear in texts and workbooks? Will a child ever come to understand the complexities and interconnectedness of different ideas if always exposed to arbitrarily fragmented and oversimplified content? Is a child more likely to become self-aware in an environment where she is permitted to explore those things that are meaningful to her, or in one in which her interests and very being are subsumed by a standardized body of knowledge that she has absolutely no control over? Will a child's individuality emerge more in a cookie-cutter, factory-modeled traditional school or in a school that is focused on the process of individuation? Where are children more likely to learn to value the viewpoints and voices of others unlike them—in a traditional school where they are grouped according to sameness (of age and also ability) or in a school where kids and adults of all ages, abilities, interests, and temperaments mix freely? Will a child become more responsible, self-assured, and committed to democratic practices in environments in which she is given a say in deciding how she spends her time, how the school operates, and how to resolve conflicts, or in an envi-ronment in which all choices and decisions are removed from her grasp? Will a child come to see learning as joyful and satisfying (and thus become a motivated lifelong learner) when lessons and tests are forced down her throat or when she gets to spend her time on things that are meaningful to her? To all these questions and more, logic seems to indicate that the sought-for characteristics and skills are more likely to emerge in schools with a progressive educational vision.

When I first read about this alternative vision for education, I was simultaneously exhilarated and dismayed. I loved its promise of a better world, but I recognized that these ideas were not broadly realized, discussed, or given much credence in the mainstream. This lack of open discussion about viable alternatives also made me wary that such ideas could really work—would students really learn anything substantive if they played a larger role in designing the curriculum? Could students actually help govern the school or would it dissolve into utter chaos? Could teachers assist students to pursue their own interests in a meaningful way? Could teaching settings move beyond the confines of the school building and be broadened to include the "real world"? Could the school day be organized in a more open-ended manner than it is now? I could not find answers to these questions in any of the traditional schools I knew of—they evinced no characteristics of this progressive vision, nor did they seem to be moving in this direction. What I needed was to see this vision enacted in a school. If I could observe how these alternative ideas about education played out in a real setting, then I could more readily understand the points the authors were making and perhaps could move on to convincing others that this was a viable alternative educational vision that ought to be embraced on a wide scale. But where would I find such a school?

CHAPTER FOUR

I FIND A SCHOOL

In my research on this progressive vision, I came across an edited collection of articles by a variety of alternative educators, entitled *Deschooling Our Lives*. This collection dealt with homeschooling alternatives, unschooling, democratic schools, and free schools. Tucked into this book was a short article by Chris Mercogliano about a place in inner-city Albany, New York, called the Free School. Mercogliano (who is the school's co-director) briefly described the school, its surrounding community, and a bit of its history. This article was excerpted from Mercogliano's book about the school, entitled *Making It Up as We Go Along*, and I promptly read the book in hopes of getting more details, for I suspected that this was a place that actively embodied the alternative vision of education. The book tentatively confirmed my initial suspicions and I sought out the opportunity to research this school as a participant observer who could experience firsthand what this alternative, progressive, educational vision was all about.

Chris Mercogliano explained that the school began in 1969 as a homeschooling situation. A woman by the name of Mary Leue had a son who was unhappy with his school, one of the "better" ones in the Albany area. He asked his mother to teach him at home and she agreed. After a bit of bureaucratic wrangling, Mrs. Leue received official sanction for homeschooling her child and he became, according to Mercogliano, "perhaps the first legal homeschooler in the modern history of New York State."[1] A friend soon asked Mrs. Leue to take on her three children who were also unhappy with their schooling experiences and thus the school was born. Over the next few years, Mrs. Leue shifted from schooling these children and others in her home to schooling them in an old parochial school building and then in a second, where it continues to this day. The school grew in student population over the years and finally settled into its present size of approximately fifty pre-kindergarten to grade eight students and about seven to eight paid teachers, a paid cook, and numerous temporary and full-time volunteer and intern teachers.

What fascinated me about this school was that it was located in and served children from Albany's inner city. These were not affluent, privileged kids whose families paid substantial tuitions. I had come across critiques of progressive, private schools that argued that such environments do not work well with students who are not enriched or privileged. It was unusual, then, to see a progressive school with this particular population of students. How could this school continue if it were not fully tuition supported, thus requiring a mostly affluent student base? The full answer lies somewhat outside the scope of this study, but some rudimentary information is applicable here. The buildings rented and then later purchased for the school were exceedingly inexpensive at the time because the neighborhood was, basically, in slum or ghetto areas (and still somewhat is, although gentrification is making inroads). Mrs. Leue had inherited a small amount of money, which she used to purchase the building that now houses the school "for practically a song from the veterans group, [which at the time owned the building and] which was anxious to flee the influx of black and Hispanic newcomers."[2] Mrs. Leue had initially financed the school's low overhead costs by utilizing her husband's university professor's salary and her inheritance. This money, however, could not cover every expense, especially with more students and teachers coming on board. Mrs. Leue, along with the other teachers who became involved early on, specifically wanted the school to have a diverse student population and not be composed only of children whose parents could afford private school. So she and the other early teachers decided that tuition would be on a sliding scale based on family income. (The current scale ranges from $0 to $75 a month for families with an after- tax income of $0 to $14,999 to $700 a month for families with an after-tax income in excess of $100,000.) Mrs. Leue and the early teachers also did without salaries for the most part, and to this day salaries are still extremely low. At different times, the school has obtained small project-oriented grants and the teachers have also made attempts at funding through such free-enterprise ventures as a college textbook distributorship and a corner store (both unprofitable), and then buying up at rock-bottom prices and rehabilitating the surrounding deteriorating buildings. To this day the school continues to receive donations for the use of these properties.

As for the school's baseline philosophy, there was no set-in-stone approach and that, too, continues. As Mercogliano's title suggests, the Free School teachers and students were making it up as they went along. That is not to say that they had no influences on their thinking, for indeed they did. Many teachers had read about and been intrigued by A. S. Neill's Summerhill School, by the Modern School (anarchist) in New York City at the turn of the century, and by the histories of various other holistic or progressive educational movements. Mrs. Leue and the other teachers were also active in the struggles for democracy and humanity that arose in the 1960s and wanted a school that typified the values of those movements—dignity, autonomy, and equity for all people through empowerment and individual choice of actions, a sense of communion with others and the natural world, and so on. According to Mercogliano, "Mary [Leue] envisioned an egalitarian model in which kids would be free of competition, compulsory learning, and social class-based status rewards. She thought that school should be a place where the students could choose responsibly from open-ended sets of options, because only in this way would they ever learn to chart their own life courses."[3]

What Mrs. Leue envisioned and what actually happened day-to-day and year-to-year were not always the same, for the school was a "terrain of struggle"[4] between competing value systems that often followed the class lines of the families in the school.[5] Working-class parents seemed to want more traditional formality, with stricter discipline and the standard school accoutrements such as desks, textbooks, tests, and so on while middle and upper-middle-class parents were more relaxed and open to experimenting with different structures. Over the years, the school's approach has shifted in small ways, with periods in which there were tests, scheduled classes, and projects to times such as now when everything is much more open-ended.

Some constants have been in place, however. They are, first, the policy of "absolute internal autonomy"—the idea "that only those actually present in the building could determine the school's day-to-day operating policy. Others were welcome to attend meetings, and to advise and make suggestions, but that [was and is] the extent of their power."[6] Another constant has been "council meetings"—the outlet for anyone (student, teacher, staff member, etc.) who wants to resolve a conflict of some sort. Council meetings are called at any time and everyone must drop what they are doing to attend. Meetings are run by Robert's Rules of Order and last for as long as it takes to resolve the issue. Another constant has been that the school encourages the children to express their emotions, whether anger, aggression, sadness, happiness, and so on. These constants represent what Mercogliano has called the Free School's "basic principles of love, emotional honesty, peer level leadership, and cooperation, which are the heart of the Free School's concept of education."[7] Such principles have resulted in a school that, if the descriptions in the book matched the reality, could be just what I was looking for—an active embodiment of the progressive educational vision outlined in the previous chapter.

I was fascinated with all this information and decided to visit the school to see if it was suitable for me to study and if the teachers and students were willing to have me around to do this research. My visit to the school on a Friday in mid-October 2002 was a bit discomfiting at first, for the school seemed physically very shabby, and I felt like a fish out of water in that I was not sure how to interact with the kids. But as the day went on, I found myself quite drawn to the students—they did not seem to exhibit the same wariness or even aversion to adults as so many kids in traditional

schools did. The Free School kids openly embraced my presence by involving me in their activities, asking my opinion on certain subjects, and so on.
I wrote in the spring 2003 issue of *Paths of Learning* that

> I was amazed at how a number of the students of differing ages
> reacted to me—an adult and a stranger. One girl of about nine years
> asked me to assist her in making some mint tea for the group that
> had gone out to the country and to take a walk with her in the
> garden, where she showed me various medicinal herbs and spoke of
> their uses. A boy of about twelve years freely conversed with me, as
> we rode in the van back to the school, about swearing, a topic that
> might be "taboo" [to undertake with a teacher or adult] in main-
> stream schools.[8]

I also wrote that I felt that the students saw me

> as a person who might be able to share with them some interesting
> information and insights and [thus] were eager to connect with me.
> This was quite a change from my many experiences with traditional/
> mainstream students, who [when meeting me, their teacher, for the
> first time] tended to somewhat tiptoe warily around me. . . . Upon
> reflection, I see that the [traditional] students' demeanor had less to
> do with their being on their best behavior and more with trying to
> figure out the power and authority dynamics in the classroom.[9]

I liked the fact that there was not any sense of this wary appraisal going
on when I met the Free School students for the first time and that I could
just be myself and act relaxed around them rather than trying to put on the
oft-encouraged professional teacher front of "don't smile before Christmas so
the kids won't think you're too nice and take advantage." I also felt comfortable around the teachers, particularly Chris Mercogliano with whom I spent
most of my visit. I closely observed how he interacted with the children and
saw that he, too, was relaxed, comfortable, and connected to the kids on a
very personal level, while never abdicating any sense of natural adult authority on issues of safety and interpersonal respect. By the end of the day, even
though I still found the physical setting somewhat daunting in terms of
cleanliness and general upkeep, I liked the idea of being at the Free School.
Perhaps this was the beginning of a realization that what is on the surface
and immediately visible is often not of the utmost importance or value.

On the basis of this visit, further communications with Mercogliano,
and continued readings of progressive writers and theorists, I decided to
commit to spending three months at the school. I started out on August 25,
2003, with the teachers and other interns for the two-week getting ready

period and began the school year with the students on September 8, 2003. The students, parents, staff, and community members knew me as an intern teacher, but also that I was concurrently researching my dissertation. Thus, they and I understood my role to be that of a participant observer.

During my time at the Albany Free School, I used multiple data-gathering techniques. First and foremost, I kept a field journal, a spiral notebook I carried with me all the time. Over the course of the day, I would jot down what activities I had taken part in, take notes in various meetings (council meetings, all-school meetings, teacher meetings, etc.), and make miscellaneous reflection comments. After school each day, I returned to my rented room, just up the block from the school, and wrote a formal journal entry for that day. In this journal I described my practices and incorporated my critical reflections on those practices.[10] At the end of my time at the Albany Free School, I had exactly sixty journal entries.

A second data-gathering technique involved interviewing. I interviewed four Free School teachers, Bhawin, Dave, Missy, and Chris—some of the teachers who have been at the school the longest (four, six, twenty-five, and thirty years, respectively). My questions included the following:

- Does the school mold the kids? If so, in what ways?

- What does it mean to be a teacher at this school?

- Which is more important in your/the school's view—the individual or the community?

- Do you think of yourself as an individual who is a part of a greater, nonhuman context? And, if so, does that belief play out in the school, and how so?

- Does this school prepare the kids to be effective democratic citizens on both a personal and societal level?

- Do you think the kids leave the school instilled with a desire to make their micro world and the whole world a better place?

- Does it ever concern you that the kids aren't systematically exposed to the academics that kids in traditional schools are?

- Do the students here face extra challenges after being in this school that traditionally schooled kids don't? And vice versa?

- Is it possible to change schools without a revolution in society? Or can substantive change come to education through gradual reform?

- Do alternative, progressive schools make a difference to the larger culture? Does this school have an impact beyond just its immediate surroundings and people?

These interviews each lasted approximately one hour, with Bhawin's being the longest at about ninety minutes. I did not engage in these interviews until I had been at the school for nearly two months. This scheduling was intentional since I wanted to have experiences at the school and thus a rudimentary understanding of its structures and functions prior to forming interview questions. I also wanted to develop a rapport with the teachers before embarking on such a personal interaction as an interview.

On leaving the Free School on Thanksgiving Day (November 27, 2003), after having spent three months there as a teacher intern, I returned to North Carolina to set about making sense of all that I saw and experienced and to think about whether this school actually did embody the progressive educational alternative vision I had read so much about. My basic conclusion was that this school was indeed actively practicing this vision, and the following chapters are explanations accompanied by excerpts from my journals and interviews that corroborate that conclusion.

CHAPTER FIVE

A VERY DIFFERENT SETUP

The Albany Free School, in its daily operations, physical settings, grouping of students, coordination of time flow, and internal governance, does not much resemble a school in the traditional sense. Rather, it is an active embodiment of the progressive educators' confluences of ideas on how a school should be run.

The Free School is located, as mentioned earlier, in an old parochial school building in a mostly residential neighborhood in the middle of a row of four-story, nineteenth-century brick houses on a quiet side street. During the summer of 2003, the school received a brand-new coat of schoolhouse-red paint with white trim and it appears quite attractive from the front with its large windows overlooking the street. Entrance is through black double doors located in the middle of the street-level floor. After entering, one can either turn right or left and thus come into the downstairs area, or proceed straight ahead up a flight of stairs to the upstairs area. The first floor, or downstairs, is broken up into distinct areas. The naming of the different rooms refers to the most regular function of the room and sometimes its physical aspect (e.g., is the biggest, hence the Big Room, is in the middle, hence the Middle Room, has a rug, hence the Rug Room, etc.).

If one had gone directly upstairs, one would encounter a single open space, about forty feet square with ceilings approximately twenty feet high. Here is the kitchen, bathroom, kindergarten room, and a flight of stairs for the single classroom that sits atop the kindergarten room that houses the seventh and eighth grades. The school also has a small backyard with a fairly extensive wooden jungle gym built on and amid a couple of trees. This backyard is separated by a fence from the neighbors on the west and south sides.

The school and its rooms are, by typical standards, quite small, but they seemed spacious enough for the number of students enrolled in the school for the 2003–2004 school year, which was about sixty. While the school building itself is "home base," school activities often take place in a wide array of local public and private community settings. Within walking distance are three public parks, and two are within one block of the school—the "Swing Park" and the "Basketball Park," so named for their contents or purpose. A football field is five blocks away. Within approximately one mile are two public library branches, a public indoor pool, the New York State Museum, and the Empire State Plaza (which mainly contains legislative office buildings, but also a large array of outdoor and indoor sculptures, a large fountain, a 42-story indoor observation tower, and a seasonal ice skating rink).

There are also many private community spaces utilized by the students and staff. For example, about three doors down is the media center—a basement apartment area devoted to a darkroom, a video viewing area, computers, cameras, and so on. Above the media center is the family life center, a birth and parenting center that the school occasionally uses for small, intimate meetings like "girls group" or "boys group." Also within one block is an anarchist collective that has an extensive library of materials and quiet space that the students, older ones in particular, can use. Most of the staff lives in apartments or houses directly surrounding the school, and on occasion classes or activities are held in staff members' homes where quiet can be more guaranteed. The school also owns property in Grafton, NY, about a thirty-minute drive from downtown Albany, where there are extensive acres of woods, a low ropes course, a teaching lodge, and a maple sugaring shack, all of which are regularly used by the Free School. Finally, individual students, mainly seventh and eighth graders, also have apprenticeships in various places inside and outside the city. As mentioned, the school building and grounds themselves are home base and students always start and end the day at the school building, even if they spend much of their in-between time in other locales.

In terms of staff and student groupings, when I left the school in late November 2003, the school had seven paid teachers, one paid lunch cook, one paid breakfast cook (although the job rotated among various people), four intern teachers who received room and partial board, three intern/full-time volunteer teachers who covered their own living expenses, and approximately sixty children. Table 5.1 may be useful as I refer to different individuals throughout this and the following chapters.

Table 5.1. Roster of Teachers

Paid Teachers	Room and Board Intern Teachers	Own Expenses Intern/Volunteer Teachers
Chris Mercogliano	Elizabeth	Mike B.
Mike G.	Michael	Alisa
Carrie	Adam	Mara
Bhawin	Jon (left in early November)	(I, too, was in this category
Megan		while at school)
Missy		
Dave		

Teachers are nominally either "upstairs" teachers or "downstairs" teachers. This nomenclature refers not just to location, but also to different ages within the school. The downstairs area is the domain of students in grades one through eight and these students are thus called "downstairs kids." The upstairs area (with the exception of the seventh/eighth-grade classroom, located above the upstairs area) is the domain of the prekindergarten to kindergarten students and those students are thus called the "upstairs kids." Downstairs kids are welcome anywhere in the school, including the upstairs. Upstairs kids, for reasons of safety, are not permitted anywhere but the main upstairs area and the backyard (with supervision). Within these broad groupings of upstairs and downstairs kids are further subgroupings of grades: a seventh/eighth grade, a fifth/sixth grade, a third/fourth grade, and a first/ second grade. While I was at the school, the upstairs area as a whole had approximately twenty-five students, about six of whom were in kindergarten—although the lines for that class are fluid dependent on interest and development of children younger than age five. Although only one teacher is "officially" assigned to each of the specific-aged classes, this is not as cut and dried as one would find in a traditional school. These teachers are simply the main contact person for the students in their classes. While the nominal teacher of the class takes care of parent contact, paying special attention to the child's progress and activities, and so on, he or she is not limited to contact only with members of his or her class. All teachers have contact with all kids and any teacher can work with any child pretty much anytime. And while the upstairs teachers and downstairs teachers mainly do stay in their "assigned" area, it is not unusual for an upstairs teacher to occasionally venture downstairs to propose or take part in a lesson or activity, and vice versa. When doing this, the teachers ensure that there is sufficient coverage in their official area so as not to cause safety or supervision problems. The seven interns and the various and sundry volunteer teachers are a bit more free in where they spend their time, though most tend to gravitate to one particular area of the school. For example, while I was there, I spent all but one afternoon of my time with the downstairs kids and thus considered myself much more of a downstairs teacher than an upstairs one. Thus, the remainder of my explanations and illustrations of what goes on in the Free School are, for the most part, limited in perspective to the downstairs area and students. As a downstairs intern teacher, I had daily contact with the thirty-five downstairs kids, listed by class in Table 5.2. (All student names have been changed to protect privacy.)

These students all have the right to mix and mingle with each other while in the school, other locales, and on field trips (although later in the year there are class-specific trips). Although nominally identified as being in the seventh/eighth-grade class, or the first/ second-grade class, and so on, this identification does not limit the students in any significant ways (other than for safety issues). While I often saw similarly aged students together (with an age range of one to three years), I also quite frequently observed vastly

Table 5.2. Roster of Downstairs Students and Teachers

Seventh/Eighth-Grade Class (Dave—teacher)		Fifth/Sixth-Grade Class (Megan—teacher)		Third/Fourth-Grade Class (Bhawin—teacher)	First/Second-Grade Class (Missy—teacher)	
Peter	Alison	Antoin	Miranda	Anthony	Colleen	Blair
Bridget	Libby	Jonathan	Corine	Allen	Ajay	Frankie
Camille	Bryan	Conner	Delia	Rebecca	Ursula	Nevin
Avalon	Daniel	Callie		Travis	Sarah	Dierdre
Lawrence	Walter			Daisy	Macon	
Grayson	Trent			Hamal (withdrew in early October)		

differently aged children interacting in ways that seemed satisfying to all. For example, at the Swing Park one day I observed Trent, a twelve year old, playing catch with five-year-old Rasheed, an upstairs kid; on another day I played a card game with a twelve year old, a thirteen year old, and a six year old. Although the six year old consistently lost, he seemed to enjoy himself and did not get mad for losing all the time. Perhaps somehow he understood that our age gave us an advantage and that he would get better as time went on.

Finally, as regards groupings of teachers and students, class sizes are extremely small. And here I am not talking about the nominally grouped-by-age classes, but about teacher–student ratio. Once all the intern and volunteer teachers are factored in, the ratio of teachers to students is around 1:4.

The school's timetable was also unique. It had some similarities to traditional schools in terms of start and end times and being on a ten-month calendar, yet other aspects of how time was attended to were quite different. The school day begins for the breakfast cook at around 6:30 A.M. when he or she starts preparing a well-balanced, ample meal for the students and staff. At 7:55 A.M., one teaching staff member, either paid or volunteer, arrives for his or her "early duty" that involves setting up at one side of the open upstairs area a buffet table with stacks of bowls and cups, a basket of silverware, quart bottles of milk, and pitchers of juice. Around 8:10 A.M. students and staff begin arriving. Parents bring students to school in their family vehicles, or students use local transit; some students (and most staff) live close enough to walk to school. At 8:15 A.M. the breakfast cook rolls out platters of food on a cart and sets them onto the buffet table. A line of students and teachers quickly forms and they serve themselves from the hot and cold items arrayed on the table. The early duty staff member serves the youngest children (ages five and under) who line up at the back of the table. Once served, adults and children sit in various chairs, or at tables, or they lean against walls or other tables, and eat and socialize. All are expected, after eating, to take their dirty cups, bowls, and utensils to the kitchen, where leftover food is scraped into the chicken bin (scraps are fed to the chickens owned by Free School community members). Breakfast is a leisurely affair, and one that I looked forward to each day, for not only was the food healthful and delicious, the conversations with other teachers and with students were invigorating, warm, relaxing, fun, and so on. Simply put, it was a nice start to the day.

Around 8:50 A.M. breakfast is mostly over and the early duty teacher wipes off the tables and sweeps the floor. Downstairs kids and teachers gather in the Big Room for the activities meeting, which is scheduled to begin each school day at 9:00 A.M., although it sometimes is a few to fifteen minutes late. Generally, one student starts the meeting by calling for order, or a teacher asks students for a volunteer. The meeting is conducted by a student, usually one of about five or six students who regularly volunteer, although teachers often encourage other students to run the meeting. On a chalkboard at the front is an hour-by-hour schedule with blanks for activities to be written in. The time from noon to 1 P.M. is blocked off for lunch and cleanup, but, aside from that, the posted hour slots are 9 to 10 A.M., 10 to 11 A.M., 11 A.M. to noon, 1 to 2 P.M., and 2 to 3 P.M. The student running the activities meeting begins by asking, "Are there any announcements or activities?" and then calling on individuals, students or teachers, who raise their hands. As the individual explains either the activity he or she wants to offer or wants to have offered, the meeting chair writes the activity on the chalkboard in the time period suggested. In chapter 6, I will fully detail many of these activities, but for purposes of explanation here, some sample activities include trips to museums, math class, reading of certain books, football or basketball games, going to the park, taking a field trip, making movies or editing movies at the media center, doing some artwork, sex education class, viewing a video, and so on. The majority of the time, activities are suggested by teachers, but about twenty percent of the activities are suggested or requested by students. The activities meeting tends to last about fifteen minutes or so and is a lively, regularly quite loud meeting, with students and teachers often taking part in side conversations, and sporadic calls for "Order!" and "Are there any other activities?" emanating from the meeting chair. Once everyone has offered or requested activities, the chair announces that activities meeting is adjourned and the students and teachers scatter to the many parts of the school. Often specific class meetings are held directly after the activities meeting and classes of kids will then gather in specific rooms.

Although specific times are suggested for certain activities, these times are not set in stone, nor are the activities themselves. For example, a teacher might ask at the activities meeting, "Who would like to read the book *The Witches?*" and four or five students might raise their hands. The teacher would then suggest a time, such as 11 A.M., asking if that time worked for the students as well. If it did, then the meeting chair would write in "*Witches* reading" in the 11 to noon time slot on the chalkboard. As would quite often happen, though, when 11 A.M. rolled around either the teacher would be busy or, more often, the students were involved in something else and not ready to stop, and so the set time for the *Witches* reading would come and go. At other times, for different activities, the meeting times were rather strictly adhered to. This was particularly true for many of the seventh and eighth graders' requested classes.

Several other events could throw activities off schedule regardless of how much a student or teacher wanted the activities to be held on time. Field trips were one. If a student or teacher wished to go on a certain trip and had a set lesson time established for some subject, the the person would inform the teacher or student(s) that class would need to be either cancelled or delayed.

Another factor that could throw time schedules off-kilter is a council meeting. Council meetings, as briefly discussed in the previous chapter, are designed to allow students or teachers to resolve conflicts or other problems (such as discussing missing items or rule enforcements). Council meetings can be called at any time by a student or teacher by going around to all the rooms where downstairs kids and teachers might be and calling out, "Council meeting! Council meeting!" On hearing that, all downstairs kids and downstairs teachers must drop what they are doing (with a very few exceptions) and gather in the Big Room. Everyone sits in an elongated oval on the floor; no one is allowed to sit in a chair or on a cushion of any kind. Once everyone is there and settled in place, one student will call out, "Nominations for chairperson?" and then call on someone who says, "I nominate so-and-so." This is done three times, so there are three students in contention for the job. A vote is taken and the person with the most votes gets the job. Surprisingly, the job of chairperson rotates quite well among the students. Although there are some perennial favorites, a good variety of individuals take on the task. Some students opt to decline a nomination, while some younger children (first and second graders mainly) generally do not get nominated since everyone seems to know that they are not familiar enough with the process to effectively chair the meeting. Once the chairperson has been selected, he or she asks, "Who called this council meeting?" The person who called it identifies him or herself, the chair asks, "What's your problem?," and the individual explains. From that point, individual students and teachers weigh in on the issue, perhaps providing evidence to counter or corroborate, making comments, offering motions, making amendments to motions, and so on. As people raise their hands to speak, the chairperson calls on them one at a time. Once someone has been recognized to speak and "has the floor," others are not to speak or raise their hands. If either of those rules is broken, or if a student is being disruptive, the chair calls out "Order!" or sends an individual to stand in the corner. If disruptive behavior is extreme, then the individual is sent upstairs to the kitchen. The meeting ends when the problem has been worked through, or motions passed, and when the individual with the problem can answer in the affirmative when asked, "Does this solve your problem?" At this point, someone will make a motion to adjourn the council meeting, a vote will be taken, and the meeting will adjourn if the majority votes that way. I observed council meetings to last as little as ten minutes and as long as six hours (split over two days). Council meetings will break for lunch and do tend to stop close to the 3 P.M. dismissal time only to be picked up at 9 A.M. the next day if the problem is not solved; however, if the issue is close to closure, the meeting can extend beyond dismissal time, to as late as 3:40 P.M. in my experience.

Time flow at the Free School is obviously a combination of some strongly scheduled and adhered to times (breakfast time, activities meeting, lunchtime, and dismissal), some semistrongly adhered to times (regular class meetings that both students and teachers commit to), and the much more in evidence fluid times (the many suggested daily activities or lesson ideas, and council meetings). Lessons can last as long as interest holds. In fact, I can recall times when I read with students for two hours straight, although most lessons or activities tended to be somewhere between thirty minutes to an hour. But even that statement is somewhat misleading, for it is difficult to easily bracket an activity and say "That's a lesson" or "That's an activity" as if they were these discrete, separate things. So many things happen simultaneously and come to natural ends that led to other things that I find it difficult to put them in terms of a schedule or timetable. What I mean by this requires an illustration. Early on, I began teaching a couple of the six year olds, Colleen and Ajay, how to play chess. They were very keen to learn since many of the older kids played semiregularly and they were intrigued by this game that so many seemed to enjoy. Once they had learned the rudiments, Colleen and Ajay often clamored in activities meetings for chess practice, which basically involved their playing against one another and me watching, correcting, and advising as they went along. In one of our first chess practices, Ajay and Colleen asked me to "keep score." Puzzled at first by this request, I told them that you do not, generally, keep score, but we could figure something out. So I wrote the name of each game piece on the chalkboard in the room, and assigned each one a relative point value (pawn 1, bishop 10, queen 15, king 100, and so on). As the children captured a piece, I asked them what piece it was and what point value it had. These were six year olds who were in the process of learning to read, partially phonetically, and so they would say the name of the piece, recognize the letter sound they heard at the beginning of the name, and then look on the board and pick out the piece that started with that letter. Then they would recognize and read out its point value and I would write that down. When the next piece was captured, I said something like, "Okay, you have four points and now you got one more for that pawn. How many points do you have now?" And so the students added in their heads or on their fingers and declared their score. Where did the activity of chess turn into a reading and a math lesson? They were all of one piece, flowing fairly naturally one from the other.

Other examples of this natural flow of activities include a child or children coming into a room where something is going on, a game or book being read, for example, and they would join in; or a lesson taking place and the child's interest getting drawn away by hearing something in the next room that he or she wanted to investigate; or a teacher either coming into a room or just being there with some students and asking in a friendly and conversational manner, "What are you doing now? Are you interested in doing such-and-such?" On a day in mid-September, I recorded in my journal the following events.

> After lunch, most of the downstairs group (except about twelve) went swimming and I stayed at school, mainly because Ajay [age six] asked me this morning to play with him this afternoon. He wanted to play the made-up money game we played yesterday, but then he pulled [the game of] Life off the shelf and wanted to play that. So we went into the Rug Room, but were promptly joined by others (Colleen, Macon, Daisy, then Lawrence, Jonathan, Frankie, and Nevin) [ages six, six, eight, twelve, eleven, seven, and seven, respectively]. We found that we couldn't figure out how to play a version that all of us could enjoy and be challenged by, and we couldn't come up with any other game we all could play (though we did try to make up a game with the Scattergories dice where you'd roll a letter and then have to say five words that started with that letter and you'd get a bonus for using that letter more than once in a word). We played that for just a little bit, but then the group sort of disintegrated. Some of the older boys went off to the park, and Ajay and Daisy and I went into the Science Room to play with blocks. There were Legos out there, too, and so Ajay and Daisy started playing with them. Hamal [age seven] soon joined them and he and Daisy got involved in a make-believe game with the Lego people talking to each other, etc. Ajay played mostly by himself with the Legos. I sat and read and wrote in my journal. It was a very cozy and quiet time with me talking with Dave and Bhawin [both teachers] some and the kids playing. Ajay commented to me as it was time to go that it was fun this afternoon with it being quiet and so on! A six year old said that!

And on November 10, I recorded that

> Colleen was back today after her sickness and hospital stay. First thing at breakfast, she came up and hugged me, saying she wanted to do chess practice. She ate breakfast with me and sort of stuck with me through activities meeting. I told her that we could do chess practice in the morning, but if Missy wanted to have class, then we could do chess after reading class. At the end of activities

meeting, Missy said to the first graders let's do class, but Colleen and Ajay somewhat resisted, saying they wanted to do chess practice. I said we could do it after reading, but then Missy interjected saying, go ahead and do it now, they want to do chess now, so let's just go with the flow. So we did chess practice with Colleen playing Ajay, and Ursula and Sarah and Delia watching. I had Sarah practice her handwriting by writing on the board the pieces' initials and their number value, and I had Ajay and Colleen practicing their math with adding their old scores to the new points they gained as the game went along. They are getting good at that, adding without using their fingers so much.

What I am trying to make clear is that at the Free School very few artificial time periods or schedules are imposed onto the school day, and those events that were regular as clockwork involved either meal and start and stop times, or things that students and teachers both held in high value and for which they committed to a regular time period. And even with those activities or lessons, they tended to sometimes stop before their "official" ending time if the student(s) started to zone out or give other evidence that they no longer wanted to do the activity.

The Free School's physical setting, how teachers and students were grouped, and the school timetable represented big differences for me. School governance at the Free School was also a change since all my schooling experiences took place in authoritarian, top-down schools. As mentioned previously, this school is governed by the policy of "absolute internal autonomy" by which all decisions pertaining to the running of the school are made only by those in the school on a day-to-day basis. Students, teachers, and staff all have an equal right to propose changes to school rules and practices and can assert these rights anytime. Each person's voice or opinion is equally valued in discussing rules and practices and there is no hierarchy of individuals. I remember being somewhat surprised on my first day that the co-directors did not come into the first meeting with a preset agenda of items. True, they each had topic ideas in mind, but so, too, did all the other staff members, and each item was given equal consideration, regardless of its source.

Prior to the beginning of the 2003–2004 school year, all teachers and intern teachers met for two weeks not only to get the school ready for the new year (painting, cleaning, and rearranging the physical space), but also to figure out new procedures and reaffirm old ones (especially for the benefit of new teaching staff). During this two-week period, several new procedures and rules were discussed at length. For example, the teachers (including intern and volunteer teachers) decided to require the downstairs kids to write their names on the dry erase board in the Big Room whenever they left the building with or without a teacher. This was so we would always know where people were. Another new policy was that children would not be permitted to play games on the computer unless the game could be proven to be one not mindlessly repetitive and thus with some educational merit. Students were not to play handheld video game devices (Nintendo Game Boys) during the school hours of 8 A.M. to 3 P.M. Another rule was that students could not pay others to do their lunch duty; they all must take their turns. A final new rule was that outside food or drink was not permitted simply because too many kids the previous year had eaten too much "junk food," which the teachers believed was detrimental to their health, and too many wrappers and bits of food were found lying about, dirtying up the school. All these rules were added to the list of rules in place from previous years, which included things like:

> The "stop rule"—if a person (student or teacher) was doing something to another person (student or teacher) that the latter individual did not like, then the latter had the right to tell the former to stop. If the person would not stop, then the "victim" could call a council meeting.
>
> Running and loud noises or activities are only allowed in the backyard as they are too disruptive inside.
>
> No cursing in the backyard, and in public in general, out of courtesy to the neighbors.
>
> No harassing the neighbor's dog.
>
> Clean up after yourself.
>
> Sign out all games.
>
> No kids in the supply closet.
>
> Respect stop signs on doors. (If there's a stop sign posted, that means a focused activity or lesson is going on and no one is to enter until the sign is removed.)
>
> Lunch duty—each downstairs kid has one day a week to take part in cleaning up the upstairs eating area after lunch is over. This involves clearing and wiping tables, sweeping, stacking plates, and so on.

The presence of these rules reveals that while the Free School teachers seek to create an environment that is free from the repressive constraints so ubiquitous in traditional schools, they do not believe in total license. These teachers' ideas about identity formation include the beliefs that human identity is a combination of characteristics that are innately present and socially constructed and that in order to allow for healthy identity development, one must provide people (children) with a social context of freedom with a few limits. Chris Mercogliano sent me an e-mail in which he argued that in the emergence of identity "there's constant interplay between inner and outer forces, and therefore [there is] an important role for the school to play." An ideal school environment, according to Mercogliano, is a space in which one can act "in ways that are true to oneself and not a means to pleasing others or avoiding unpleasant consequences" and where one can "express one's beliefs and emotions without fear of retaliation." A free environment, one that allows children's identities to fully emerge, is one that lacks tight controls over how people act or spend their time. Some control mechanisms *do* exist to prevent freedom from turning into unchecked license, and the governance mechanisms of council meetings and the previous rules are some examples of this. Students at the Free School are not free "to abuse the safety, rights, or sensibilities of others,"[1] and the school is set up to teach the idea that "freedom always includes being held accountable for the effects of your actions on those around you."[2] Bhawin, another teacher, also agreed that freedom is not the same as license. He stated that, "kids have freedom to do what they want to do, but once they start interfering with other people's freedom to do what they want to do, or the school's freedom to have a window or, you know, not have a door that's kicked in or a wall that busted in, then there's a problem and then the kids have to be held responsible." Part and parcel of identity formation, Free School teachers might argue, is this going up against social limitations.

On the first day of school, the downstairs teachers and students all sat down together in the Big Room and discussed these old rules and the new ones. There was a bit of grumbling on the part of the kids about some of the new rules, but on hearing this, the teachers were quick to assert, "There are no victims here. If you don't like a rule, then you know that you can call an all-school meeting at any time and attempt to change the rule democratically."

Whereas council meetings are, for the most part, specifically designed to deal with individual and interpersonal problems, all-school meetings address school operations and policies. And while council meetings are mandatory for all downstairs students and teachers, all-school meetings are not. All-school meetings are called in the same manner as council meetings— whenever an individual wants to call one, he or she goes around the school declaring that an all-school meeting will commence in such-and-such a room. An all-school meeting can also be planned in advance by announcing it in activities meeting. When the other students and teachers hear that an all-school meeting is going to take place, they make a choice whether to attend. The all-school meeting begins with the selection of a chairperson much like in council meetings. Once chosen, the chair asks for agenda items and lists them on the board. Then each item is discussed one at a time, is voted on, and so on.

During the three months I was at the Free School, only one all-school meeting was called and it was in regard to the rules banning handheld video games and outside food and drink. In this meeting, only about six students initially attended, whereas nine teachers came (mostly interns curious about how such meetings were run). As the meeting went on, some teachers left and other students joined in. This flow of students and teacher continued throughout the meeting. After much discussion of rationales for allowing or forbidding handheld video game playing and outside food and drink consumption, a vote was taken on certain motions and amendments and two new rules were passed: (1) handheld video games could be played between 2 and 3 P.M. and (2) candy and gum consumption would be allowed in school. Both rules had student-suggested amendments attached that imposed some limits or consequences (if candy or gum wrappers were found lying about, then the ability to have gum and candy would be suspended for two weeks for the whole school; if handheld video game playing occurred prior to 2 p.m, the game would be taken away from the individual for a week).

Motions and amendments stemming from both all-school meetings and council meetings are binding and enforced by both teachers and students. If a violation of one of the rules (new or old) occurs, anyone has the right to call a council meeting to discuss what happened and decide as a whole school what should next occur. Power of governance (rule making and enforcement) is thus held equally in the hands of both students and teachers at the Free School. While some students and teachers might exercise this power more than others (by opting to attend and participate in the all-school meetings), the power *is* offered to all.

The Free School, in my opinion, is embodying the confluences of progressive educators' ideas on how the learning settings and timings of a school should be coordinated. The terms "efficiency," "uniformity," or any other industrial or factory-influenced terminology are just not relevant here. In every way, the Albany Free School asserts its philosophical grounding of seeking to help create individuals who are unique, not uniform, and questioning, not acquiescent.

Classrooms in this school in no way resemble the "egg-crate" setup of most traditional schools. In fact, the school building itself is not often the only site of classes or activities, for as individual students pursue their own nonstandardized curriculum, the traditional walls of school dissolve. Children are learning and growing not just at the Free School building, but also at many public and private community locales, and all the different field trip destinations.

How the children and staff are grouped at the Free School further emphasizes individuality. While a child is nominally assigned to a "touch base" teacher and class according to age, that is the extent of any sort of age grading or age segregation. Children of all grades freely intermix and students have contact with all the teachers. Groups form and reform around activities for which children have an interest and few limitations are placed on who (i.e., what age child) can take part. Certain children form especially strong relationships with teachers who are not their "touch base" teacher and instead are just persons with whom they seem to have a certain rapport. Class sizes are exceedingly small when compared to traditional schools, which further forwards the end of developing individually unique people. When a teacher does not have to work or interact with a large number of students at one time, she can truly see the person rather than the group.

Honoring the individual person and assisting his or her growth also occurs through the school's timetables. Because the school has very few set-in-stone, committed time periods, teachers and students are able to recognize and attend to each child's learning paces, rhythms, and cycles. Students thus do not feel pushed or prodded into staying "on schedule," for their own internal schedules are respected.

Lastly, students and teachers at the Free School have an equal say in coordinating and governing the school's policies and day-to-day operations. Students thus become active participants in their own learning and active democratic citizens in the school. They do not easily succumb to outside manipulation or authoritarian rule. They do not become boxed-in victims of some faceless bureaucracy, but instead are empowered individuals who recognize the rights and responsibilities that come with living or working in a community.

CHAPTER SIX

A VERY DIFFERENT CURRICULUM

As I mentioned in chapter 3, the assumptions by traditional schools that knowledge exists outside of and distant from human consciousness and that learning is the transmission of this knowledge to students have far-reaching repercussions for what is studied in traditional schools, what roles the teachers and students play, and what resources are used. Progressive educators strongly disagree with traditional visions of education on many levels and have set forth their own ideas on the content of curriculum, materials to be used, and roles to be played in teaching this curriculum. The Albany Free School, with its unique curricula, is enacting these progressive educators' vision in many ways.

The Albany Free School does not have a formal curriculum in the sense of a standard course of study that students all follow. What the school does, instead, is allow each child to do what he or she wishes to do, within certain limits. Those limits involve safety issues and respect for others in the community. If a student wishes to do something that interferes with another's rights or with some other aspect of the running of the school, then the student is not permitted to do that thing until he makes some compromises or adjustments. As A. S. Neill phrased it, students in the Albany Free School have freedom, but not license.[1] Students are free to pursue those activities that interest them; they are not compelled to study certain subjects, nor are they required to attend any classes. But this in no way means, as many critics argue, that the Free School students "don't learn anything." Simply, the Free School students learn (make meaning about) those things that hold interest for them—in other words, what they feel a connection to. This freedom to pursue their interests and make meaning from these interactions with the world leads to growth and change in the students along their own personal paths and potentials

In the process of interacting with the world and making meaning from those interactions, the Free School students *do* come into contact with those subjects or skills that make up the curricular content in traditional schools, but they experience little of the sense of disconnection, unreality, or alienation that is so much in evidence for students in traditional schools. In other words, the Albany Free School students come to the traditional academic subjects, disciplines, or skills on their own terms and for their own purposes, and thus the subjects and skills are meaningful and more than likely will stay with them much more solidly throughout their lives.

Not only do the Free School students have exposure to traditional academic subjects through their individual curricula, they also get to experience a different, social and emotional curriculum—one that is largely missing for many students in traditional schools.

The Albany Free School students experience democratic governance and diversity, they're actively involved in the "real world" (the world outside the school building), and they encounter opportunities to develop their skills of interpersonal interactions and intrapersonal understanding. Both curricula—the academic and the more social/emotional—work in tandem to gently guide students to an understanding of what it means to be fully human. Students learn that each person is unique and should be valued equally, that we must seek to understand ourselves and the world in which we live, that people have responsibilities to be just, equitable, and caring toward their fellow humans and to their environments, and that sometimes one needs to actively challenge limit situations to increase levels of social justice. In this chapter, I will use my journal entries and interviews of teachers to illustrate these two different curricula at the Free School.

ACADEMIC CURRICULA

Students at the Albany Free School come into contact with the traditional academic subjects and skills in several different ways: (1) when they explicitly choose to, (2) when a teacher suggests it, and (3) when the subject they are interested in has a natural connection to one of the traditional subjects or skills. The first way occurs more frequently than most people might expect, particularly with older students. Since the school only goes up to the eighth grade,[2] almost all the students will attend traditional schools for their high school years. Because the Free School students realize that in high school they will be required to take classes in certain subjects, many of them want to arrive prepared and so they begin, in seventh grade especially, to request classes in the traditional subjects. At the beginning of the school year, Dave, the seventh/eighth-grade teacher, held a class meeting in which he asked students what classes they wished to have offered over the course of the school year. On the list were a large number of the traditional disciplines, subjects, and skills that one might find in traditional schools. These included math subjects such as algebra, geometry, and arithmetic (multiplication and division especially); the skills of handwriting, spelling, and read-

ing; social science subjects, including history and geography; language subjects, including literature, creative writing, journalism, and poetry; science
subjects, including biology and sex education; and art subjects, including
pottery, carving, drawing, painting, and so on. Once this list was developed,
Dave and the students sought out teachers for these classes and then the
students and teachers individually planned meeting times and goals. Sometimes these classes were formally set up and scheduled and at other times
they were more informal, catch-as-catch-can, so to speak.

Not only did the seventh and eighth graders explicitly request exposure to the traditional subject areas, but so, too, did many younger kids. For
example, a number of the fourth-grade girls worked with me, for a while
quite regularly, on memorizing their multiplication tables and doing long
division. I also worked through some math workbooks with several younger
children in a more sporadic fashion. And nearly all the students worked on
reading in some way or another, either by a phonics class, like the ones Missy
often taught to her first- and second-grade students, or by being read to and
practicing reading oneself in various settings.

Exposure to or contact with traditional school subjects comes about not
just through student requests, but also by teacher suggestion. Teachers frequently ask students if they wish to read something, or practice some skill, and
also quite often bring in materials or suggest activities in certain subjects that
might pique the students' interests. In October, Missy proposed a spelling bee,
which excited and involved a number of the students. Teachers make such
offers out of their own personal interests in the subjects, but also from interactions they have with the students that indicate that the student may also be
interested. For example, a seventh grader named Lawrence and I were speaking
one day and he mentioned that he had recently purchased a survival kit at an
Army Navy surplus store. I, too, am interested in survival gear and stories and
I asked if he had ever read this great survival story called Hatchet. He said he
had not, and initially did not show much interest in reading it with me, but
I occasionally raised the idea at later points in conversation with him and he
ultimately expressed some interest in reading the book, which we (and other
students who were intrigued by the topic) proceeded to do. We later went on
to read the sequel to Hatchet, called Brian's Winter, and another survival story
called The Cay. Another example of connecting traditional subjects and skills
to an individual student's interest involves Trent, a twelve-year-old seventh
grader at the school. Trent, an African American boy, has attended this school
since he was little (first grade or so), but never developed great reading skills.
The teachers wanted to really work on that with him during his seventh and
eight-grade years so that he would transition well to high school. Through
their interactions with him, teachers discovered that Trent has an interest in
and talent for acting. So Chris, an upstairs teacher who has a strong relationship with Trent, hit upon a possible personal connection that might draw
Trent into reading more. Chris told him about Sydney Poitier, an African

American actor who was illiterate well into his adulthood. Chris showed Trent and other interested students a number of Poitier films and then asked Trent if he wanted to read Poitier's autobiography, which he did. The two of them, at around 10:45 A.M. each day, read that book together and others that Chris knew would connect to Trent's life. One last example of linking the traditional subject of reading to student interests or life experiences came when about four of the fourth- and fifth-grade girls built themselves a clubhouse in a little woodsy area across the street from the school. Megan, the fifth/sixth-grade teacher stumbled across a book entitled *Tree Girl* and decided to offer to read this book with those girls. They readily agreed as the topic of the book deeply connected with an activity that was currently giving them a lot of satisfaction.

Student requests for and teacher offerings of the traditional subjects and skills, although somewhat frequent, are not the main ways that students come into contact with the traditional school subjects and skills. Rather, the holistic manner in which this school approaches curriculum provides the students with the majority of their exposure to the traditional academic subjects. Because the school makes no major value judgments on what a student does with his or her time (aside from safety and interpersonal respect judgments), students are free to take part in play and through this play gain exposure to traditional subjects and skills. In the previous chapter, in explaining the natural time flow of one activity to another, I offered the example of chess practice, an activity often requested by the six year olds with whom I had become quite close. Chess was the actual "subject" of our time together, but we also drew in reading practice, as well as some arithmetic lessons. Aside from what I have already described, these "math lessons" went beyond simple adding and moved into comparisons of value. For example, one day when we were having chess practice, Colleen and Ajay had each captured a number of pieces to the point where both of their scores were in the thirties, but they were uncertain as to who was ahead. They seemed to be struggling with the fact that both their scores look the same since they started with the same number. I explained to them, in a very rudimentary way, the idea of place value, that if the first digit is the same, then they needed to look at the second number to determine which was higher and which lower.

Chess was not the only game that was good for integrating play with traditional subjects or skills. The school has an excellent collection of games that give kids practice in math, spelling, word formation, handwriting, creative writing, categorization, and so on. Besides such standards as chess and checkers, the school has the games of Life (which involves a lot of counting and analysis of possible options) and Scrabble (great for spelling, vocabulary development, and math for keeping score), and then unique games such as Quiddler (a card game somewhat similar to Scrabble that involves spelling, word formation and vocabulary development, scorekeeping, and logic for strategies), Blink and Set (both are visual perception/categorization games), and the games of Once Upon A Time and Dungeons and Dragons (detailed, creative storytelling games). There are also some computer word games such as Text Twist and Word Racer, and both math and reading games found on certain Web sites. Then there are strategy games and logic puzzles that help students to develop critical divergent thinking skills. Free play unconnected to games also develops academic skills. For example, playing with Legos builds students' spatial understandings and artistic senses; playing pretend games develops students' imaginations and verbal skills.

Free play also means free interaction with others, including adults, and a great deal of academic learning goes on in such interactions. Kids simply stumble into these secondary exposures to the academic subjects in the basic interactions they have with one another and with teachers over the course of the school day. For example, one morning in early November, I was sitting at the computer in the Science Room writing a letter to be sent home with students regarding some apple pies that a group of students and teachers were planning to make in order to raise some money. One of the eighth-grade boys, Walter, wandered over and was just watching me as I typed away. Apparently he was reading over my shoulder, for he made some comments about the contents of my letter, quibbling over certain points and arguing that I should phrase something differently. This got us into a discussion of semantics, and of composition. We talked about run-on sentences, the effective and ineffective uses of repetition, and so on. In essence, we had a mini-composition and grammar class from this, perhaps twenty-minute, unplanned interchange. Another example occurred when I asked six-year-old Sarah if she wanted to help me do lunch setup duty, which she did. She came upstairs with me and I had her write up labels for the vegetarian and nonvegetarian foods and also had her count out silverware for each table. At one point, she ran out of forks at one table; she had only one fork but six were required, so I asked her how many were needed. This required her to do a bit of subtraction. So, just in helping me set up lunch, Sarah got practice in handwriting and mathematics skills.

Field trips also provide the students with opportunities to come into contact with traditional academic subjects. As mentioned in the previous chapter, the students have ample opportunities to leave the school building and go on field trips both to places within walking distance and those farther away. I frequently accompanied students to the New York State Museum, which is a quick five-minute walk from the school. It contains extensive displays on such things as the 9/11 tragedy (which teaches history and reading in that students have to read the descriptions, or be read to), the Iroquois and Mohawk Indians who are indigenous to New York (again teaching history, cultural studies, etc.), the minerals and gems of New York (which teaches science, and geology), the birds of New York (which teaches science/zoology), fossils found in New York (which teaches prehistoric botany and zoology, and geology), neighborhoods of New York City (which teaches social history and cultural studies), and so on.

The downstairs teachers also plan frequent hikes and nature walks to various locales both inside and outside the city and the teachers quite often give little explanatory lectures on the botany, geology, and zoology of an area as the field trip progresses.

More mundane field trips occur as well that also provide the kids exposure to traditional subjects. For example, shortly after the school had made a trip in October to glean apples at a nearby apple orchard, a group of students and teachers decided to make applesauce. We had the apples, but we also needed some spices and sugar. So a group of three children (one aged six, and two aged eleven) and I walked to the neighborhood grocery store where we did some comparison pricing and addition to figure out what we could afford and which was the best deal, thereby having some math practice. We also did a bit of reading practice as we tried to locate the aisle that held the items we were seeking to purchase. In addition to this minor field trip, other teachers and I often took students with us on errands to various neighborhood locales, such as the post office or library, which again gave students some exposure to the traditional academic subjects and skills (most especially reading and math).

These field trips, the informal interchanges, free play, and the requested classes have meaning for the students; they are connected to them in some way and thus the students are constructing knowledge around them, knowledge that will stay with them rather than be forgotten quickly (as often happens in traditional schools). And in the free choice of activities, free play, field trips, and simple daily interactions the students come to value many ways of knowing. They are not made to believe, as so many traditionally educated students are, that something, some knowledge, is only valid if it comes to them through rational means. Instead, the students viscerally understand, I believe, that knowledge or meaning can come to them through their bodies, through interpersonal relations, and through their emotions and feelings. The Free School students *are* learning the traditional academic subjects, although not in a systematized, prearranged, uniform manner and not just through rational methods. This lack of systemization and occasional lack of explicit rationality gave me pause at times, for I am a product of the traditional conception of education, and lifelong habits, values, and beliefs are not exactly easy to overturn. But even as I questioned the absence of a systematic academic curriculum, I realized that this very same lack allowed the Free School students to focus on constructing their own meaning and knowledge and thereby grow. I also realized that this lack opened the door for other, nontraditionally valued curricular content to come in. This nontraditional content included a greater emphasis on physicality and the arts, emotional health, "real-world" issues (issues that connect to the students' daily lives), and issues of democracy and diversity.

SOCIAL/EMOTIONAL CURRICULUM

Physical activities make up one aspect of this nontraditional social/emotional curriculum. In traditional schools, some attention is paid to the students' physical bodies, but not a great deal. For example, students do have physical education classes, but the time devoted to this is relatively minimal compared to the amount of time students are expected to remain largely stationary. There is little recognition in traditional schools of how important physical movement and physical expression are. Physical education and recess notwithstanding (and recess is only available to elementary students, and even that is going by the wayside), traditional schools, broadly speaking, do not emphasize the body; in other words, they place little value on the concept that one can learn a great deal by focusing on and using one's body. Traditional schools exhibit a significant mind–body split, where the mind is valued much more than the body. The hidden curriculum in traditional schools teaches children to ignore the needs of their bodies; thus, these children become alienated from their own physical selves.[3]

Progressive educators, on the other hand, challenge this mind–body split and argue that all knowledge is body-mediated and thus we must question where the mind actually is.[4] In schools, we should allow for a great deal of physicality and the Albany Free School does just that. Free School students have the freedom to move their bodies and experience things kinesthetically all the time. They can wiggle, and dance, and run, and lounge, and stretch, and stand, and sit whenever they like (with the main exception of council meetings and within the limits of safety and respecting the rights of others). Free School teachers believe that a child's free movement is necessary to growth and emotional well-being. If they were to suppress the child's physical expression, they believe, then they would be stunting the child's growth.

Thus, I saw a great deal of physical movement in the kids themselves, in terms of moving freely from room to room and while in a class setting. I want to make clear here that the free movement of the students was not frenetic or chaotic, as many critics assume. Such frenetic movement, I believe, only occurs when children who are tightly reined in are given rare moments of freedom. Then, bodily expressions virtually explode out of these children for they have been so bottled up prior to this moment of freedom. At the Free School, in contrast, the movement of the kids was very "natural" in appearance, and by this I mean the movements were expressions of the children's ages, their temperaments, the activities they were involved in, and so on.

There is a strong recognition at the Free School that physical play is vitally important to children's growth, and opportunities abound for the kids to take part in somewhat organized physical games (such as basketball, football, soccer, baseball, ultimate Frisbee, etc.) and in many other not so organized movement activities (such as riding skateboards or scooters, hiking, walking, tumbling, swimming, gardening, playing dress up, running around the parks, playing on swing sets or jungle gyms, etc.). Horseplay, an example of a nonorganized movement activity, is not discouraged at the Free School (except when it is overly disruptive, but, in those cases, kids are told to just go outside) because the teachers recognize that connecting one's body with another's is healthy and normal. This recognition of the healthiness of using bodies in concert is perhaps the reason why the school built a low ropes course on their woodland property. Here the teachers recognize that students can learn a great deal by using their bodies in teamwork activities.

One can see, I hope, that at the Free School the body is far from being ignored or denied. The children integrate their physical selves into everything they do, and their bodies thus become a source of learning as well as the content of that learning. Physicality is both a subject itself and a manner in which subjects are learned.

The arts are another of those subjects or approaches to learning that show up to a small degree in traditional schools, but infuse progressive educators' visions of schools. Progressive educators value the arts as a means of expression and a vehicle for personal growth. While many traditional schools do have classes in the arts, these classes tend to be valued below the more academic core courses (as evidenced by cutting funding to the arts first when budgets are tight). Progressive educators, on the other hand, believe that schools should equally embrace and value the arts, including movement, music, crafts, sculpture, performance, and so on.

The Albany Free School embodies this progressive educational belief in the value of the arts and provides plentiful opportunities for artistic endeavors. There is an art room in the downstairs area filled with materials for drawing, painting, sketching, sculpture, pottery, collages, and so on. Students do need to request supervision for use of the supplies, but most any teacher is happy to oblige them. Teachers also frequently offer activities in the art room, such as making junk-item or nature-item sculptures, pottery classes, plaster carving, printmaking, sewing, knitting, origami, mask making, and so on. Students also take part in filmmaking with the school's digital camcorder and software for editing movies.

The Free School also offers opportunities for students to be musical. On occasion I would sing songs with students as we sat doing another activity, like drawing, knitting, or sewing. Around the holidays, one of the parents establishes a chorus and practices with them. There is a piano in the Big Room, which kids are free to use, and two of the seventh/eighth graders had piano lessons as one of their apprenticeships. Some teachers play the guitar and could often be found playing and singing and offering to teach the instrument to those who showed an interest.

Music and movement also become integrated quite often at the Free School. A number of the teachers are into drumming and will frequently bring drums with them to school and they and a group of students will sit down to an impromptu jam session. While they are drumming, students will often get up and move their bodies to the rhythms, particularly the younger children.

Free School teachers also provide the students with many opportunities to observe professional and amateur artists in action. While I was at the school, we took numerous field trips to plays, dance performances, art museums, outdoor and indoor sculpture parks, and so on.

Another nontraditional "subject area" that shows up in the curriculum at the Free School involves emotions and needs. There is a tremendous amount of emphasis on the students becoming emotionally whole—in other words, being able to name their feelings and act truthfully on them, learning how to deal with inter and intrapersonal problems, and so on. The council meetings are perhaps the most obvious way of learning these skills. Council meetings exist as a means for students to assert their rights by naming their problems and working through conflicts, as well as an opportunity for developing in students an ability to work in concert with others to solve problems.

The school offers other activities for developing emotional wholeness. In the Big Room downstairs, half of the chalkboard is called the Problem Wall. Here, the only things that can be written are problems particular students are having. In most cases, these are problems over which students do not wish to call council meetings, but are still bothering them nonetheless. The problem remains written on the Problem Wall until it is somehow resolved. For example, a young six-year-old student named Ursula was having trouble getting along with another six year old named Sarah. Apparently Sarah had shoved Ursula. Ursula did not want to call a council meeting (possibly because she was intimidated by the setting), so I suggested that she write her problem on the Problem Wall. She told me what she wanted to say and I helped her to spell the words as she wrote them on the board. Later that morning, Sarah recognized her name on the board and asked someone what was written. On hearing it, she got mad and wanted to have it out with Ursula. A teacher intervened and they had a mini-council meeting, just the three of them, to resolve the problem.

Understanding and acting on one's emotions also emerge during "boys group" meetings and "girls group/goddess" meetings. As a female, I was not permitted to attend the boys group meetings, but I did find out that the sort of things they talked about involved issues of stereotypical gender roles, how pressures to conform to a certain definition of masculinity made them feel, and so on. I was allowed to attend one of the girls/goddess meetings and the topics were a freewheeling range of the girls' dreams (during sleep), fears (of death, loss of parents, etc.), and also gender roles (how they behaved around one of the eighth-grade boys who exhibited characteristics of hypermasculinity). This was an interesting meeting, a bit new agey for me (singing songs about goddesses, doing Runes—a sort of advising stones, holding hands to transfer energy, etc.), but it was also a good space for the girls to just talk about deep issues and express themselves freely.

Touching on one's emotions comes out through nearly all the traditional and nontraditional subjects mainly because the activities the students get involved with are outward expressions of their interests and needs. If a student chooses to attend a film like *Whale Rider* because she is intrigued by the female lead, then the film and postviewing class discussion help her, perhaps, in understanding her own feelings, needs, and opinions. Emotions and needs arise from the books the students read, in the classes (especially classes like sex education), and in their free play. No separation exists between what the student does at the school and his or her emotions—they are inextricably linked.

Another aspect of the social/emotional curriculum involves "real-world" issues, including democracy and diversity. When students do not have a standardized, mandated curriculum that they are forced to "learn," opportunities then are opened up for their interests and life concerns to enter their school studies. Although traditional teachers often try to relate the standardized curriculum to the lives of their students, a significant disconnect still exists between the two. This is mainly because the traditional teacher has a large group of students to work with at one time, all of whom do not live identical lives and thus do not have identical real-life concerns, and because the traditional teacher is under significant pressure to get students to absorb or memorize the standardized curriculum and thus perform well on standardized tests. These two factors serve to largely prevent real-life student concerns from becoming one of the true focal points of the curriculum.

As mentioned, this is not true in progressive educators' conception of education. They believe that real-life and real-world experiences of the students should be the curriculum that the students study. They believe that the problems and resources of the world should be brought into the school or that the student should be taken out into that world to interact and deal with those problems and resources.

The Albany Free School, I believe, achieves this vital wholeness or connection between the school world and the world "outside." It is not just a place where one learns the "3 Rs," and never how to truly live in the world. The Albany Free School provides opportunities for students to learn practical living skills and study subjects that will aid them in understanding their world. If students show an interest in cooking, automobile repair, bicycle repair, or gardening, then the teachers help them seek out opportunities to practice and develop these skills. Students also explore the world outside the school through many field trips, including the ones already mentioned and others such as to the local soup kitchen, the city dump, the police horse farm, a nearby bird sanctuary, and so on. All the students also get practice in economics by planning, organizing, and raising funds for their various class trips. (Parents are generally not asked for a lump sum amount to pay for their child's class trip; instead the class works as a group, putting on dinners, bake sales, movie nights, and so on, to raise the funds needed for everyone.)

Students thus learn what is in the world around them and many of the skills needed to negotiate that world. They also learn a great deal about politics, both in terms of their democratic interactions in the school and the wider political picture in the country as a whole. The council meetings, all-school meetings, and activities meetings give the students a great deal of day-to-day practice with democratic structures and interactions. And the teachers, many of whom are activists for a more participatory democratic system, often try to further raise awareness of and interest in issues of how people in our society often have no voice in making changes or in decisions that affect their lives.

Another real-world subject students are exposed to at the Free School is the issue of diversity. Not only does the school itself have a diverse population of students and staff (in terms of social class, gender, and ethnicity), the teachers also actively try to bring in people with varied backgrounds and orientations. In addition, teachers offer activities that further kids' exposure to this aspect of the real world. What is key about all the diversity-related activities or interactions that get offered is that they connect in some way to the lives of the students and their interests. These are not decontextualized, one-shot-only "multicultural" activities, but ones integrally related to the students' lived experiences.

The social/emotional curriculum that exists for the Free School students is unique and serves to accomplish many of the goals of progressive educators: it helps students to understand themselves and the communities and world in which they live, it helps them to know and understand their bodies, and it helps them to express their thoughts and emotions—all of which are sorely lacking in so many traditional schools.

These two curricula, the academic and the social/emotional, combine to form an overall curriculum that is about liberation, about meeting our "ontological vocation" of becoming fully human.[5] A liberatory curriculum is what progressive educators seek; as discussed in chapter 3, progressive educators want students to discover who they are as individuals and how they should live with others in community; they want students to learn to use traditional academic skills and topics to critically examine and question the world and their immediate environment; and they want students to learn how to break through personal and interpersonal obstacles in a quest for justice and equity. Neither of these two curricula that make up this overall curriculum is of higher value; both are necessary and exist symbiotically. As illustrated in this chapter, they are taught both through explicit means, such as a teacher introducing lessons, as in traditional schools, but also, perhaps more frequently, implicitly through how the school is organized and run, and through its daily structures and practices. The following discussion of the different components of a curriculum for liberation explains how the Albany Free School delivers on this progressive vision through both implicit and explicit means.

DEVELOPMENT OF CRITICAL CONSCIOUSNESS

A number of progressive educators, particularly those known as critical pedagogues (Paulo Freire, Maxine Greene, Henry Giroux, to name just a few),
believe that an education for liberation must involve the development of
students' critical capacities so that they can begin to realize and name limitations and obstacles in their own lives and in their communities. Education,
in these authors' vision, should provide students with the critical methodological and conceptual tools needed to undertake this examination of their
world.[6] The Albany Free School delivers on this vision both through the
implicit lessons the students learn from the very structures and practices of
the school, and through the explicit actions of the teachers to foster the
development of critical consciousness.

Critical consciousness is composed of a set of other characteristics or actions, all of which are geared toward being critically aware of oneself and one's
world. Critical consciousness includes the practice and ability to question and
challenge, to name one's problems or obstacles, to self-evaluate, to be resistant
to suggestive leaders or demands for hyperobedience, to be able to debate, discuss, probe, compromise, and thus to see or imagine other possibilities.

The Albany Free School environment, I believe, implicitly aids in the
development of children's critical consciousness. This school has structures
and practices in place that encourage questioning, challenging, and other
critical habits. These structures and practices include the council meetings,
the Problem Wall, the all-school meetings, the nonauthoritarian relationships between the teachers and students, the diversity of the student and
teacher body, and the abundance of resources (human and other) that are
available for developing one's intelligence and academic skills.

As mentioned earlier, council meetings exist as a means for students to
assert their rights by naming their problems and working through conflicts.
In the process of these meetings, students develop critical consciousness
habits such as questioning and coming to understand one another and oneself, seeking out the core or root of problems, challenging ideas if they seem
wrong or false, debating the efficacy, reasonableness, or justice of certain
motions or amendments, probing to find out more, compromising with others if one is at an impasse, and so on. Examples of these behaviors include
the following council meetings.

> *October 15:* After lunch, I called a council meeting. On my way
> up to lunch, I had found a wrapper to one of those Vitamin C
> drinks that the kids had been eating like candy all morning. The
> rule about candy was that if wrappers are found, then they all lose
> the privilege of eating candy at school for two weeks. I went up to
> Dave at lunch, showed him the wrapper, and asked if I had to call
> a council meeting to put the consequence in effect, but he said no;

all I had to do was make sure everyone knew. So, I went around to the different tables at lunch and told the kids that the gum and candy privilege was lost again. At almost every table, the kids protested that the Vitamin C stuff was not candy. My argument was that they had been eating it like candy, so it was, for all intents and purposes, and should have the same consequences. But the kids, particularly Walter and Grayson, protested so much that I said that we will just have to call a council meeting after lunch to sort it out. So at the council meeting, it came out that Rebecca and Miranda were the ones who brought the stuff, because, they said, they had colds. But I challenged them on why they had brought so much of it and others challenged them on why others were eating it (and some even snorting it), and that both of these things lead to the conclusion that it WAS like candy in how they were consuming it. Walter made a motion that if anyone needs "medicine" like that, then they must take it to a teacher as soon as they get to school and that the teacher needs to supervise its taking, and it must be taken properly (in this case mixed with water and drunk, not eaten or snorted). This motion passed.

October 28:   The day started with a council meeting regarding lunch duty jobs needing to be done better and lunch crews needing to be shifted around so that they are more even across the days (some crews have a lot fewer students or some crews have too many younger kids, not enough of a mix). Allen made a motion that if you whine and complain about doing jobs, then you have to do dishes for two days. Walter said that you can't make such a motion because people can say what they want as long as they do the work. And Daniel exclaimed, "Free speech." Allen ultimately erased his motion. Bryan complained that it is basically the big kids doing the work because the little kids either get in the way or complain that they don't know what to do. Dave said that this is often a ploy to get out of doing something, and that the big kids are doing a disservice to themselves and to the little kids if they don't hold them (the little ones) accountable and teach them. Peter agreed, saying that the little kids CAN do the work, but they just have to be taught. There is going to be a seventh- and eighth-grade meeting to rework the crews. Dave said that all are invited to come, especially those who want to put in for jobs on a particular day.

All-school meetings serve the same critical consciousness ends as council meetings. They also allow students to realize that they have an equal voice in how the school is set up and run, which leads to a realization that one's environment is not set-in-stone and unchangeable—that, in fact, one can work to alter it. Here is an integral part of critical consciousness, this being able to imagine and work for alternatives.

The Problem Wall is also a means for students to name and work through problems. As described earlier, the Problem Wall is a chalkboard on which students write a problem they are having. This does not have the immediacy that council meetings have to work through problems, but students make a conscious and critical choice to use the Problem Wall rather than call a council meeting. This assortments of choices—council meetings, all-school meetings, and the Problem Wall—for expressing one's concerns and obstacles constantly and implicitly send the message to students that they have the right to question and challenge things and the right to imagine their future without the problem or obstacle constantly hanging over their heads, unresolved.

Critical consciousness is also about self-evaluation. At the Free School, students are not, like traditionally schooled students, constantly bombarded with outside evaluations. In other words, the hidden curriculum lesson of constant evaluation, which I detailed in an earlier chapter, was not present. The students are not graded or tested; teachers have no autonomous power to withhold privileges, and thus students do not learn to try to curry favor with "superiors" (for there really are none) to garner rewards, nor do they learn to abdicate their definition of self to others. Instead, Free School students are strong self-evaluators, recognizing when they have mastered something or are ready to stop or start an activity, recognizing (perhaps with the help of others) how to resolve conflicts or personal challenges, recognizing when they have a strong argument to make, recognizing their true motivations for doing something, and so on.

I was frequently amazed that as a teacher I could not often get students to do me a favor such as run a quick errand ("Please go get so-and-so to come here"). My students in traditional schools used to jump at that chance. Perhaps they wanted to have a break from routine or were trying to score points with me; whatever the reason, I never had a shortage of volunteers for such errands. But at the Free School I did. The students had no need to curry my favor for I had no privileges or punishments to mete out. Students at the Free School were often considerate, kind, and loving to me, but those feelings, I believe, were sincere and unconnected to any power I, as an adult, could wield. I noted in my journal as early as the fourth day of school that "most of these kids seem to like adult presence and attention," and I truly believe that this was due to the more equal balance of power. Because the students do not feel subordinate in a power dynamic between teachers and students, they are helped in coming to critically know themselves. It also helps them to more carefully think through problems and challenges and arrive at decisions that are meaningful to them rather than dictated by others. For example, in mid-September I was sitting in the Science Room doing some embroidery with a couple of girls. Sitting on the couch about six feet away were four boys (ages ten–fourteen) talking about what I gathered were off-color Web sites. This caught my attention and I asked,

> "Where is this?" and Grayson sort of nastily said, "None of your business." To that I sarcastically responded, "Well, that makes me feel really good" and then I didn't say anything more. Lawrence looked at me sort of sympathetically and then they sort of talked to each other about how they couldn't get in trouble for talking about a Web site that they only look at home, so after a bit of this, Lawrence turned to me and explained what the Web site was.

Here was an opportunity for us to talk about a subject that if addressed in a certain way could help these boys negotiate the issues and challenges of adolescent sexuality, but that in a traditional school environment would be taboo for teachers to overhear students discussing. These boys did not have to fear a negative evaluation from me for having heard their conversation, and thus we could discuss the topic in an honest and straightforward way.

Another example of how this lack of outside evaluation helps the students to self-evaluate and learn about themselves and thus develop their critical consciousness came in early October. At council meetings, students are not allowed to play with objects, write, fiddle with one another's hair, or fidget excessively; if they do, the chairperson calls them to order or sends them to the corner. Since the beginning of the school year, I had taken notes during council meetings. Everyone knew I was not just an intern teacher, but was also there as a researcher and I thought that no one ever bothered me about writing in council meetings because of this fact. However, after one council meeting an eighth-grade boy, Avalon, came up to me. In my journal that evening I wrote the following:

> After the council meeting was over, Avalon told me that I have to stop writing during council meetings, that if the other kids were called out for playing with anything in their hands, even if it wasn't disruptive, then I had no right to write during the meeting. I tried to explain to him that I was keeping track of what was said, but he said it didn't matter. I initially tried to pull the researcher trump, that I was allowed because it was a special situation, but he didn't agree with that either. I think conceivably I could have appealed to Chris [co-director of the school], but I thought maybe I needed to work this out with Avalon. I explained to him that I wanted to get down as much of what was said as possible, and so had to take notes because I couldn't remember it all. He said that he can remember it all. So, I said, would he be willing to sit down with me after every council meeting to go over what had been said. He said yes. I said, would he also agree to seek me out, not make me go hunting him

down to do it, and he said yes. I also said that if he ever did not seek me out, then that was a breakdown of our agreement and from then on I could take notes without his hassling me about it, and he said yes to that, too. We shook on it. This was an interesting interaction. He did not let me off the hook just because I was a teacher and it showed evidence of his being confident enough to approach me about this and help deal with the situation in a way that would solve my problem, but also his at the same time.

To me, this interaction provides evidence that Avalon recognized the strengths of his argument and that he could work out this conflict with me in a satisfactory manner. Again, the lack of a teacher authority dynamic fostered this student's ability to critically self-evaluate and act on that confidence of self. [Avalon never held up his side of the bargain, and so I continued to write in meetings without getting hassled by him.] Some other examples of this ability to self-evaluate and not fear teacher power authority in acting on those self-evaluations included the following, which occurred at one of the council meetings:

> *November 12:* At one point in the council meeting, Missy was summoned upstairs to take delivery of something. Trent questioned why she was allowed to leave but kids are not—he felt it was a double standard. Dave countered that kids are always allowed to leave for important things and gave a couple of recent examples. He stated there was no double standard. What was neat about this was that Trent felt empowered to bring this up and not just sullenly and silently stew over it. [Later in this same meeting the following interaction occurred.] Bhawin saw a lot of kids acting in a somewhat disruptive way and he asked, "Do you care that people are going into book bags and taking stuff?" He wanted to hear from the kids. Walter made a point that although he did care, he was bothered by the fact that at all other council meetings the teachers always tried to keep the discussion to the specific problem raised and that they discouraged generalizations of problems (like if a kid was punched, the teachers always focused on the victim and perpetrator and discouraged others from bringing up their problems with the perpetrator, saying, "If that bothers you, then call your own council meeting"), but when teachers feel that the general issue is a problem, then it is okay to generalize and force people to stay and solve the general problem (like stealing). This was a good point, I thought. Dave and Missy responded saying that the reason is that this problem has been going on for some time and kids aren't addressing the specific problem (kids aren't calling council meetings over thefts of their stuff), so we (teachers) have to step in and address the problem on

a general level. This was also a good point, I thought. Dave said, "It's really a good distinction you're making, Walter, but in this case we have to deal with the bigger picture." Just like with Trent's earlier challenge of what he thought was a double standard, this is another instance of a kid feeling empowered to really challenge the teachers on an issue they feel strongly about and not just hold it in.

Both examples give support to the idea that the nonauthoritarian relationships between teachers and students implicitly encourage students to critically examine a situation and how they truly feel about it and then speak out if they oppose something about it. The students do not mindlessly conform themselves or their opinions to what an adult says or does but instead speak their minds.

The lack of powerful outside teacher evaluations is not the only factor that allows the students to self-evaluate. The council meetings also help them to truthfully examine themselves. There were a few council meetings called on students for some wrongdoing, such as hurting someone (physically or mentally), disrespecting school or neighborhood property, and so on. At these council meetings the emphasis was rarely on punishment from outside sources (teachers), but rather on the student's "owning" the problem, devising a consequence (that the group would agree with) or a plan that would preempt him or her acting in a similar manner in the future. An excellent example is the council meeting that occurred on October 30, 2003. I quote at length from my journal.

October 30:   No activities meeting today; instead there was a council meeting called by Bridget because someone had written on the upstairs bathroom wall that "Bridget likes sex." She accused Corine, saying that Delia had told her that Corine had done it during the after-school program yesterday. Bridget said over and over throughout the meeting that she just wanted it gone, that her main beef was that it was up there. At different times she said she didn't care who did the writing, she just wants it gone, but then later she wanted Corine to admit she did it. Peter said, "Corine, do you have anything to say? We're never going to know either way if you don't say anything." Corine denied doing it. In what I consider a great intuitive fashion, Missy unearthed the animosity that existed between the girls (asking them if they were troubled in their relationship) and offered herself as a mediator between the two should they want mediation. What it boiled down to was that Corine (we all think) wrote it up there because she was mad at Bridget's constantly rebuffing her attempts at friendship. (Corine claimed that she had tried to talk to Bridget a number of times and had been pushed away. Bridget said it was always at a bad time when others were around. Missy pointed out that Corine's approach may not have been what Bridget wanted, but that they were attempts to make friends.) Corine said she'd paint over it, even though she didn't do it, "just to get it off her chest." Bridget pushed and pushed for Corine to admit doing it, but she never did. Missy also asked Bridget if she would be satisfied with Corine's agreeing to paint over it, that this was, in essence, the admittance of guilt, but not in so many words. Bridget made clear that if people don't like her, then she would rather they tell her to her face, so that she was aware of it.

In this council meeting there was much emphasis, from both teachers and students, on dealing with the root, rather than the symptoms, of a problem. I believe that this helps the students better understand themselves and the role they play in their community and the world.

Critical consciousness is not limited to just being able to self-evaluate, question, and challenge. Being critical also means having an understanding of the world and possessing the skills necessary to negotiate that world. Having "academic" skills and knowledge allows a person to function effectively in society. As discussed earlier in this chapter, at the Albany Free School, students have access to all sorts of resources that will help develop their academic skills and create knowledge about the world. Students can interact with and learn skills and information from the human resources available at the school, such as the many teachers, volunteers, and visitors who all come to the school with unique skills, bodies of knowledge, and interest areas. The students also have access to a wide array of books, games, artistic materials, equipment such as computers, microscopes, musical instruments, and so on—all of which can be utilized if one seeks to develop one's skills and abilities. These resources are generally not foisted on the students, but are there and available if the students decide to utilize them, and thus they add to an environment that implicitly fosters a critical consciousness.

The Albany Free School seeks to develop in students a critical consciousness not only through these implicit means, but also through deliberate actions taken by the teachers. During my time at the Free School, I saw what I have interpreted to be explicit steps the teachers took to help students name their obstacles, examine, and understand their world. These steps included real-world exposure, teacher-initiated dialogue to raise consciousness, teachers pushing or gently prodding on academic subjects, and aesthetic encounters.

Teachers at the Free School plan a large number of activities that offer students exposure to the world outside the school building. Their purpose, I believe, is to provide students with knowledge of a diverse array of people and environments so as to aid in the development of children's critical consciousness. When children see or interact with different people and different environments, they begin to understand that certain ideas are not all embraced equally by all people. They come to realize that some taken-for-granted ideas they have are not shared by others. This creates a cognitive dissonance and an opportunity for students to really think about the situation and wonder if their previously held beliefs are indeed valid or appropriate. For example, the teachers required that seventh- and eighth-grade students set up a weekly apprenticeship in an area of their interest. These get the students out into the world, interacting with a diverse array of people, which helps them obtain a real sense of what certain occupations are all about (through hands-on experience, not just hearing or reading about it). The teachers also plan field trips that encourage a deeper understanding of the world in which they live. Some field trips that occurred while I was at the Free School included a trip to an organic farm to understand how food is grown and why organic might be better for our environment, to the city dump to understand the implications of our "throwaway" culture, and to a local soup kitchen to get a more accurate picture of the cross section of people in our society (thus making poverty visible to those students for whom it is not a daily reality). Teachers also brought in slide shows of trips they had taken to faraway locales, such as Malawi and Afghanistan, in order to expose the children to the lives of people the world over. I believe that the Free School teachers who proposed such trips and activities felt that children will tend not to question or challenge ideas and ways of being unless confronted with some sort of evidence that these ideas might not be universal. The Albany Free School teachers, by providing students contact with diverse peoples, environments, and experiences, add to the means by which the students can see such evidence, and then reflect, question, and challenge. This is not to imply that the activities always had the desired results of students questioning and challenging, but the opportunities were there.

The teachers also take part in extended dialogues with students on all sorts of matters in many different ways. One way is through certain classes or activities that are designed to raise the students' consciousness or awareness of certain taken-for-granted ideas. For example, in our society, masculinity is generally defined in a very narrow, specific way—that boys and men have to be "tough," strong, unemotional, and so on. Through discussions in boys group meetings, teachers help students see that masculinity so strictly described is damaging and that, in fact, masculinity can be defined in many other ways. Challenges to definitions of femininity occur in the girls/goddess group meetings; and issues of sexuality and misconceptions about sex are openly discussed in the coeducational sex education classes that are held approximately two times a month. The teachers at the Free School purposefully bring these topics to conscious awareness, knowing that children receive all sorts of misinformation and one-sided views in the greater society. This is part of the reason why some teachers invited students from the Queer Youth group at the high school to be interns. In my journal on October 20th, I wrote about the discussion at a teachers meeting when we decided to issue that invitation:

Mike B. talked about his idea of getting some Queer Youth from the Albany High School Gay Student Association to come into the school to show that people are just people. He raised the question of what would be the best way to have this issue broached so that the most kids would be exposed to it, but at the same time they wouldn't feel that stuff was being pushed down their throats. He didn't want there to just be this one class in sex-ed class about this topic and then everyone would think, "Oh, they've been exposed to the ideas and so now there is no longer any homophobia here." What he and other teachers felt would be the best thing was to have those high school kids become a part of school somehow, say, to intern here one afternoon a week, etc. to really start to establish relationships and have their radar tuned to homophobic statements and then maybe call council meetings on them, or even teach a sex ed class after they have established relationships. The feeling was that a constant open presence of some openly homosexual individuals might help to solve the problem, not just talking about it in one class meeting.

Another way teachers attempt to initiate dialogue is in their responses to student comments. These responses are done to purposefully awaken in the students the realization that events and situations are not set in stone. On the first day of school when some of the students griped about a couple of the new rules, Missy shot back with the statement: "There are no victims here. If you want to change things, call an all-school meeting and challenge it." Teachers' responses to students' comments in council meetings, all-school meetings and other environments within the school also serve to help the students probe deeper, to get under the surface. For example, in mid-October, Dave called a council meeting about Grayson speaking much too colorfully within hearing distance of the street. In the course of the council meeting, the teachers asked Grayson to look deep within himself to try to figure out why he might behave in a certain way and to find the root of the problem himself. In countless other council meetings the teachers tried to help students seek their deeper causes for behaviors. Teacher comments or responses in various meetings and interactions also help students to see various sides to issues. For example, during the all-school meeting in which we were discussing whether to lift the ban on handheld video games, the kids got to hear full rationales for why these games had been banned in the first place; they were thus hearing a side of an argument that they had, up to that point, not been completely aware of or considered.

Sometimes teachers make statements on their own that are not in response to student comments and these statements are attempts to challenge students' definitions and ideas. An example occurred in mid-October at lunchtime. Intern teacher Michael made an announcement about how concerned he was about food wasting at lunch, that if meat or vegetables are left on the table (meals are served family style at lunch) and are largely untouched, then this food should not be put into compost but should be saved so that people could eat it later. He said, "We are so blessed with so much good food. It just kills me to see so much of it go to waste." Up to that point, the kids had apparently been unthinkingly tossing into the compost bucket full bowls of perfectly fine food simply because it had been dished out and put on the table. Michael's comments were an attempt to spur them to reconsider their definition of trash. I also tried my hand at prompting redefinitions. On October 21, the following interaction occurred between six-year-old Ursala and me.

> After lunch I was in the big room with Callie, Sarah, Daisy, and Blair where the girls were doing beauty shop and putting makeup on each other. Ursala came in and wanted Sarah to put lipstick on her. Ursala then asked me if it looked good. Instead of just saying yes, I thought about how she is being socialized to feel that her looks improve with makeup, so I said to her, "Do you see lipstick on me? I think you can look good without lipstick."

And on October 31, I made the following observations in my journal.

> Daisy was dressed up as a princess [for our Halloween parade], and she said to me, "Do I look pretty?" The girl is only eight years old, but is so focused on how she appears; she wears a lot of makeup and has frequently asked about how she looks. Can kids her age be worked on to see that their focus on superficial things is harmful to themselves? Or is her family and the greater culture too strong to counteract? Then again, if she never hears an alternate message, then the stronger culture will, of course, prevail, so maybe it certainly wouldn't hurt for her to get some "deprogramming" at school even if it won't have a lasting effect.

Teacher-initiated discussions also helped students challenge and discuss events in society. For example, in August, a proposal went before the Albany City Council regarding a daytime curfew for children that would limit them from being outside school grounds during the school day. Because this would have serious repercussions for the Free School students' mobility, Dave raised the issue with his seventh- and eighth-grade class. Together they probed why such a proposal had been put forth, what their specific points of contention were about it, and what they wanted to do about the situation, if anything. Another example concerned the Free Trade Agreement of the Americas (FTAA) meeting held in Miami in November 2003. Intern teacher Adam initiated discussions on what this was all about and what results such agreement might have globally. A further example, again with Adam being the initiating teacher, was his offer of an activity of listening to the radio program "Democracy Now" and having a postprogram discussion on it. In many ways, these teacher discussions with students can be seen as the critical pedagogy method of dialogue. In these conversations, the Free School teacher is not imposing ideas on the students or "banking" ideas into them but is re-presenting concepts and ideas and asking them to examine them in a different way.

In addition to real-world exposure and teacher dialogue with students, the Albany Free School teachers also explicitly guide development of critical consciousness through pushing or gently prodding the study of academic subjects. As I mentioned previously, critical consciousness involves not just being able to question and challenge, but also having the skills to negotiate in the world. By being available to student requests for academic teaching and gently prodding the students to develop their academic skills, the teachers are explicitly working to develop in students another aspect of critical consciousness.

The last way in which I have identified the Free School teachers as explicitly or actively working to develop the students' critical consciousness is in their use of aesthetic encounters. Free School teachers take the children to live performances, show them films, and share literature with them that challenge status quo beliefs. For example, while I was at the Free School, students had the opportunity to attend a handicapped dance troupe performance and the plays *Anne Frank* and *Dr. Faustus*; they had the choice of viewing such films as *Whale Rider, A Raisin in the Sun, Look Who's Coming to Dinner, Billy Elliott,* and *Flatliners;* they could watch such documentaries as *Bowling for Columbine, This Is What Democracy Looks Like, The Devil's Playground,* and *Media Coverage in a Time of War;* and they could also listen to readings of Native American stories, the books *Dude, Where's My Country?* and *Roll of Thunder, Hear My Cry.* What all these artistic productions have in common is that they raise topics or present viewpoints on issues that are not often fully present in mainstream culture. For example, many of these productions raise issues of race, religion, or gender inequity or injustice. Or they present a point of view that many had never considered (e.g., *Bowling for Columbine, This Is What Democracy Looks Like,* and *Media Coverage in a Time of War* argue that our media greatly influences the development of misperceptions). Or they depict stories of groups of people or situations that are not broadly understood in society (*The Devil's Playground* teaches about the *Rumspringe* period in the life of Amish youth, *Dude, Where's My Country?* presents several alternative arguments about the September 11 tragedy and the Bush presidency, *This Is What Democracy Looks Like* illustrates that the World Trade Organization protests in Seattle were much more peaceable than the mainstream media presented them, and the handicapped dance troupe performance showed that society's assumptions that people in wheelchairs can't dance is absolutely untrue). After each of these activities, the teachers attempted to initiate discussions of students' reactions to the production and the issues raised.

Even with all these explicit guiding steps to developing critical consciousness in the Free School students, some progressive educators, particularly critical pedagogues, might argue that these teachers are not going far
enough in helping the students problematize their world, and that what they
are doing is not intentional and concentrated enough to effectively debunk
power and inequity or help the students develop a language for understanding who they and others are. That may be true, and there are no guarantees
that the Free School students' critical consciousnesses gain in development,
but it seems to me to make sense that if the opportunities are there and the
students take them, there's bound to be some positive effect, however
infinitesimal. This may not satisfy some critics, but what the Free School
teachers are doing is so much more than many traditional teachers do to
raise their students' awarenesses about the world that I thus feel secure in
stating that the Albany Free School is embodying, at the very least, the spirit
of progressive educators' beliefs about critical consciousness.

DEVELOPMENT OF DEMOCRATIC IDEALS AND SKILLS

In progressive educators' vision, the development of critical consciousness is
a necessary component of an education for liberation; another vital component is the development of democratic ideals and skills. Such ideals include
having concerns for social justice, and such skills involve being able to act
on one's critical understanding of justice issues in a politically active way.
The Albany Free School's liberatory curriculum works to develop these democratic ideals and skills in their students and, just as with the development of
critical consciousness, the school itself strives both implicitly and explicitly
to develop these sensibilities and abilities.

The Albany Free School environment is one in which children's concerns for democratic social justice can begin to emerge, simply by virtue of
the school's day-to-day structures and practices. Social justice concerns, in
my mind, encompass caring for and respecting not only other humans, but
also the natural environment, and the Albany Free School implicitly encourages the development of both aspects of democratic citizenship. The council
meetings, the nonhierarchical relationships between students and teachers,
the diversity of people in the school, the circle ceremony, the absence of a
mandated curriculum, the many field trips out into nature (particularly out
to the school's woodland property), and the composting/recycling practices—
all foster these ideals.

Council meetings not only serve the development of children's critical
consciousness, they also help develop empathy and the ability to truly hear
and value the voices of others. At council meetings, the children hear about
others' life situations and about how they feel about events, interactions, and
so on. Because the school is composed of a diverse body of individuals,
people from different social classes, of different genders, different sexual

orientations, different ethnic, cultural, and racial backgrounds, and different ages, the stories and experiences that the children hear in the council meetings (and elsewhere at the school) are not homogeneous or identical to their own. The council meetings provide safe opportunities for people to speak openly and thus offer children opportunities to consider other points of view and life circumstances. An example of a council meeting in which students were able to put themselves in another's shoes occurred in mid-September. Six-year-old Blair had called this meeting about eight-year-old Anthony aggressively putting his hands around Blair's throat in an attempt to get the baseball bat from her. Blair explained over the course of the council meeting that this triggered memories of her father doing that to her and her mother and that it scared her and made her feel very bad. The children, especially Anthony, got to hear about Blair's past home situation, and about how certain actions made her feel. As mentioned in chapter 4, during council meetings one person at a time "has the floor" and, as Blair spoke, she had everyone's attention (for the most part). Anthony also had the opportunity to speak and both children's voices were equally valued and heard.

Children at the Albany Free School not only have opportunities to hear the voices and concerns of their peers, but also the chance to hear from adults. Teachers at the Free School, because they do not hold excessive authority and power over students and thus do not need to create a false persona of "hardness" or "a thick skin" to maintain this power, can speak of pain they experience from students' treatment or from certain circumstances that occur. For example, both Michael and I called separate council meetings about Rebecca, Miranda, and Delia, eight- and nine-year-old girls who consistently refused to clean up their messes. And Adam, in late October, called a council meeting concerning some boys he had taken to the museum who had disrespected his requests for them to be safe (i.e., not ride escalator handrails, not go in the street, etc.). Instead of punishing these children for their actions, which might occur in traditional schools, teachers called council meetings about them and were able to voice grievances about the situations. In all three meetings, Michael, Adam, and I explained how we didn't want to approach the kids as police officers. And in Adam's meeting he went on to say, "If I make you mad when I ask you to be safe or to do something, then say so instead of just being disrespectful to me, because that disrespect feels so bad. I don't want to be just some authority figure to you." The kids were thus able to hear some of who we were and what our intentions and desires were in regards to how we wanted to relate with the students. There is certainly no guarantee that hearing others in council meetings automatically leads to a development in empathy in all children, but the opportunities are there for children to develop a degree of hearing the voices of others and learning to care for others, critical aspects of developing social justice mindsets.

Another practice at the Albany Free School that, I believe, works to engender caring for and empathizing with others is the circle ceremony.

Whenever a person is sick, going through a troubled period (e.g., experiencing a death in the family—human or animal), getting ready for surgery, leaving the community, and so on, the circle ceremony is held, usually at the beginning of the day, after breakfast. Everyone gathers in the upstairs big room and forms a circle, with some of the upstairs kids sitting on the teachers' or downstairs kids' laps. The ceremony begins with an explanation of what the circle is about, and then moves into a visualization process when someone (usually a teacher) asks everyone to hold hands and imagine healing going on or sending out good thoughts. The ceremony generally ends with the singing of "Dear Ones"—the lyrics of which are "Dear Ones, Dear Ones, shall I tell you what I know? You have given us your treasures and I love you so." The song is sung two or three times and then everyone hums it another time. Once done, everyone disperses. While I was at the Free School, we had a number of circle ceremonies.

> October 2: There was a circle today for Elizabeth. It began by lighting three candles and asking Elizabeth to tell her story, which was that she has a tumor on her eye and that is causing her to lose her sight. She is going to have surgery next week, and she explained what that would entail and that her eye would be very red when she came back, but that it was just a sign of her healing. Then Missy had us all hold hands and imagine Elizabeth healing, seeing well again, etc. Then we sang "Dear Ones" and then it was over.

> November 3: After activities meeting we had a circle for Colleen in which we talked about where she was (intensive care) and what the problem was (major asthma attack), then Chris and Mike both did some positive visualization, telling the kids to close their eyes and imagine Colleen's lungs filling up and the cilia filling with blood, and her being able to blow up a balloon. Then we sang "Dear Ones," but before we started Walter questioned why we sang it, I think saying that the past tense of "you have given us your treasures" didn't apply in that she wasn't dead and also questioning what treasures meant. Chris, Nancy and Missy answered him saying that treasures could mean anything, not necessarily something you buy in a store. So then we sang "Dear Ones" and it was over.

Two others were farewell circles, one to an intern named Jon who left early on in the year and one for me in late November.

In my teacher interviews I asked about this ceremony and its meaning for the teachers. Dave responded that

> I feel like some of the things we do, what I guess you would call our ceremonies, or our rituals that we have at school, that typically

come up when someone has died, or something has died, a goldfish, you know, anywhere from a goldfish to a parent has passed away, we have a ceremony where we sit in a circle and we light candles, we sing a song. And I feel like that is connecting kids to something bigger than our human context. But also, we do things like that when someone's going in for surgery, you know, and I know there are scientific studies about prayer and things. And we don't call it prayer, but I think that with the candles and the singing, the sitting in a circle, and the fact that the whole school comes together at that time, creates this feeling of, well that person's miles away in a hospital, but we're here supporting them and we're still contacting them. And, you know, we see it come true, we see the effects of it, I mean, I just can't tell you how many times people have responded quicker than they thought they were going to, and I know that you can't totally attribute that to our presence, but, but, people do feel a part of a community here. People's grandparents, people's parents are included, because it's such an open and loving place, I think they know that we're singing for them, they feel supported.

Chris stated that

The times I think that it [connection to others] comes out and I think are very important, are when somebody's seriously ill, like Colleen was in the hospital the other day, with her breathing trouble, or some one of the kids, some of the kids' family, is going to die, then we'll all come together, the whole school, and light a candle, sing "Dear Ones," send positive thoughts, feeling thoughts, or what- ever, you know, toward others in need, you know. There's no ques- tion that one of the things that we're doing there, other than we believe it works, is, you're modeling praying for others, thinking outside of ourselves.

The Albany Free School teachers clearly believe that this ceremony, this practice of the circle, is a way for school members to feel connected and care for one another's emotional and physical well-being. Thus, I see it as a way to develop social justice concerns.

One last aspect of the Albany Free School that I believe implicitly emphasizes caring for others is the lack of a standardized, mandated curricu- lum. Children's voices and choices are honored and this comes out most especially because they are free to spend their time as they choose (with the exception of council meetings). When one's dignity, autonomy, and basic humanity are so acknowledged, I believe one tends to then honor that in others. The school's lack of compulsion and other discussed structures and practices imply to children that each person at the school is worthy of respect and is a valued individual.

Not only do I believe that the Albany Free School structures and practices implicitly encourage the development of caring and concern for other humans, I also believe that the structures and practices lead to caring and concern for the physical environment. Although the Albany Free School is in an urban environment, the children spend far more time outdoors than many of their traditionally schooled counterparts. In addition to visiting and playing in the many parks within walking distance, the children also have many opportunities to go hiking and camping, visit nature preserves and other parks, use the school's low ropes course on its woodland property, and garden both in a lot by the school and at the woodland property. Such opportunities develop a sense of connection to and appreciation of the natural world. Connection and appreciation, then, in turn I believe, translate to concern and caring for the physical environment.

Other practices that leads to concern for the physical environment are those of composting and recycling. At the end of each meal, every child is responsible for taking his or her plate to the kitchen to scrape it—placing compostable items (those that can be fed to the chickens, which belong to Free School community members) into a bin, and separating out what cannot be composted (meat, milk). The school also has several recycling bins so that kids can sort those "trash" items that can be sent to recycling and those that must go to the dump. These two practices implicitly place a value on the physical environment and thus encourage the children to develop a similar mind-set.

Not only do the basic structures and day-to-day practices of the Free School implicitly work to develop in students the democratic ideals of social justice, the teachers at the school also engage in deliberate, explicit actions to this same end. The Albany Free School teachers' actions to develop their students' critical consciousness simultaneously develop students' democratic sensibility for social justice. In addition to the teachers' explicit actions to raise students' awareness of inequity in our society, discussed earlier, the teachers do other specific things to raise awareness of the anti-democratic, dehumanizing, and anti-environment forces at work in our society. The things I noticed the teachers doing to help develop in the students habits of caring for others and the environment included enforcing the many respect-related rules, calling council meetings on or discussing within the council meetings issues of respect for others and issues of the school's physical environment, suggesting specific activities or behaviors that manifest caring behaviors, and offering activities that show the value and beauty of nature.

In chapter 5 I detailed the school rules that the teachers enforce at the Free School. Many directly concern developing behaviors of respect for others: the stop sign rule, the rule about not running around and screaming indoors, and the rule about not cursing in the backyard or out in public. These are all attempts to help students realize that their actions can offend or disturb others and that when one is part of a community, one must be sensitive to the rights and sensibilities of others. Dave explained such rules to me.

Part of our view of what it means to be an individual is the relationship to the people and the community around you; that's a big part
of being a whole person, being interrelated, and you know, to use
the seventh and eighth-grade as an example, to know that your
classroom is above the kindergarten, where kids sleep, you do not
have free reign up here to do whatever you want. You know, you
can listen to music, but to a certain level. You can't stomp around
up here after lunchtime, kids are trying to sleep, you know, I mean
it's related. So, I hope we're getting that across to them.

A final rule to make students aware of their effects on others concerns
committing to activities. Apparently, in past years, teachers had suggested
activities, particularly field trips, and certain students had enthusiastically
signed up. But when the time came for the trip or activity, some students
would opt out. The teachers had counted on the students and made reser-
vations or obtained prepaid admissions and when students backed out at the
last minute, the person running the activity was put into a difficult spot. So
the teachers imposed a rule this year that if a student agreed to do some
activity or go on a particular field trip, then the student had to do it. This
was an explicit attempt on the part of teachers to say to the kids, "Hey! Your
decisions affect other people's actions and so you must be courteous and
thoughtful to others and truly think through the decisions you make."
    Another method for developing habits of caring is for teachers to call
council meetings when students are unkind to each other, or speak up within
other meetings or in various interactions when they observe kids manifesting
uncaring behaviors. The following examples illustrate this practice.
    On the third day of school, Missy observed Delia, Callie, Rebecca, and
Miranda excluding Daisy from hanging out with them. Because Daisy did not
get mad and call a council meeting regarding this, Missy called a council
meeting on Daisy for not standing up for herself. In my journal that day I
wrote the following.

> After lunch, Missy called a council meeting on Daisy for not calling
> a council meeting of her own about Rebecca, Callie, Miranda, and
> Delia excluding her. Missy said that she was here at this school to
> learn open-heartedness and caring and that these were more impor-
> tant than things like the ABCs, and that she is here to notice and
> to care. And if that is not what these girls want, then maybe they
> should go someplace else. As the meeting progressed, the four ac-
> cused girls defended that they were not being exclusionary, but
> Dave and Missy and others explained how through body language,
> etc. they were. The kids were all given a chance to talk and some
> (the four accused) were especially encouraged to talk. The meeting
> seemed to have no resolution. Bhawin suggested a boycott against

the girls' "store," but then it came back to the fact that the meeting was called about Daisy not standing up for herself and that if she doesn't start calling meetings then Missy and others would call council meetings on her.

Another example of a teacher pointing out the importance of caring occurred on the fourth day of school when Dave asked me to keep an eye on the seventh and eighth graders' gossiping and being catty. He had noticed on a computer that someone had changed the screen saver to read, "Camille likes Peter" and this raised his concern over the kids talking behind one another's backs. He changed it to read, "Gossip Sucks" and was thus trying to communicate to the kids the importance of their being nicer, kinder, more caring people.

Yet another example occurred on October 9 when seventh grader Alison called a council meeting on Bryan alleging that he had broken into her locker and taken some things. In the course of the meeting, which was supposed to stay specific to that one crime, other students started bringing up particular beefs they also had about Bryan. In my journal I noted the following.

Missy said that she didn't like this turn, that it was beginning to sound like a lynching against Bryan, and that she didn't want that. She said that they should all call their own council meetings about Bryan if they had had it with him. She was empathizing with Bryan and said that if she were in his shoes that she would be feeling really attacked and ganged up on. [A bit later] Missy again reiterated that if she were Bryan right now she would feel really defensive. She again said that each person should call their own council meeting, that they should "eat whatever he gives them until they're done." She was REALLY opposed to the ganging up feeling.

Another example occurred on October 16 when I observed a seventh/ eighth-grade class meeting in which the topic of discussion was their somewhat out-of-hand behavior. The kids all started to blame it on Conner, a sixth grader; they were talking about his being annoying and a pest and causing their negative behavior. I noted the teacher's response.

Dave said even if Conner truly is annoying that they were not doing anything effective to deal with it, rather they were allowing the situation to create more problems. He said that they need to get creative with how they deal with Conner, and not let his behavior have power over theirs. Dave also tried to get the kids to see that Conner is lonely and that they should have compassion for him, but that they should also confront him for his annoyingness.

A final example deals with encouraging children to be respectful to the neighbors. Megan called a council meeting on October 23, for she had gotten word that some of the eight- and nine-year-old girls had been playing "Ding Dong Ditch" in the neighborhood (ringing doorbells and then running away). The teachers (and several students) expressed real concerns about how disrespectful and uncaring such an activity was and that the girls needed to do something to make amends. A motion passed saying that the girls had to write apology letters and then come up with a consequence for themselves.

All these council meeting discussions were specifically geared to making students aware that uncaring behaviors were unwelcome at the school, and that one should behave in ways that are just, kind, and respectful toward others. Albany Free School teachers, to emphasize those behaviors, also planned a number of activities that involved caring acts. On Halloween, the teachers handed out UNICEF boxes for kids to take with them while trick-or-treating, thus opening their eyes to the needs of people in other communities and countries. The school also has a strong connection to a Buddhist nun who lives in a temple on land adjacent to the school's woodland property. Several years ago, the Free School teachers organized construction crews of students to help in the building of a Peace Pagoda near the temple. To this day, teachers still plan activities in conjunction with the nun, Jun-san. For example, while I was at the school Jun-san participated in a peace walk and Megan arranged for some students to accompany her. The students also took part in the tenth anniversary celebration of the Peace Pagoda by performing a dance and making origami paper cranes. These happenings always explicitly (and implicitly) concerned caring for others, promoting world peace, and so on. Similar activities that teachers planned included going to the hospital to visit six-year-old Colleen, and having a "grooming activity." What precipitated this latter activity was that Carrie (upstairs teacher) commented in a teachers meeting one afternoon that eight-year-old Rebecca was looking a bit haggard and messy lately, and didn't seem as "sparkly" as she used to. Someone suggested that maybe she needed some physical affection, perhaps in the form of hair brushing. The next day, Missy brought out a suitcase of combs, brushes, hair clips, and so on and began brushing Rebecca's hair. Other students got into it and a whole barber shop/beauty parlor activity emerged. I myself got a brush-through by a couple of girls and it felt wonderful. Surely any student who received a similar treatment felt the same and thus knew that caring for others feels good and right.

Teachers also work on actively drawing the students into showing concern for their physical environment. They do this by enforcing certain school rules, calling council meeting when the physical environment was abused, and suggesting activities that would underscore the value and beauty of nature.

As mentioned in chapter 5, certain rules were in place regarding maintenance of the physical space—cleaning up after oneself, fixing things that one broke, not leaving food or food wrappers lying about, and doing one's weekly lunch duty. By holding the students responsible for all these things, teachers were working to get the message across that, as part of a community, one has responsibilities to uphold and care for the physical environment.

Teachers emphasize these responsibilities when they call council meetings about certain messes they find in and around the school. When Megan and I noted in early November that some of the apples we had picked had been thrown around and crushed, I called a council meeting to point out the inappropriateness of that action and the importance of those who did it to clean it up. And back in September when many of the kids had been making forts in the vacant lot next to Missy's house, Missy called a council meeting to announce the she was closing down access to the lot because it was such a mess and needed to be cleaned up.

Teachers also emphasize the importance of having respect for the physical environment by planning activities that explicitly point out the beauty and value of the natural world. Dave occasionally offered classes on animal rights discussions and issues; Bhawin showed some nature films, including a great one on insects entitled *Microcosmos*. The teachers also frequently offered nature arts activities in which individuals would go out into parks or the woods to collect natural materials and create sculptures that emphasized the natural beauty of these items. Teachers also talked about the wonder of being out in nature. In his interview, Dave recounted his experience.

> I feel like the whole world is alive. You know, sort of the Gaia concept, and I'm just one manifestation of it. It's probably my deepest spiritual belief, it's how my spirituality expresses itself. It's hard to, it's hard to teach that. I try to, but I want to be careful not to impose my value structure. . . . So, I try to talk about that, but the way I do it, typically, is not so much through a class setting, although if things, when we were talking about animal rights and things like that, you know, I'm able to express my beliefs about our place as humans in the scope of things. But I more get to express that in informal conversations with kids. I'll tell the kids about a story of being in the woods, you know, sort of feeling like you disappear, you can just become still and watch and be part of something bigger than yourself. And kids are more likely, and this is just my personal experience, more likely to hear it in that setting than if you are sort of preaching from the pulpit in the classroom, even if you're doing it in a non-pushy way. You can feel them resist that, so it's in my awareness as a teacher, but I'm careful not to impose it, but give examples of how I see it happening.

Again, as with critical consciousness, these actions on the part of the teachers to develop the democratic ideals of social justice in students come with no guarantees that they will get the desired results. But I truly believe that an effect in this direction is bound to occur.

In both implicit and explicit teachings of the democratic ideal of social justice at the Albany Free School, the message is sent that every person and the physical environment is of ultimate value and worth. Because students get practice in sympathizing and empathizing, they experience what it means to interact with others as fully human beings and come to appreciate the value of such interactions. Educators at the Free School attempt to instill in students as part of their critical consciousnesses an in-depth concern for the plight of others, an understanding of the dehumanizing forces in society, and a desire to make all of greater society a place where every person and voice is valued equally.

According to progressive educators, particularly critical pedagogues, developing critical consciousness and awakening concerns for social justice are only part of the characteristics or factors necessary for a liberatory education. One more crucial element is still needed—a desire for and skill in taking political action. Paulo Freire, in *The Pedagogy of the Oppressed*, wrote about the process of praxis: it has two elements and both are required for achieving our ontological vocation to be fully human. The first part of praxis is reflection—critically looking at society and situations—here is where critical consciousness comes in. The second part of praxis is the action component—acting against society's dehumanizing forces in a manner guided by one's critical awareness. Both components—reflection and action—are necessary, for without action all you have is verbalism or idle chatter, and without reflection all you have is activism, which is just action for action's sake. Freire believed that to be fully human, to play a role in one's identity formation and thus take part in the quest for freedom, requires that one is able to both name the world (using one's critical consciousness) and act to change it. Thus, to Freire and other critical pedagogues, a very strong connection exists between education and politics. An education that serves to develop one's critical consciousness also needs to encourage, model, and illustrate past examples of people taking action in the world.[7] The Albany Free School provides just such an education, again through both the implicit means of the school's day-to-day structures and practices and the explicit actions of its teachers.

The Albany Free School environment, in addition to implicitly encouraging the development of critical consciousness and social justice concerns, also implicitly develops skills in taking political action. The Problem Wall, the stop rule, all-school meetings and council meetings all give the students practice in democratic citizenship skills, and in having a voice that is heard and respected regarding the governance of the school.

As discussed earlier, the Problem Wall is a means for children to express concerns and conflicts. Simply writing up one's problem on this board is an example of a politically oriented action in that the child is seeking to create different conditions. The stop rule is another standard practice that the children can employ to change their situation. As mentioned briefly in chapter 5, whenever a person is doing something to a student that the student does not like, then the student can tell the person to "stop" and if the person does not stop, the student can then call a council meeting. This simple action is a model of the first steps that politically active persons take when they want to change events in society. They say "stop" and then work from there.

The council meetings and the all-school meetings offer the Albany Free School students opportunities to directly influence how the school is run. The one all-school meeting that was held while I was there, which I described in chapter 5, gives specific evidence of the students voicing their opinions by voting on new rules for the school. And at the council meetings, the students can express their opinions on motions or amendments, they can take part in debating, compromising, and seeking out facts, and so on. From both types of meetings, the children are gaining practice in the thought processes that are necessary for democratic citizenship in our society and in the steps one takes to push one's own agenda within a plurality.

Progressive educators, particularly critical pedagogues, have argued that educators interested in helping students quest for freedom need to model and show past examples of people taking action in the world; the Albany Free School teachers certainly do this. These teachers, simply by virtue of who they are, model for the students what being a politically active citizen is all about. Teachers at the Albany Free School tend to be people who are generally interested in challenging the status quo (as evidenced by their mere presence in such an alternative educational environment), and so, simply by being themselves, are modeling what political activism involves.

Not only do the teachers model taking action in the micro-society of the school when they voice their own opinions or think through actions in council meetings or all-school meetings, they also model taking political action in the wider society. For example, some teachers, during school hours, listen to a radio program called "Democracy Now," they attend protests and support rallies at the state capital building (a quick walk from the school), they prepare for other actions at various locales by making posters, pamphlets, or flyers, and they get their opinions out in other means such as publishing 'zines, making films, going to community meetings, and so on. The teachers also take part in peace walks, they utilize the Infoshop (the lending library at the nearby anarchist collective), they talk about current political issues, and they discuss past political actions they took.

In all these actions, the teachers invite, but never compel, the students to participate. When I interviewed some of the teachers, they explained this fine line between modeling and compelling.

> Dave: Most of the teachers that are at the school are active in working for social change and it's part of the reason why we're in a

school like this, but we're careful not to impose that on the kids. I do think, though, that they learn how you protest, how you voice your opinion, how you go about it.

Bhawin: I've never once coerced a kid to doing anything active; I think that's the worst thing you could do, to teach them that you have to be coerced into being an activist, that's horrible! You know, you should feel it.

Missy: I do think it is subtle, I think that it's, I don't think that you can negate the fact that whenever you're in anybody's presence that they have, you have an effect and they have an effect, I guess it depends upon your perspective, but I always feel like whatever space I'm in with someone, I would hope that my, my essence to live and to move on, and to reach for the light, to reach for whatever it is that I'm questing for, I, I hope it has an effect. . . . I prefer to lead a horse to water, but I won't make him drink.

Through all these actions, teachers are modeling how a person effectively participates in a democratic society. They demonstrate how people inform themselves on issues, how they formulate opinions, and how they act in ways they give force and voice to their opinions. A Mexican teacher's saying sums up the point I'm trying to make about Free School teachers modeling political activism: "El maestro luchando, tambien esta ensenando"— "the teacher in struggle is also teaching."[8] Because the Free School teachers are often politically active themselves in terms of standing up for what they believe in, they are modeling the very kind of critical thinking and democratic processes that politically active people employ.

The Albany Free School seems, to me, to be embodying the progressive educators' vision of a liberatory education. With all their emphasis on creating the right type of environment in which children can think through issues, particularly those concerning equity, justice, and personal problems, and with the training or modeling they provide of political actions, the Albany Free School teachers appear to be saying that they want students to take part in a quest for freedom in which students realize, name, and take action against their obstacles. I have also observed countless times what I have interpreted to be the students' quests for freedom. And I heard from Free School teachers words that suggest that they define freedom in this way as well. In other words, rather than treating critical consciousness, social justice concerns, and political action skills as separate entities, teachers and students showed me evidence that they put these all together into one process—the process of praxis.

Many things that the teachers say to the students give evidence that they see the process of praxis as one of the key concepts they teach. Over and over I heard teachers telling the kids to "use their words" or "stand up for themselves"—in other words, critically express (name) their concern (obstacle) and figure out how to solve the concern (take action). The teachers consistently encourage the children, especially during council meetings, to confront their deeper motives for doing things (reflect and name) so that they will know how to act differently in the future.

And I believe the students learned from the teachers' implicit and explicit lessons about praxis. I observed students take action by calling council meetings, or writing their concerns on the Problem Wall, or confronting someone about some trouble. I saw students critically think through problems and come to compromises or envision other solutions and realities. I observed the students act in caring ways toward others and take stands against unkindness and disrespect. Certainly, some students had a better grasp of this process of praxis than others, but what I noticed was that the kids who had been at the Free School the longest tended to be the ones who realized, named, and acted against their obstacles the most. The Free School teachers whom I interviewed agreed. When I asked if they believed that experiences at the Free School made a positive, liberatory-type difference in who the students became, they all answered in the affirmative:

> *Dave:* I think there is sort of a Free School personality that develops in kids. I think the kids who come through the Free School are really good at expressing their emotions, they tend to be pretty good problem solvers and they recognize situations, they're creative in situations about coming up with real solutions. I just see kids that I know that are now twenty or twenty-five years old that went here, they're all very confident, very self-possessed. They really know who they are. They're very clear and articulate. [The students] know what they want, they know how to get there, they recognize obstacles and they find effective ways to deal with their obstacles, and they get what they want. And they have good relationships and, you know, they're really prepared emotionally to deal with what life presents them. I see people that leave here that are beautiful people, that have good relationships, and, you know, when they become parents are great parents and they have healthy family lives. To me, that's the heart of social change, is people that do that. I see them living in community elsewhere, they learned that, too. They're healing and they're changing some of the things that are the biggest problems we have, you know, family divorces, bad parenting, things that kind of cause the other problems, like crime and things like that, so, I see them really dealing with it on the most basic, mundane level. They have positive relationships, they raise a generation of good children, you know. I suppose, you know, that that's making a difference, you know, that's giving them skill[s] that [aren't] necessarily made a priority in other places, so we're providing something unique.

They're getting something here that they're not going to get at very many other places.

Missy: [The school] encourages them [the students] to use whole body thinking, mind, heart, spirit, truth. I'm going to encourage them to problem solve, to look at what they love and do things that make [them happy]. We acknowledge the kids having a sort of knowing nature, that is, if anything derogatory or negative is being said toward them, they don't have to eat it, they can challenge it, and I think that's the beginner stage and it grows and develops as they go up to seventh and eighth grade. I think if they [the students] can tackle their own pollutants of their own mind, and I think that's what we help them work with, maybe it will give them ground for knowing that they can stop someone from the outside, someone in the outside that is having an effect on your world.

Bhawin: If anything I think that we're just, we're teaching kids to be real, we're teaching kids that who you are matters, and who you are is important and you can be whatever you want to be, you know, as long as you're honest about it and you feel good about it and you're not hurting other people. I think that it's kind of like the bedrock of what we do here, is teaching kids to just be real and be who they are and be able to act upon that and not feel like they can't say something when they feel something's wrong or when something is great. And some people argue that that's not a good thing because you get out in the real world and, you know, you've got to just do what people say. I don't buy that, I mean some people buy that and they're like, okay, we've got to teach kids to be sheep, you know, 'cause that what's they're going to be anyway. I like to think, and from what I have seen from kids coming back, I really believe that the kids that come out of here are very, you know, are very confident people that have a really strong sense of who they are, they know their place in the world, they feel comfortable being, you know, who they are and what they're doing, they don't have to feel like they need to be, you know, whatever, doctors or lawyers. . . . I see them being very comfortable with who they are, being happy doing whatever and some people are really successful and some people are just kind of doing, maybe working in a restaurant or something, being a cook or whatever, you know, just pretty basic, service jobs or something. And they're happy, because they're comfortable with who they are and I think that's really important. And I think, I notice a lot of kids are very mature and I think that goes along with the sense of knowing who you are, they don't have to be anything, they don't feel like they have to play a role. And I really feel it's a big part of the school, I don't think that it's something that's written down anywhere, but I think it happens because all of us realize, as individuals that in our culture or a society or whatever you want to call it, there's a lack of that. And I think especially in kids 'cause kids aren't, you know, they're not treated as individuals, they're not respected for their, for their unique talents and their unique way of being and, you know, I think that's something that they get here.

Chris: I think there are many, many sorts of core values that we want to encourage children to develop. . . . We want kids to think for themselves, not to be followers, to be original thinkers. [We also want to encourage people who will do] something about [their] problems, not just put up with a bad situation or run from it or just rebel against it, but face it head on, honestly and, you know, try to muster [their] resources and do something about it, change it, if [they] don't like it, change it. [And because this has] been their experience all the time in the school, you know, taking some measure of responsibility for the, for the larger whole and I think that transfers over to them as adults. The world at large, the world around them, not being passive about things, involved, being active about it, building an active connection. So. I'm not sure they all vote, they had a lot of practice doing that at school. But beyond that, I think they just, they'll tend to, not all of them, but you'll see them tending more to want to get involved in things and make some, make a difference in one faction or another, in a directly political way or, you know, maybe they're not going to be directly politics bent. Still, you see them being engaged.

These teachers' words clearly express that they see the purpose of education and of their curriculum at the Free School as being liberatory—that students should be encouraged to develop skills, abilities, and ideals that will allow them to become whole, self-determined people within a democratic society.

When many people first hear of a school in which the students are not mandated or compelled to learn anything specific, they assume that the school has no curriculum and that the students never learn anything. I hope that, through this chapter, I have shown otherwise, that there is, in fact, a very full and rich curriculum in place at the Albany Free School. That curriculum is a multidimensional intertwining of academic and social/emotional curricula, and these combine to create an overall liberatory curriculum that is both greater than the sum of its parts and an active embodiment of what progressive educators had in mind in their alternative vision for education.

CHAPTER SEVEN

VERY DIFFERENT STUDENTS AND TEACHERS

In the previous two chapters, I explored how the Albany Free School seems to embody the progressive educators' alternative vision of education in terms of learning settings and timings, curriculum, and materials used, and, by association, the role students and teachers play in this very different school. I now turn my focus to an explicit examination of the role of students and teachers in this school, and again argue that the Albany Free School is actively embodying progressive educators' visions of what education should be about.

THE STUDENTS

As discussed earlier, in most traditional schools students are expected to be passive recipients of information and experiences, to compete with one another for scarce resources, to submit to evaluation by others and largely abdicate their responsibility to evaluate and work on themselves, and to obey authority on issues of school governance and operations. Conversely, students in progressive educators' visions of schools are expected to be active shapers of experiences and curriculum, to cooperate, not compete, with one another, to critically evaluate themselves (an aspect of the student's role fully explored in the previous chapter's discussion of the development of critical consciousness) and work on their problems and challenges, and to aid in the school's governance and operations.

The Albany Free School students create their own individual curriculums based on what is most meaningful to them and that they have an interest in. Students are not compelled to attend classes or to study a specific canon of subjects, and thus control of learning rests squarely in their hands. Free School students do not passively receive an education; instead, they actively make their own education by constructing meaning through their chosen activities. Students request that certain classes or activities occur (either at the daily activities meeting or in one-on-one conversations with

teachers or other students), and sometimes teachers propose certain activities, which the students have the right to accept or reject. The students are
thus the sole decision makers as to what they do at school (again, within the
limits of safety and interpersonal respect).

While I was at the Free School, I constantly observed students initiating their own activities. I often simply watched students interacting with
one another. Frequently, they were playing games, showing each other how
to do something, or talking with one another, and so on. The majority of my
journal entries, however, relate how the students interacted with me, a teacher.
I recorded how students often asked if I would do something with them,
perhaps going with them to the museum, library, or park, or playing a game;
or they asked if I would help them to figure out something, or look up
something, or teach them how to do something. Or students would simply,
again on their own initiative, join in on an activity that was already going
on, such as a game, lesson, book reading, or film showing.

Examples of student initiation of activities abound in my daily journal
entries; a few are excerpted as follows:

September 24:   After breakfast I was cornered by Lawrence again to
play Quiddler. Around 10:50, I did some sewing with the some of
the young girls at their request.

September 25:   After activities meeting, Lawrence asked me if I
wanted to play Quiddler, and then asked me if I wanted to play
Dungeons and Dragons. I told him I did not know how to play, but
was willing to learn, so Antoin and I both learned at the same
time. Lawrence gave us character sheets (already made up) and we
went into the reading room to play. So it was me, Antoin, Jonathan,
and Marshall. It seems a creative game that requires imagination,
but is very difficult to pick up, I find. It requires use of special dice
and a guide book as well. We played until 10:00 when I had
promised to take Jonathan and others to the museum. It was 11:00
when we got back and time for math class with Miranda and
Callie. I found Miranda and tested her on her 6s and then put up
the 7s for her to learn. She, too, is picking them up fast. I think
maybe we should do two tables a week. Then Callie joined us and
she reviewed her 7s tables on the board. While she did that, I
checked her "homework" and graded it (she said she wanted me
to). She got 98 out of 100 correct, and she said it only took her
about ten minutes to do all 100. At 11:35 we stopped for the day,
to continue tomorrow. Callie then wanted to play Set, and Bridget
joined us and wanted to as well. So I got out Set and we played
for a bit, Lawrence joined in, as did Daniel, and Travis. Then
Lawrence wanted to play Quiddler, so we branched off from the

Set game and started to play Quiddler (Lawrence, me, Avalon, and for a bit Anthony). Then lunch was called.

October 7:   After activities meeting, Callie, Corine, and Colleen wanted to do knitting. After about forty-five minutes of this, I got out *Hatchet* to read with Lawrence. We were going to read in the Middle Room, but no one else came and Lawrence wanted other people to hear it, too. So we went into the Big Room where there were a couple more people and began to read. At the end we had read two chapters, and Marshall, Ajay, Anthony, and Jonathan had all been listening at some point or another. After lunch, a bunch of kids, Jon, and I went to Lincoln Park to play soccer. We played for about thirty minutes and little by little kids drifted away to play on the monkey bars and jungle gym. At 1:50 we started back to the school so that we'd get back in time for the 2:00 spelling bee. On the walk back, some kids asked me to quiz them on their spelling words, which I did. When we got back, Ajay wanted me to read some more to him from *Hatchet*. So, I read to him a couple more chapters while the spelling bee was going on.

October 8:   After lunch, Bridget found me and asked me was I doing anything that afternoon. I told her no, and asked her what she was interested in doing. She wanted to paint the downstairs bathroom. So we first cleaned the bathroom, and then asked Missy if we could paint it. She said to come up with a plan and show it to her first, which we did. Basically, we are going to put up a border of geometric shapes, and do a mural on the back of the door, and put a "Bathroom" label on the front of the door, with some polka dots. We cut out the stencils we would use for the geometric shapes. After we showed Missy the plan, we got to work. I showed them (Camille had now joined us) how to use a level to draw a level line for writing, then wrote "Bathroom" in bubble letters in pencil. Camille and Bridget then painted these letters in, while I copies the stencil shapes onto the wall in pencil. While the two girls worked on the door, I started in on the border painting itself. We stopped at around 2:40 when Bridget seemed to lose some interest. Hopefully we will finish it over the next few days. It does look nice.

October 16:   I attended a seventh/eighth-grade class meeting and then when it ended at 10:00 stuck around in the classroom to observe the math class, too. The kids wanted to do algebra. Bridget, Peter, Daniel, and Grayson were there. Dave asked what and all they could do as far as algebra was concerned. It appeared that Bridget needed very basic level algebra while the boys had had a bit of experience with it and could do more advanced stuff. I grabbed an algebra book off the shelf, and then suggested to Dave that I could take the boys to another room and give them chapter end tests to see sort of where they were as far as knowing how to do stuff. At the end of working thru stuff (we had been at it all for about forty-five to fifty-five minutes), they asked me if we could set up something regular to teach this, and after thinking about their sched-ules/apprenticeships, etc., we agreed to do the class at 10:00 on Mondays, Tuesdays and Thursdays.

In addition to creating their own unique curricula, Free School stu-dents actively cooperate with one another in working through personal challenges. This is mainly done in the council meetings. Granted, these meetings are mandatory and thus the students do not choose whether to attend, but participation is a different story—that is not mandatory. In other words, the kids could just sit mutely through the meeting (which some do), but I found that many actively participate in helping their fellow students work through their issues. The following detailing of a council meeting I observed and took part in illustrates how the students actively challenge one another. This meeting was a personal one in that I called it. I had been reading a book to a group of girls who were notorious for being uncoopera-tive in cleaning up. While I read to them, they sewed pillows and clothes for their stuffed animals. Things went well until it came time to clean up. The girls, Rebecca, Miranda, and Delia—all of whom were around eight or nine years old—tried to run off when I asked them to help put away the sewing stuff. This was not the first time I had had trouble with these girls not taking responsibility, and I was fed up and mad and so I called the council meeting. In the course of the meeting, eighth graders Libby and Daniel worked ac-tively to get the three girls to see that they have to assume responsibility for their messes.

> *October 3:*   At the council meeting I explained that I was mad that Rebecca and Miranda and Delia did not clean up their mess and I felt like I had to be a policewoman about it and it wasn't right, that they needed to take responsibility. . . . I was feeling frustrated and angry at being disrespected and these feelings led me to start crying. While I was crying, Libby said to the girls that they were being jerks, that sometimes she cleans up messes that she doesn't even make and that it comes with being a part of the school, that some-times you just have to pitch in and clean up, even if you weren't one hundred percent responsible for the mess, and that she felt they were also being totally uncompassionate for my crying. Daniel put forth a motion that if those three girls made a mess and didn't clean it up, then they couldn't be in that room again for a week. Bhawin

asked me how I was feeling about that and the whole meeting. I responded that I still felt pretty bad about it most especially because Rebecca would not take any responsibility for her actions, whereas Delia and Miranda seemed to have (because Miranda had admitted to much of the mess being hers, and Delia did rightly defend that she had not been doing much of the sewing and so could not have made a big mess). I also talked about how messes sometimes need to be attended to communally, unless it is clear that someone made a particular mess. So, Daniel amended his motion saying that if the girls didn't clean up a mess together, then they would lose the use of that room for a week. I was satisfied by this because of the communal focus. The motion passed.

Though the teachers did talk some in this council meeting (and all the others I attended as well), the students were also actively engaged in challenging the three girls and me to work through our problem.

Interpersonal cooperation also extends to respecting one another's rights in the school. Students know that their rights to pursue their own curricula cannot infringe on another's rights and were not often disruptive of other students' activities and lessons. Occasionally a class or activity got interrupted by someone not heeding the stop sign on a door or by a young child being noisy, but the students, just as much as the teachers, involved in the activity asserted the right of the group not to be disturbed.

Interpersonal cooperation showed up in other ways in the school besides assisting others in council meetings to work through their problems and in respecting the rights of others to pursue their interests. Interage cooperation was also much in evidence. I frequently saw children of different ages playing together, or older children acting in nurturing ways to younger children. Another form of cooperation that I quite often observed was a tremendous level of resource cooperation or sharing. In late October, I noted in my journal that "I went to the basketball park with Ajay, Daisy, Macon, and Sarah. They were riding on a skateboard and I noticed that the kids do a good job of sharing the skateboard, taking turns, and I do not have to mediate. They have some tiffs about it, but nothing extended and major." Such free sharing of a coveted object was not something I had often seen in my years teaching public school, and so I made note of it because it seemed so anomalous at the time.

In addition to being actively involved in their own education and cooperating with others, students also take an active role in the governance and operation of the school. Already discussed has been the role of students in council meetings and how they help to enforce school rules and govern one another, and the role of students in devising new school rules at all-school meetings and undertaking operational tasks such as lunch cleanup. Students also play a role in keeping the school tidy by helping (if they choose) the Cleanup Committee—those who pitch in about once a week to straighten up and sweep the downstairs. The students are not forced to help out, though those who do get an immediate reward (such as cookies or ice cream), which alleviates some of the resistance to doing an unbeloved task. Students are also responsible for cleaning up their own messes and fixing any damage done to property. For example, in mid-October seventh grader Trent and sixth grader Conner were roughhousing in the Big Room and Trent pushed Conner into the wall. The force of the impact broke a hole in the Sheetrock, which then needed to be repaired. Since I had learned how to do such repairs during the two-week getting ready period, I offered to teach Trent how to fix the hole, which we finally did to great success on Halloween morning.

The role for students in the Free School is clearly an embodiment of many progressive educators' visions. These students are not passive or dependent recipients of education for it is they who are choosing what they study and when and how. And while they receive assistance and guidance from teachers, they are not controlled by teachers to the same degree as students in a traditional school. The students at the Free School get to focus on the process of constructing meaning and connections; they are not constantly pressured to "perform" to outside mandated standards. This shift in focus from products to process allows the students in the Free School to be more cooperative than competitive. Part of this cooperation is in the area of helping others to understand themselves. And, with the help of others, students at the Free School become adept at self-evaluation. Lastly, the students play an active governance role in the school that further develops their self-reflection skills and makes their school experiences highly meaningful.

THE TEACHERS

As discussed in chapter 3, progressive educators critique traditional education wherein the teacher's role is very fixed and focused on "transmitting" information to students. In traditional schools it is the teacher's job to slowly feed the preorganized, precategorized canon of knowledge (skills and content) to students bit by fragmented bit, and then check (through tests or other performance evaluations) to see whether this information has been successfully transmitted. Progressive educators argue that this "bank-deposit" approach to education objectifies the students, encourages them to be overly dependent on others for what, when, and how to do things, forces students all into one mold, and discourages them from developing their critical consciousness.

Progressive educators, again as discussed in chapter 3, envision the teacher's role very differently. Because they view knowledge as individually structured and created, progressive educators want teachers to create environments in which students are allowed to make their own personal meanings, rather than having meanings made for them. In these environments, students would be free to find and pursue ideas and activities and work through problems that interest or connect to them, rather than being made to study a preset canon of subjects.

In this environment, it is necessary for the progressive teacher to seek to know the students, to find out what interests them, troubles them, and connects to them. Doing this is no easy, one-dimensional task; rather it involves a multifaceted approach that one must take with the child, an approach that involves close and distant observations, informal and formal interactions, and a great deal of empathy. In all this, the teacher must be herself with the child and seek to connect with the child's interest and struggles. Once the connection is made, once an interest comes to the fore, then the progressive teacher must think carefully about what she knows about the child and determine how she can best serve that child's quest to make meaning. Depending on the child, the teacher, and the activity to be pursued, the teacher will either take an active or a passive role. In other words, sometimes the teacher will simply step back and be supportive, loving, and trusting, and at other times the teacher will actively instruct, guide, or push, and so on. The progressive teacher, in that she has no set body of knowledge to transmit, is not interested in the students' "performance" regarding knowledge retention; rather the teacher is more interested in the process of meaning making, which in her mind signifies growth and change.

At the Albany Free School, the teachers embody all these progressive ideas of what the teacher does. The teachers also have specific operational duties that assist in the creation and maintenance of such environments. My discussion of the details of this embodiment integrates my observations of and interviews with other teachers at the Free School and my own actions as an intern teacher there.

Teachers at the Albany Free School have ample opportunities to find out who their students are, what their home life is like, with their interests are, what concerns them, and so on. The absence of a standardized, mandated curriculum provides a space for the teachers and students to come together with nothing between them to get in the way of real interactions. In other words, at the Albany Free School, no major intermediary comes between the students and teachers; there is no object (i.e., a mandated curriculum) to which the students and teachers must both turn their attention. Teachers at the Free School are not burdened by having to impose a curriculum on the students and students are not burdened with the expectation of unquestioningly accepting what is imposed on them. Teachers and students can thus be themselves and interact in a real, face-to-face, rather than a face-to-mandated curriculum-to-face manner. While teachers in traditional schools often try to get to know their students mainly as a means to facilitate an easier and smoother transmission of the mandated curriculum, teachers at the Free School get to know their students both as an end in itself and a means to help them grow.

This getting to know the students occurs in several different ways, all employed simultaneously. Teachers at the Free School seek to know their students by direct and indirect means. Direct means include specifically asking about interests or concerns, offering classes, interacting at council meetings, activity meetings, or all-school meetings, and in scheduled classes. Indirect means include hanging out with students, playing with them, taking part in games or other spur-of-the-moment activities; indirect means also include watching the children from a distance as they directly interact with others, reading into their comments or actions (trying to delve for deeper meaning), and speaking with other teachers about the children. An example of how the teachers directly work to know the students follows.

One September afternoon, eighth grader Grayson and some younger boys were sitting in the Rug Room, speaking loudly and using graphic language. Because the windows were open, people passing on the street could hear quite clearly what these boys were saying. The seventh/eighth-grade teacher, Dave, overheard them, deemed it highly unacceptable, and called a council meeting. Dave had two main concerns: (1) that such overheard conversations makes people think ill of the school, and (2) the boys could be spending their time in some other way, one not only more socially appropriate, but also one that would assist them in their personal growth. As an attempt to point the boys in the direction of seeking out their interests, Missy stated, "We just want you doing what you're passionate about at the school, that's all. If it's not classes, and it's not apprenticeships, what is it? What do you love to do? And let's help you." Missy then made a motion that everyone had to come to school the next day with a list of ten things about which he or she is passionate.

Such a motion was somewhat out of the ordinary, but the questions Missy asked and what the motion represented are quite common at the Free School where the teachers often seek to directly find out from the students what their interests and concerns are. In addition to comments like those, I often heard other teachers ask, or I myself asked, "What are you interested in doing?," "How do you feel today?," "What's bothering you?," "Would you like to do such-and-such?," or "Why do you seem unhappy?" These are explicit, or direct, attempts by the teachers to understand who the children are and how the teachers might assist the children in their growth/meaning making process.

Based on the answers kids give to these questions, the teachers offer activities or ideas that would address the interest or concern areas. The main venue for the direct offering of activities and learning further about the students' interests is the activities meetings. During activities meetings, teachers offer certain activity ideas and ask which students would be interested in taking part. The students also can request certain classes or activities at activities meeting. From these requests and the interest shown to teacher-suggested activities, much can be learned about the children. For example, on the fourth day of school I asked at the activities meeting if anyone would be interested in doing any math. Nine-year-old Callie responded that she was interested and so we set up a time to meet that day. What started out as a one-time class doing some multiplication and division developed into a fairly regular math class that generally met around 10:30 A.M. two or three times a week and lasted anywhere from twenty to fifty minutes. In the course of these classes, which were often one-on-one, I came to know Callie as a bright, energetic, lovely child prone to breaking out into song or dance steps while in the midst of doing multiplication tables. I learned about her dad, her sisters and brother, her mother, that Callie was into sports and all sorts of other things. From our conversations, I also found that she had an interest in reading mystery novels and so sought out books for us to read together or for her to read on her own.

Other suggested-by-teachers classes added to my knowledge of the students. For example, former teacher Nancy, who still lives in the community, held occasional goddess/girls group meetings, one of which I discussed in the previous chapter. Activities like this and its complement, boys group, help the teacher know the students intimately; teachers learn about the kids' hopes, fears, misperceptions, interests, and so on. The occasional class meetings and whole class activities worked in this regard as well. I attended several seventh/eighth-grade class meetings, whose topics ranged from discussion of the film *Whale Rider*, to their class trips, to their apprenticeships. Through all these teacher-suggested activities, I gleaned bits and pieces of information that allowed me to build activities and interactions around the students and who they were.

Not only did I learn about the students from activities that other teachers or I suggested, but I tended to learn just as much, if not more, about them from activities they suggested. For example, eleven-year-old Jonathan was a frequent student suggester at activities meetings. On the first day of school, he requested a trip to the New York State Museum (within walking distance). I volunteered to be the teacher chaperone and took Jonathan and four other boys to the museum that afternoon. Thus began my understanding of this particular student based on his interests in a certain activities. I learned that Jonathan was highly inquisitive and liked to dabble in all sorts of different things. He early on showed an interest in creating a school newspaper, he helped establish clubhouses, he offered magic shows to the other students and to the teachers, was eager to explore areas like the Empire State Plaza, and liked to read books, such as *Holes*.

And through the oft-requested chess practice, I learned an incredible amount about Ajay and Colleen, two of the six year olds. I discovered that they were both eager to try out new things, that they had great senses of humor, that when they were trying to concentrate they did not appreciate interruptions, but at the same time they were more than willing to teach and advise others who interrupted out of a desire to learn what they were doing.

A last example of this learning about the students came from the eighth-grade–student-requested algebra class. Peter, Daniel, and Grayson asked that I offer them a regular algebra class, a request to which I readily agreed. We ended up meeting maybe five times total between October 6 and when I left in late November. This taught me a great deal about these boys. First, because we met only five times over a four-week period when the boys had originally requested a three-time-a-week class, I learned that adolescents need some sort of strong motivation to keep them coming to class when other, quite interesting, activities are simultaneously occurring. I also learned about the specific boys. I realized that Grayson does not cope well with frustration. In the second class he became so frustrated with solving one problem that he threw his hands up and left in a huff. No matter how often I later implored him to rejoin our group, he would not. From this I learned that Grayson needed to work on recognizing that his low threshold for frustration and his tendency to give up could hurt him as he tried to tackle new subjects and interest areas. This algebra class also taught me about Daniel, that he was incredibly bright and picked up math skills with ease. And it taught me about Peter and how his math skills, particularly in multiplication, were weak and that he needed to practice. About Daniel and Peter I also learned that they enjoyed friendly competition in solving problems, but that they just as easily shifted into a more cooperative mode. This showed me their senses of humor, and their feelings of friendship toward one another.

Besides the activities meetings with both the teacher-suggested and student-suggested activities, teachers also learn a great deal about the students from the council meetings and the all-school meetings. How the children conduct themselves in these meetings (whether engaged, participating, attentive, and involved or disengaged, disruptive, withdrawn, and in the case of the non-mandatory all-school meetings, absent) tells the teachers a great deal about who the children are, what interests and concerns them, and so on. For example, I learned early on that eighth grader Walter was greatly interested in governance, seeking out loopholes, and solving problems in a manner that tended toward the conservative, as indicated by his actions and comments in the council and all-school meetings. He was a frequent chairperson of council meetings, was the chair of the one all-school meeting that occurred in my time there, and could be counted on to make relevant and often hard-nosed motions at these meetings.

I also learned about children's home lives from the council meetings. For example, six-year-old Blair called a number of council meetings, for reasons ranging from a boy grabbing her around the neck to not wanting to do her lunch duty tasks. During these meetings, she or her sisters revealed personal aspects of her home life, including the fact that her father was abusive in the past (he is no longer part of the household), and that chores at home were often closely connected to punishment. Another example involved Anthony, an eight-year-old boy with tremendous anger management issues. In council meetings, information came out about Anthony's somewhat toxic home life and the factors he had to deal with there.

Council meetings and all-school meetings also revealed students' ways of dealing with problems—did they speak out and stand up for themselves or were they more passive and willing to take abuse or the imposition of rules without defending themselves or having a say in the matter? For example, Conner was an eleven-year-old boy who was perceived by many students as a pest and was thus very often treated badly. He had an annoying habit of interacting with the kids, the older ones in particular, in a way that did not discourage the abuse. He smiled and laughed when they teased or poked at him and somewhat jokingly said that he would call a council meeting, but never did. When he finally had his fill and called a council meeting, all this came out and he and others learned that he habitually sent mixed messages, saying one thing with his words and another with his body and facial expressions. Such information helped the teachers (and students) to know Conner better and thus they were more able to help him grow and progress in his interpersonal skills.

Direct means of seeking to know the students were quite effective. By the time I left the school in late November I felt that these means had served me well in getting inside the students' heads somewhat, understanding their interests, concerns, and so on.

While direct means of getting to know the students were highly effective, I would argue that indirect means were even more so. Perhaps this was because indirect means happened with more frequency or because when one approaches an individual in a more subtle fashion, that individual's true self shows through more.

The primary indirect means of getting to know the students was simply that of "hanging out" with the kids. Hanging out was generally not scheduled or planned; rather it just arose over the natural course of the day. I might walk through a room and a student would ask if I wanted to play a game, or vice versa. Or a student might be involved in a task or activity and I would inquire what he or she was doing, or vice versa. We would get involved in doing the activity jointly and then converse on topics ranging far and wide. If one listened carefully to what the students were saying, one could learn a great deal about who the students were, their interests and concerns, and so on.

The following are some examples of this getting to know who the kids were by simply hanging out with them.

October 8:   I started to sew covers on the couch cushions in the Rug Room, as the sheet was always getting messed up. So I got out everything I needed and began to work. At this point the room was empty. Within ten minutes, the older girls (Camille, Bridget, and Libby) came in and were hanging out, talking, on the computer, etc. Camille asked if she could do some embroidering, and I told her yes and to go get the stuff, which she did and then embroidered a pillow cover for her dog. We were just working and talking companionably. I talked to Bridget and Camille about whether or not they wanted to go to college or what they might want to do as adults. They both said that they didn't intend to go to college. None of their parents had, or siblings, I discovered, and they said they didn't want to do the hard work that was involved. Bridget said that she wanted to be a Navy Seal, or get involved in dance (go to dance college, she said).

November 17: After reading with Sarah I went into the Art Room where Paul, Ryan, and Austin were and I hung out with them for a while. We talked about *South Park* and they talked about some other television shows and films, etc. These boys totally rip on each other, at one point teasing each other about their reading skills. Avalon admitted his inability to read well. Bryan has some real reading problems, but he has an entirely different reaction than Avalon. Whereas Avalon sees his deficiency and wants to work at it, Bryan sees his deficiency and wants to avoid any contact with working at it. Could this be due to the fact that Bryan's years in public school so damaged his self-esteem regarding academics that he has been convinced that he is totally incapable of getting better? He already plans to go to a vo-tech school.

I have countless other examples of this sort of informal interaction leading to learning information about who a student was. What is key is that the initial purpose of these interactions is not to seek this information, but simply to *be* with one another doing an activity that is mutually satisfying. Such indirect means of coming to know the students happens everywhere—in the school, at the parks, on field trips, on the walks or drives to field trips, at mealtimes, and so on. There is no separation between interacting with the child as a person and interacting with the child as a teacher seeking to aid the student's growth; it is all one and the same.

Another indirect means for understanding students involved distant observation. I term this an indirect means for different reasons than that of hanging out. Hanging out is an indirect means in that it is not directly intended to gain knowledge about the child's interests. Distant observation is intentional for those ends, but is indirect in that it does not involve face-to-face interaction. Dave, early on in the school year, counseled me and other intern teachers not to feel pressured to constantly directly interact with the kids, that we could learn quite a bit from just sitting back and observing how they interact with others or how they spend their time alone. And so I tried to follow this advice on the rare occasions when I found myself at loose ends. What I observed taught me a great deal about particular students and about children in general. For example, on September 25, I wrote in my journal that "I watched Macon play this reading game on the computer. He was on a PBS Web site where a voice said a word, and then the player had to read and then pick that word out of three choices. Macon was playing very well, and he also chose to write each word on a piece of paper." No one was helping Macon or asking him to do this, he simply chose to do it. I thus learned something about Macon and his interests and also saw confirmation of many progressive authors' arguments that kids do not need to be coerced into learning or constantly watched by teachers to ensure that learning occurs. Instead, if left to their own devices, kids will frequently seek out activities that challenge them and help them to grow as learners.

Another time when I observed students from a distance occurred on October 17.

> I went into the Big Room where some kids were wrestling, being watched by Megan. They have very specific rules about wrestling. Shoes must be off, you must stay on the mat, a teacher must be watching, the teacher times the rounds and referees the match, etc. Daniel was going around challenging people to wrestling matches. I watched kids wrestling each other and it is a great, supervised, controlled way of letting the kids be physical with one another without it getting out of hand. And all the kids were having a blast, and rooting on others while they wrestled.

From this I learned about specific students who had an interest in wrestling, and I also learned that students can be physical with one another without going too far, that kids are not these powder kegs ready to explode if given the slightest spark, as so many traditional educators would have one believe.

Teachers sometimes do distant observation to see if a child is ready for a certain privilege or responsibility. For example, when teachers determine that a child is sufficiently responsible, the child is permitted to sign out and go to the two nearby parks without a teacher chaperone. The child must still inform a teacher where he or she is going, but does not need a teacher to supervise at the destination. All of the youngest kids, up to age eight and a half or so, require a supervising adult if they go off school grounds, but at around age nine, students start to evidence some responsibility for being out on their own. If a teacher has some question about whether a particular child is ready for this step, then she will quite often give the child permission to go to one of the parks when asked, but then quietly follow the child at a distance to see if the child was, in fact, able to handle that responsibility. Thus, this distant observation shows the teacher a great deal about who the child is.

Distant observations also allow teachers to see a child in a different light from what they may have gotten used to. For example, eight-year-old Rebecca was somewhat my nemesis at school—she drove me crazy with her obstinate refusal to clean up after herself and her tendency to be somewhat snotty in her interactions with me. But one day in late October I sat for a while and simply watched her. In my journal that evening I wrote:

> Rebecca and Delia had picked up a wounded pigeon today and were "nursing" it. It was sort of disgusting [unhygienic], but sort of sweet, too. I feel like my relationship with Rebecca in particular has improved, but maybe we're just having a good couple of days. I looked at her today while we were reading and saw not just a disheveled girl who has issues with power and adults, but as sort of a pretty and sweet and curious and spirited girl.

I also used distant observation of other teachers with students to understand the students more. For example, on Halloween, a costume parade around the block was planned and most students brought their costumes to school in preparation for this. At 1 P.M. all the students were allowed to get into their costumes, and there was much excitement and high spirits, except from Blair. Six-year-old Blair had gotten really scared by Jonathan's zombie costume (it was quite effective), but then, in my opinion, she just carried on and on. I was rather annoyed at her after listening to this for some time, but then noticed that another teacher pulled her aside, quietly questioned her, and then took her to get a Hawaiian shirt and grass skirt from the teacher's house. Blair's main problem was that she was feeling left out because her mom had forgotten to send her in with a costume. Once she was set up in the Hawaiian outfit she was just as happy and jolly as she could be. From observing the teacher interact with Blair I learned that she could become very upset when feeling left out and I also learned that one needs to look below surface behaviors to really understand students.

This reading deeper of students, empathizing with them, is another indirect means of seeking to know the students. I observed many teachers being empathetic and thus teaching themselves and also teaching me about a particular student. An example of this again involves Blair, who refused to do her lunch duty when I reminded her. While I saw this as a power issue between Blair and myself, Missy viewed it differently. She probed Blair's reasons. Missy asked if she felt comfortable doing jobs. To this question Blair finally said that she was not exactly sure what she was supposed to do and no one would help her. Missy's empathetic approach showed me a child who was unsure of herself and needed guidance in carrying out a task, something that I did not see at all prior to Missy's involvement.

After such examples, I tried to be more conscious of empathizing as a way of getting to know the students better and in early October noted in my journal when I had a chance to employ this particular indirect means.

> After activities meeting, Ajay wanted to do a chess lesson, so we went into the Middle Room and set up the board and started to

play. Then Callie came in sort of looking like she wanted to do something, so I invited her to be the referee of our game. Ajay sort of got a funny look on his face and started balking a lot when it was his move in the game. I wondered about it, but didn't ask him about it. Then Camille and Bridget came in to get knitting stuff to take with them to Grafton, so I got sort of sidetracked with helping them get stuff down and doing the casting on for Bridget. Again, I noticed Ajay glowering a bit. Then he sort of stalked away and then, before I could talk to him about it, a council meeting was called. After that council meeting, I went up to Ajay and told him I was sorry that I let people keep interrupting our game (I figured that was what he was mad about). He said that he just wanted it to be him and me playing and no one else. I said, okay, just be sure to tell me when you want that and I will make it so, but it was important that he be sure to tell me (use his words). I said, "So you don't want to play anymore right now, right? So, will you help me clean up the chess board and put it away?" Which he happily did.

This interaction taught me that Ajay sometimes just wanted to spend time one-on-one with me and I somewhat empathetically picked up on that (although I was a bit slow in figuring it out and acting on it).

A final indirect means of teachers seeking to know students was that of sharing information about students with each other. Although this teacher-to-teacher sharing occurred in and out of school, Monday's after-school teachers meetings and the once-a-month board meetings were the main venues. At these three to four hour meetings, individual teachers raised concerns they had about individual students and requested others' advice or assistance on how to deal with the situation. Although they were long and draining, I learned an incredible amount about specific children from these meetings. I discovered information about students' physical disabilities, such as Ajay's hearing loss in one of his ears. I learned about students' home lives, such as abusive conditions or other family troubles. I learned about conflicts between kids that I did not directly observe. I heard about students being annoyed with me or other teachers. I learned about students' bad habits, such as stealing, or being irresponsible, or being homophobic. I found out about students' interests in certain subjects. I learned about learning difficulties that particular students had and how best to work with them. And I learned of specific difficult situations that arose between kids and teachers. Had these meetings not occurred, I would venture to say that I would not have known the students half as well as I did by the time I left in late November.

All this work to seek to know the students through direct and indirect means is done to help the child figure out who he or she is and thus construct knowledge and pursue personal meaning. Therefore, knowing the child becomes an end in itself. But seeking to know the students is also done as a means to help the teacher figure out how best to be of service to the individual students in this quest for meaning. As mentioned earlier, using the knowledge of the student gained through direct and indirect means, the teacher then chooses to take either a passive or active role in assisting the child's quest for meaning. These determinations are the next major aspect of the teacher's role.

A Free School teacher passively supports a child's interests or concerns by simply evidencing a supportive demeanor, but not actively taking part in the activity or helping to move it forward. A supportive demeanor can include being a good listener by validating the student's interest or concern, praising the child's interest or progress in pursuing something, and simply helping to maintain the environment in which the child has the space and time to follow individual interests. "Passive," in this case, is a bit of a tricky word, for being supportive can be construed to be active. I am using the term more as a contrast to more active involvement in terms of teaching a child formally, or pushing and guiding or prodding the child along a meaning-making path.

At the Albany Free School I observed other teachers and participated myself in this passive support for the students' pursuing their own interests and concerns. As I mentioned earlier, teachers make conscious efforts to listen to and empathize with students. Sometimes children just need teachers to be sounding boards. For example, I spoke on separate occasions with twelve-year-old Camille and thirteen-year-old Daniel, and as we were talking they expressed to me some frustrations they were having over council meetings being called for what they saw as frivolous reasons. I recognized these statement as concerns, but also realized there was little I could do so I just listened and, essentially, validated or supported their concern as being something they had a right to be bothered by. I suppose I could have suggested that they take active steps like calling an all-school meeting to propose a motion concerning the calling of council meeting, but I sensed that they knew this and just needed someone who would listen.

Teachers also give support by praising the students' approaches to solving their concerns or pursuing their interests. Whenever a student called a council meeting, teachers consistently praised the student for doing so, thus encouraging the child's attempts to work through a problem on his or her own. I also observed teachers frequently praising students for their artwork or other accomplishments, thus supporting their actions of pursuing their interests. I, too, even though I had some difficulty at first, became a frequent praiser. One day I was in the Science Room and overheard someone playing a beautiful piece on the piano in the Big Room. When the person was done, I stuck my head into the room, saw it was eleven-year-old Corine, and praised her for her playing. She pointed out that the piece was of her own composing, to which I added further accolades for her originality. At other times I found myself walking around the downstairs, seeing works of art (pottery, drawings, etc.) or construction (birdhouses, benches) and praising their creators for their work. In all these activities, I knew, and I think the other teachers knew, that the students did not need a teacher's active assistance in dealing with their concerns or pursuing their interests. It was enough that the teacher was there to listen and support and help maintain this unique educational environment.

While this passive support is a constant undertone in the teacher–student relations, the teachers also take active steps to serve the children in their quest for personal meaning and pursuit of interests and concerns.

As discussed earlier, teachers offer classes or activities to students or respond to their requests for classes or activities. In these responses to students' interests or concerns, teachers do not all provide the same kinds of active support; instead the teacher carefully considers the activity itself, who the student is, and who they themselves are, and comes up with a tailor-made active response. For example, Callie responded to my offer to teach math and so from there I needed to consider the topic (math), Callie and what I knew about her from direct and indirect means (what skills she already had, what she was interested in working on, how long she could handle focusing on a task, what her learning style was, what time of day she was most amenable to instruction, what things gave her difficulty, and so on), who I was (what teaching style I preferred, what method ideas I had in my teaching "toolkit," what I was seeking from this activity), and what resources were available (manipulatives, games, Internet access, quiet space, etc.). Depending on the teacher and the child and all the other factors, a teacher might be very traditional in his or her active support of the child (mini-lectures, paper and pencil work, use of texts or workbook, etc.) or nontraditional (methods that value nonrational ways of knowing, kinesthetic and tactile methods rather than just visual and auditory ones, unconventional grouping, using games to teach reading or computation skills, etc.). In the case of Callie's math lessons, I had found through direct and indirect means that she could focus for thirty to forty minutes, but when she consistently broke out into song or dance steps, she was close to having had her fill of math for the day. I knew she had a positive self-image and so could warmly tease her a bit when she missed an easy problem. I knew she was bright and caught on fast, so I could move quickly. I knew she liked to touch things and play games, so I tried to come up with activities and resources that would allow for this (multiplication card games, Internet games, etc.). I knew that she occasionally wanted to have homework and so at the end of many classes I asked if she would like an assignment. And I knew that I wanted her to memorize her multiplication tables and so used timed repetition, fast computation quizzes, and so on. In the case of eighth graders Peter and Daniel and their requested algebra class, I had to do things differently. Because this was a class with more than one student, I had to think about how the two of them and their interests, needs, and skills would intertwine. After one class, I spoke with Dave, the seventh/eighth-grade teacher, and got a sense that Daniel was much stronger in math than Peter and thus could move quicker and more independently through the content. Dave also told me about Peter's reading disabilities and his difficulty transferring information from the board to his paper. I had to factor all this into my thinking about how I would teach the class and what materials I would use. I knew from my own interactions with the boys that they were quite high-spirited and hard to pin down for a long period and so any lessons needed to be in short spurts or entail several different activities. I also knew that I could joke with them and keep a light atmosphere in the classroom without their losing focus.

Acting to support the students' pursuit of interests and concerns does not always involve a teacher's taking the initiative. Sometimes teachers' active steps are simply that of being a participant in the children's activities. For example, many of the six year olds like to make up their own rules for games, and they often requested that I play with them. Ajay and Colleen frequently wanted me to play a "bank" game using checkers, the Scattergories letter dice, paper money from the game of Life, and cardboard folders. Although I never fully understood their rationales for the game's rules and process, I played along in whatever way they requested. They needed some participants, they were using their imaginations, and I was happy to join in. Another example of participating in a student-designed activity was when seventh grader Bridget wanted to paint the downstairs bathroom. She needed a teacher to help in getting supplies and approving plans. And although I assisted her, she pretty much made all the plans and decisions. Other examples of this sort of active involvement were the many times students requested I go to the museum with them, or accompany them to the park, and so on. Even though I was not setting the agenda in these activities, I was still an active participant and thus was serving the children's needs in a way that seemed best at the time.

Lesson planning and participating in student-designed activities are not the only ways that teachers actively serve the needs of children in their quest for meaning. The teachers also take some very subtle, but active, steps as well. I would term such steps as "gentle prodding" wherein the teacher recognizes (through direct or indirect means) who the students are along with their interests or concerns and then works somewhat (but not completely) behind the scenes to help propel the children along their meaning-making path. Gentle prodding has the force of teacher or adult guidance behind it, but not the full force. In other words, gentle prodding contains no element of compulsion. Instead, it is just a teacher helping the child along, aid that derives from the fact that the teacher is an adult with more years of worldly experience in working through similar issues.

I observed other Free School teachers and I myself took part in gently prodding the students. Council meetings are a place of considerable gentle prodding. While students generally initiate these meetings from a concern or problem they have, the teachers often guide a student down the path toward resolution. For example, a number of council meetings were called about Anthony's lack of anger management skills. He tended to harass other students, sometimes physically, sometimes verbally. In late September, seven-year-old Hamal called a council meeting concerning this harassment. In my journal on September 29 I detailed this meeting and noted how the other teachers gently urged Hamal to deal with this problem and also prodded Anthony to try to come up with ways to check his negative behavior.

> Hamal called a council meeting because Anthony was messing with him. Walter put forth the motion that had been suggested at a previous council meeting about Anthony that the next time Anthony messes with a student, even after that student said to stop, that he should have to go home for the day. The idea was that maybe that would make Anthony think twice before messing with kids, but Missy and other teachers (like Dave and Elizabeth) were strongly opposed to that motion saying that it is too harsh and that Anthony would probably get in a whole lot of trouble if he got sent home and that home may be part of the problem, and he would just come back even angrier than ever, and the problem would still need to be dealt with. Dave put out a couple of suggestions of what to do about this situation: (1) that Anthony can't be in the same place as anyone who he has messed with—but that it is up to that person to make sure Anthony stays away—that they should define the parameters of what they will accept; (2) that Anthony should get the sitting-on treatment (that way there would be more of a direct impact on Anthony, and it would keep the problem in the school). [The "sitting-on treatment" is something used rarely at the school, and I never observed it. Basically, it is a way for the kids to deal with a bully situation. If a child bullies and bullies and will not stop, then the victim seeks out a teacher and asks if he or she and other students smaller than the bully can sit on the bully, immobilizing him until he agrees to not harass or bully again.] Missy probed to see what the root problem was and asked Anthony was there anything he came to school today mad about, but he would not respond at first, then a bit later he said he was angry. Missy told him that he has options of what he wants to do with that anger and he needs to make choices that won't end him up in constant council meetings. Some of his choices are to work out his anger with a punching bag, going to the park, etc. Teachers volunteered to work with him on that (take him to park, hold punching bag, etc.) Dave pointed out that since this is the second meeting about this problem that we need to have clear consequences so that Anthony will know what will happen, that Hamal (and anyone else this happens to) needs to make a clear statement like, "If you do this again, then I will. . . . "

So, Hamal said, "The next time you mess with me, then I will call a council meeting to impose the rule about you not being allowed anywhere where I am." Dave said to Anthony: "We care about you, Anthony, and we do understand why you come to school mad, but Hamal has a right to come to a safe place, and he is doing what he has to do to protect himself at school."

Without such prodding from the teachers, it is possible that both Hamal and Anthony would have been stymied for where to go with their problem. The teachers, I believe, feel it is part of their role to actively guide the students toward problem resolution.

I tried my hand at gently prodding a problem to resolution that same day.

I was on the computer in the Science Room when Blair came in and asked me to help her resolve a conflict with Macon over a ring of hers that she says he took from her. We got him in the room, and I had them start talking to one another and tried to prevent them from getting into a fight (Blair especially). Blair claimed that Macon took her ring from her backpack and wouldn't give it back. Macon claimed that the ring was his and he had one just like hers, but hers was at home (although not siblings, Macon and Blair's families live together). They went back and forth a while, and Macon's story started to deteriorate and it became clear to me that Macon *had* taken it from her, but I did not accuse. Finally, Macon asked Blair if she would share the ring with him, and I made clear that it was *her* ring to share and would she be willing? She said yes, he gave the ring back along with some Yu-gi-oh cards and we went to activities meeting. In this interaction, I made a strong point of letting them do the talking, and trying to keep myself on the periphery and only making occasional remarks. It seemed to work pretty well.

Gentle prodding happens a great deal around trying to get the students involved in activities that would give them contact with traditional academic disciplines (reading, math, science, etc), but mainly after the student expresses some initial interest. Teachers see a student show a spark of interest in something and from that encourage the child. For example, both Trent and Peter, seventh and eighth graders, respectively, expressed a desire to work on their reading skills, perhaps realizing that they would soon be attending public high school and that these skills needed some developing. Teacher/Co-Director Chris volunteered to work with the boys, but he had to be persistent in getting them to meet, not necessarily chasing them down, but almost. He was just gently prodding the boys to follow their personally initiated quest to improve this necessary skill. In my interview with Bhawin, he spoke about Chris's actions.

I think like what Chris is doing right now with the reading with Trent and Peter, is that that's his responsibility, he's taken that on. I think there is a responsibility for us to push kids to a certain degree and say, "Listen, Trent, I'm really concerned about your reading, why you don't you want to do it, when are you going to learn how to read? You're eleven or twelve." I mean, that's a concern, that's genuine, I don't feel comfortable with sending a twelve year old out into the world not knowing how to read. I think that's irresponsible, you know?

Teachers also gently encourage students to take part in academics by offering exciting activities or lessons on the traditional disciplines. Missy, in her interview, spoke about how she did this.

Sometimes I get extravagant because I want to teach something and I make it extremely attractive and fun because I want to let these kids know that everything can be joyful on some level, I want any kid I work with, to start out with a pleasurable kind of place. I want them to know that reading or whatever it is I'm teaching is fun and that you don't have to do it "by the book." I want it to be, I want to have a good time, too, and my energy can be just as high as a kid's, and I feel like that is one way I teach; I look for a pleasing way to do it, that's my mission, and it's challenging to me, you know? Sometimes that's not always what I want to do, but I think that there's a part of me that believes that if I do a little bit every day and something of it is playful, it'll start to sink in that this is a fun, this is a pleasurable thing for them to have in their lives.

I, too, got into the habit of gently prodding kids to work on traditional academic disciplines, mainly when they first expressed an interest, but then didn't follow up. I have mentioned the case of Lawrence being interested in survival themes and how I finally led him to read *Hatchet* with me after numerous offers on my part. This process of gentle prodding took a number of weeks, as I detailed in my journal.

September 12:   Yesterday, Lawrence had said he was interested in doing survival stuff, and I enthusiastically suggested he read *Hatchet* and that if he brought his library card tomorrow that I would walk to the library with him and show him some books that are about survival. I asked him this morning if he had brought his card and he said no. He doesn't seem all that interested in reading the books I suggested, even though they are on a topic that he purports to have an interest in. Is the interest a real and deep one, or is it more fleeting?

September 16: After lunch I tried for a long time to get Lawrence to go to the library. He *had* brought his library card, but then changed his mind about walking so far to the library. I don't understand this. He says he is interested in going, to the point that he brought his library card, but then he backs out.

October 1: At activities meeting I talked about reading some of *Hatchet* (I had checked it out at the library myself the other afternoon) but we did not end up doing any reading today as each time I saw Lawrence he did not want to.

October 3: I was in the Middle Room doing some knitting and some of the younger girls were doing some sewing. I asked them if they would like to hear some of *Hatchet* while they sewed. They said yes and I started reading and about two pages in I got up to close the door, and saw Lawrence in the Reading Room and invited him to come in to listen, too. At the end of chapter 2, I said I would stop there and we would pick it up again maybe next day of school.

October 7: I got out *Hatchet* to read with Lawrence. We were going to read in the Middle Room, but no one else came and Lawrence wanted other people to hear it. So we went into the Big Room where there were a few more people and began to read. At the end we had read two chapters.

October 15: At activities meeting I proposed reading *Hatchet* at some time today. After the meeting, I went and got *Hatchet* and tried to drum up a group of students to listen to it. The timing was bad as many kids wanted to take part in Megan's treasure hunt.

October 17: After activities meeting, I took Alison, Bridget, and Callie to the library. We went upstairs to the Juvenile Fiction and I saw that they had books on tape, so I checked out *Roll of Thunder, Hear My Cry*, and *Hatchet*. Hopefully now with a tape I can set up regular times for reading with them. This afternoon I arranged to read with Lawrence from 9:30 to 10:00 on Mondays, Tuesdays, and Thursdays.

October 20: After the activities meeting I was going to read with Lawrence, but he had his apprenticeship.

October 21: At around 9:30 most of the seventh and eighth graders went to the museum to work on the haunted house, but Lawrence didn't go so I tried to get him to do some *Hatchet* listening, but he did not seem to want to. So, with no classes to teach, I went down-stairs to the Reading Room. Lawrence walked through at one point and I fussed at him about always dissing me on reading the book. He said that he wasn't dissing me, that he wanted to read something else, which I agreed to and then also asked, "So, do you want to give up on *Hatchet*?" to which he said no. Lawrence then left. After lunch, I ran into Lawrence who said that he wanted to do *Hatchet* reading then. I got the book and tape player and we headed into the Middle Room to do our listening, and were joined by Ajay, Frankie, Nevin, Blair, and Ursula. We listened to a total of fifty minutes of the book. Ajay, Nevin, and Lawrence stayed the whole time and said they wanted to continue tomorrow.

October 22: At activities meeting I suggested reading *Hatchet* at 1:00 P.M., to which the boys who had been listening yesterday agreed. After lunch, I listened with Frankie, Nevin, Lawrence, Ajay, and Michael to another hour of *Hatchet*. The boys all seem to be pretty into it, and I am enjoying it, too.

October 27: At activities meeting I suggested reading *Hatchet* at 1:00 P.M. again. At 11:00 Ajay was saying to me, "*Hatchet, Hatchet*" and since I wanted to see the movie in the afternoon, I told him to go find Lawrence, Frankie, and Nevin and we would listen to it this morning rather than at 1:00, which we did. We are down to just an hour to go before the end of the book.

November 3: At activities meeting I suggested reading *Hatchet* at 1:00 P.M. again. At 1:00 P.M., I went into the reading room and played the rest of *Hatchet*, mainly to Lawrence, but Nevin did come in later. Lawrence is now interested in hearing *Brian's Winter* (the sequel), so I will go to the library for it tomorrow. I tried to get him interested in *The Cay* and, if I can get the tape, we will listen to that, too.

When gentle prodding does not work, teachers tend to pull back be-cause they believe that the student's lack of commitment perhaps indicates that the activity is not really an authentic interest. But Free School teachers also recognize that some kids need more than gentle prodding—that, in fact, they require a push. This was especially evident with the seventh and eighth graders. In past years, the older students tended to not want to take part in many activities or pursue interests, and often did not respond well to gentle prodding (i.e., they continued to resist doing things that *they* had expressed an interest in). They preferred to simply hang out and socialize with one another. To some degree, this is acceptable since learning does occur with socializing and game playing, but this hanging out also sometimes got out of control and became disruptive to teachers and students involved in an activity or pursuit; it also gave the other, younger students a bad model to follow. At the end of the 2002–2003 school year, the teachers decided among themselves to go beyond gentle prodding as an active means to serve the seventh and eighth-grade students' quest for meaning, and instead start to push the students and compel them to actively pursue subjects and interest areas. The teachers mandated that each seventh and eighth grader choose an adult "Guidance Counselor" from the school community and meet with that individual once a week. The seventh and eighth graders also had to come by the school (or call) the week before it started with a list of interest areas and apprenticeship ideas; they had to commit to setting up and attending some classes and setting up and going to an apprenticeship. The teachers knew full well that this pushing violated, in many ways, the Free School's core philosophy, but they also felt that not to do something would harm these particular children's quest for meaning. In my interview with Dave, he stated that:

> That's the most interesting difference for this year is that we are doing that. And the reason that came about was because we were seeing that the older kids, that this really was becoming just a place for them to hang out and that was the exclusive activity of the older kids. There was boredom creeping in, there was destructiveness creeping in, and they acted like there was nothing to do. But the culture of that older class was becoming so strong that it was hard for kids that, you know, a kid who really wanted to have a class, but ten other kids around him weren't doing classes or weren't doing apprenticeships created this situation where what it meant to be in seventh and eighth grade at the Free School was to hang out, wreck it up, and not do much, and by the end of last year, the 2002 and 2003 school year, we said we just can't keep going on this way, we're starting to see it creep down to the younger ages. The kids who are in fourth, fifth, and sixth grade this last year were starting to say, well, that's what I'm going to do when I go to seventh and eighth grade. We just had to make a decision, again, you know the decision was made and imposed sort of institutionally, we were saying, this is what it is going to be like to be a seventh and eighth grader. But it was also matching the personalities of the kids we had. You know, we were factoring that in, it wasn't an abstract decision. It was okay, what do these kids need to get them motivated? And I know that is tricky, it is a slippery slope, but we said "I think they need a kick in the butt, you know, they need a little bit of like, wait a minute, no, you can't do this," . . . the level of disruption of other activities that were going on was becoming a problem, we as teachers weren't comfortable with the fact that kids that were about twelve or thir-

teen years of age were just hanging out 'cause there's so much cool stuff to be doing. So, there was a value judgment there, but we were also saying, "This is a really cool group of kids and we can break them out of this pattern, how are we going to do it?" And we talked about it a lot and we just said, "Well, we've got to get tough with them, but if we put it this way, I think they'll respond." And I would say that ten out of the twelve, eleven out of the twelve have responded really well to it, it did work and that came from us really knowing these kids and going, okay, we've got to, we've got to come up with something that's going to work, what is it? Is it getting softer or getting tougher? Getting tougher has mostly worked, but if it had been a different group of kids, we might have come up with a different strategy, we may have told them they couldn't be here or, you know what I mean? It could have been anything.

And in my interview with Chris, he stated that he sees this situation as a form of active guidance. He stated,

I think it's guidance, is what I would call it because it has to do with learning and them not just wasting their lives, you know, wasting their time, setting a lousy example to the younger kids. And that's part of what we were reacting to, was that they've been really changing the culture of the school away from its true nature, almost demanding that they be treated in authoritarian ways, because they're so pissed off, you know, they don't want to, they're bringing all their negativity to school and acting it out and making the rest of the school pay the price. I hate it, I feel lousy, I feel terrible, I think, I hate having to do it, that also goes against the school's basic, it's a contradiction, I didn't know what else to do, what else were we going to do?

The teachers really struggle with this idea of pushing or compelling the students; it is not something that comes easily to them. In part, they justify it by equating themselves with parents. Bhawin, in my interview with him, stated that part of being a Free School teacher is being "someone that's sort of a guide, someone that's somewhat a parent." And Chris stated that,

in the Free School we, you know, it isn't just laissez-faire, we don't, kids just don't do whatever they want. See the other big piece of the teaching role in the school is that we do a lot of parenting, what I would call parenting, it's flat-out parenting. Don't eat so much candy or your teeth will fall out. You know, whatever, just the things that parents would do. Because otherwise, you know, this school would be a madhouse and the kids wouldn't get what they need.

The teachers have a keen intuitive sense of when this parenting, this pushing, is working and when it is not. As Dave stated, the kids were not terribly resisting the compulsion of taking some classes and doing an apprenticeship, and thus his conclusion was that the school is best serving a child's quest for meaning by instituting a small degree of compulsion. Compulsion also seems to work regarding both the lunch duty tasks that each child must do once a week as well as the safety rules. Students, though pushed to follow these rules, found them to make sense; the teachers thus were helping the kids make meaning. The students always knew that they had the right to challenge any rules and so perhaps this pushing is not truly a violation of the school's philosophy. In the following example, Bhawin seemed to know when compulsion was unproductive.

> *October 21:*   I went over to the media center to catch the tail end of the discussion about the film Bhawin showed called *Independent Media in a Time of War*. Nearly all the seventh- and eighth-grade kids watched the film with Bhawin and Adam. But Bryan, Libby, and Camille did not stick around for the discussion. Bhawin said that he felt like trying to "make" them stay (plea the case of the importance of the film), but saw that it would instead be counterproductive. He and I discussed afterwards how this is a tension in bringing forth these issues in a free school (that he feels funny saying to the kids that "this is something you *should* know about")— that the kids who most need to have their worldviews challenged tend *not* to be the ones who show an interest in discussing these topics. Makes you think sometimes that maybe there is something to compelling the kids to look at these issues that could be argued to be something that is *so* important for them. But when you get into compelling them, then you are sort of violating one of the tenets of criticality and independence that you are trying to instill!!!

I, too, had an experience when I learned when it was okay to push. On Thursday afternoons some teachers take whichever kids want to go to the "Public Bath"—a city-owned indoor swimming pool. For twenty-five cents for kids and one dollar for adults, we could swim during the afternoon. On October 2, two male teachers and I took a group of seventeen students to the pool. In my journal that evening, I wrote:

> When it was time to get changed back into our clothes, Sarah [six years old] was acting all whiny and saying that she needed help drying off and getting dressed (she had been that way when she got there, too, saying she needed help getting into her swim suit, which I did help her). I thought she was a big girl and said so to her, and that I needed to get dressed myself and that she could dress herself

and dry herself off. I said it pretty firmly and went back into my changing room. She sort of whiny cried a bit and stomped her feet, but then I didn't hear anything more for a while, so I assumed she was either sitting there pouting or was getting dressed. When I got done dressing, I checked in on her and she was all dressed and was just putting her shoes on.

In essence, I pushed Sarah to dress herself; I did not gently prod her at all, in fact, I was quite firm. But apparently that is what she needed to work through her baby acting. Had she not been dressed when I checked back with her, I would have helped her dress and I would have realized that apparently she was not ready for such pushing. Sometimes, it seems, one way of finding out if pushing is an appropriate means to serve the child's needs is to try it and see what happens, but one must be careful, for if used too much it could turn into an authoritarian situation, like that found in many traditional schools.

Through active or passive means, the Free School teacher tries to help the students move forward in their quests for meaning. This is a subtle, delicate, and quite intuitive dance on the part of the teachers for they must weigh all sorts of information about what they know of the individual child, what the activity or situation is, how the child initially reacts to the teacher's actions, and so on. The role of the Free School teacher in figuring out how to best serve the child is exceedingly complex and it is folly to believe that by allowing children to pursue their own interests that the teacher has no role to serve, for, indeed, the role is pivotal.

The teachers also have some ancillary responsibilities that round out their roles as teachers at the Albany Free School, and include attending and participating in various meetings, supporting one another, maintaining the school, miscellaneous duties, and enforcing school rules.

Attendance at and participation in meetings is a major responsibility. Two weeks prior to the first day of school, the meetings began. Starting on August 25, and culminating on September 5, all teachers, intern teachers, and volunteer teachers met at the school each day at around 9 A.M. From then until either noon or 1 P.M., we discussed school operations. Topics included school rules, how to group the kids this year, teacher duties, working as a team, information on individual students, and so on. Part of what went on in these discussions was explanatory for the new teachers or interns, the other part was ironing out details so that everyone was basically "on the same page." Once school started, teachers attend once-a-week teachers meetings. These occur three times a month and begin at 3:30 P.M. and last, on average, three and a half hours. On the fourth Monday of each month, the teachers meeting is called a board meeting and begins at 7 P.M. and lasts about the same time. The main difference about the Board Meeting is that community members also attend and weigh in on issues concerning the school. Community members include former teachers and some parents of current or former students, but mostly the meeting is attended by current teachers. At the beginning of all these meetings an agenda clipboard is passed around and individuals jot down those topics or concerns they want to discuss. Once the meeting begins, the teachers basically work their way through these agenda items, spending as much time as necessary on each one. As mentioned in the section on seeking to know the students, a major topic of discussion concerns particular issues connected to individual students, but other topics include maintenance and operation of the building, use of the school van, field trips, and so on.

At these meetings, but not only there, teachers offer support to one another. Teachers come to these meetings with concerns about particular students and other teachers offer suggestions or give moral support. And this support is often quite in-depth, not at all cursory. Support during meetings is always evident, but is especially noticeable at the teachers meeting on the third Monday of each month. On this day, teachers meeting begins as usual with the discussion of "business" items, but the teachers try to move through these quickly so they can get to the "Process" or "Feelings" part of the meeting. This is when the teachers go around the circle and each person reflects on how he or she is feeling about how school is going. Do we feel good about things? Were we resentful about something? And was something giving us joy? My brief notes from the teachers meeting on the third Monday in October (the week of the process meeting) illustrate some of the issues touched on.

> We moved into the Feelings portion of the meeting. We went around in a circle and talked about how we are feeling things are going so far this year. Mike B. was talking about his relationship as "Enforcer" to many of the little kids and that he didn't like this. Missy suggested that he try to think up activities to do with the kids to connect with them. This is a hallmark of this school, thinking about the specific kids and then planning from there, rather than having everything all set and planned before you even know who the kids are (like I would do in traditional school). I talked about liking the relationship building time and really getting to know the kids that this school's structures allow. I also talked about liking being able to be physically affectionate (give and receive), and that I liked how I could really see how other teachers are with the kids and thus develop myself (rather than being stuck in my own classroom with no contact or exposure to how other teachers work or deal with kids). I feel like I am able to see some great teaching, which is allowing me to become a better teacher. Chris spoke about how he appreciated how everyone is really being like a team, that there is no major hierarchy, that everyone is stepping up, being

present with their whole selves. Jon talked about seeing a lot of misogyny and homophobia at the school and that he wants some ideas on how we can battle that.

Support between teachers also occurs at other times, other than the scheduled meetings. At breakfast and lunch, as well as at any other time during the day, teachers talk with one another and share concerns or troubles, and offer one another ideas on how to work through these issues. The teachers also agreed to having "creative days"—each teacher gets two days a month that he or she does not have to come to school, but instead can spend in a way that nourishes his or her soul and reinvigorates creative "juices." The only "rule" is that the teacher cannot spend these days doing chores like laundry or house cleaning; the day must be devoted to some creative endeavor. In this way, the teachers are thus supporting one another's emotional and intellectual well-being and growth.

Because the school has no janitorial or maintenance staff, the teachers serve "double duty," so to speak. During the two weeks prior to school starting, the teachers spend their mornings in meetings, as previousaly described, but then use afternoons to do maintenance and cleanup. The following listing includes some of my activities during this two-week period.

August 26:   Before lunch, I started work with Dave organizing the supply closet. Later I did work on cleaning up the room right outside the closet and then in the Computer Room.

August 27:   After lunch, I scraped some more paint and plaster off the wall. Then, I went downstairs into the Rug Room and dusted the bookshelves and organized the books, putting all fiction in that room and moving the topical books to the Big Room or the Reading Room. After organizing the books in the Rug Room, I started work in the Reading Room, organizing stuff.

August 28:   After lunch, I set about tackling the Reading Room. Again so much dirt and disorganization. I grouped things according to topic (reading, math, social studies, handwriting, spelling, etc.) and I rearranged the room somewhat and cleaned.

August 29:   In the afternoon, I helped to clean the upstairs. Dipped the blocks in bleach water, swept, helped Carrie go through stuff for the kindergarten rooms, etc.

September 2:   I painted the wall and ceiling where I had scraped off damaged paint last week. Then I started work on the seventh/eighth-grade classroom. I pulled all the books off the shelves and started to sort them by category (for nonfiction) and then by author's last name for fiction. I also washed two loads of the upstairs kids' dressup and other clothes and hung to dry.

September 3: We worked today almost all day—from about 9:30 A.M. til 3:45 P.M. I worked upstairs in the seventh/eighth-grade classroom, totally organizing the bookshelves and cleaning up all the other miscellaneous stuff that was up there. Then I went looking for a job and ended up scrubbing the downstairs bathroom on my hands and knees.

September 4: Meeting was very short and then we got right to work. I did the following: Sheetrock patched a hole in the wall, plastered over it. Moved stuff out of the Rug Room (had to take all books off shelves) and swept it to get it ready to be cleaned the next morning. Helped Missy move shelves around in the Reading Room. Washed two loads of laundry for the upstairs folks and hung them on clothes line, put labels on the pink tubs/cubbies, swept off the cubbies shelves, inventoried the kitchen supplies, helped put up chalkboard in Missy's room.

September 5: Changed light bulbs where needed, painted trim in the Art Room (around windows and doors), replastered hole in wall and then painted over all the plastered areas, straightened up and swept the big room, re-set up computers and bookshelves in Rug Room, fixed bookshelves and cabinet in middle room, straightened up the middle room, moved shelves into art room, painted a bookcase.

Teachers also take on a large part of the school's daily maintenance. Although the students are responsible for cleanup of their individual messes and lunch cleanup, and can volunteer to help the once-a-week Cleanup Committee, teachers still do a lot of tidying up each day. No one really enforces this process—teachers just do it depending on how much of a mess they are willing to tolerate. Missy and I tended to be some of the more neatnik-minded, and so we could be found on occasion sweeping or straightening up things.

Teachers also have regularly assigned duties that they sign up for at the beginning of the school year. They include early duty, lunch setup duty, "baby table" lunch duty, and closing duty. I listed descriptions of each in my journal on September 3.

Early day: When you have early day duty you come in at 7:55 A.M., and you are here to watch the kids who come in early (8:00). Everyone else comes in at 8:15. You help the cook to bring out dishes and food and set up breakfast. And you serve breakfast to the little kids. We were told to be aware that we should always give the kids *less* than what they ask for (small portions), to help prevent food wastage. Also some kids have some real food issues, like they take more than they really want, or gorge themselves, or hoard, etc. Chris said that we just can't look the other way when kids have dysfunctional food issues. We need to be mindful of kids' attitudes toward food, so we can attend to them.

"Baby Table":   At lunch, there are three "baby tables" (tables of little kids—upstairs kids) and each table has an adult who is in charge of serving out initial portions, pouring drinks, and basically teaching the kids how to eat communally (pass the food, etc.)—this teaches the kids some independence (rather than the teacher doing everything for the kid, the kids do have to pass food, etc. and it also teaches cooperation). This teacher is also aware of what the kids are eating and tries to make sure the kids eat balanced meals. At the end of the meal, the kids clear their spots themselves, even the littlest kids. No one gets out of this chore.

Lunch Setup Duty: For this job, you come upstairs at around 11:15 or 11:30. You go into the kitchen, pull out all the plates, cups, etc. You set up the tables and chairs. Mainly it is communicating with the cook to see when lunch will be and getting everything set up for it. Must be mindful of keeping things quiet 'cause the upstairs kids are having story time while all this is going on.

Closing Duty: For this job, one teacher goes through the whole downstairs at 3:00 turning off lights, shutting down computers, and shooing kids outside to be picked up or go upstairs for after-school care. This teacher also locks the doors to downstairs so the kids cannot come back in once they have gone outside or upstairs.

The last ancillary responsibility for teachers at the Free School is that of enforcing the school rules specifically connected to issues of health, safety, and community respect. In my journal I wrote of enforcing the "no candy" rule, the "no video games" rule, the "no crossing the street without a teacher" rule, the "clean up your mess" rule, the rule about "everyone doing assigned lunch duty," the "no cursing in public" rule, the "no playing on jungle gym during lunchtime" rule, and so on. In the early part of the school year, we discussed the importance of all teachers equally enforcing these rules and thus providing a "united front" on these important issues.

Clearly, the teacher's role at the Albany Free School is incredibly multifaceted and complex. In everything they do, ranging from seeking to know the students to determining the best way to serve each student to their ancillary responsibilities, these teachers embody the progressive educators' visions of what a teacher should do and who a teacher should be. The Free School teachers honor the dignity and autonomy of each student while also maintaining standards of community respect. They do not take part in the "banking" concept of education in any way. Instead they create an environment in which children can find and pursue ideas and activities that interest them, and thereby allow them to create their own knowledge and grow as human beings. I found the teachers at the Free School to be incredibly devoted to the students and to the school as an entity itself. I learned so much from them about how to be a whole person who exists alongside others (children and adults alike) and who can help those others to grow and progress. Being with these people made me redefine what a "good" teacher is and I feel that I became a much stronger teacher during the short time I was at the Free School.

Living out the progressive educators' alternative vision of education through being a teacher who interacted with these very differently acting students and experienced varied learning settings and timings, as well as the Free School's unique curriculum, challenged and transformed me in a multitude of ways. My experiences at the Free School offered me a systemic answer to the discomforts I felt both as a student and a teacher in traditional schools and in many ways helped me to unlearn the hidden curriculum lessons that I had absorbed and taught so well. The following chapter details the unlearning of those lessons.

CHAPTER EIGHT

A TEACHER TRANSFORMED

As explored in chapter 1, I experienced significant discomforts as a traditional school teacher, discomforts that I initially blamed on personal shortcomings and that later, after my exposure to critical educational theorists during my doctoral course work, I came to see as being caused by the traditional system of education in our society. I reexamined, in chapter two, my time as both a student and teacher in the traditional system in light of these systemic critiques and came to understand that much of my unease emerged as a result of certain hidden lessons I had been taught and was, in turn, teaching to my students. I sought out a school like the Albany Free School to determine if, when one removed the conditions that seemed to demand the teaching and learning of these hidden curriculum lessons, one could also be relieved of the discomforts I had experienced. What I found at the Albany Free School was that in this new setting, a setting where the ideas and vision of progressive educators were carried out, I became a very different teacher—one who unlearned the lessons of the hidden curriculum and lost many of the misgivings connected to being a teacher that I had been feeling for so long.

UNLEARNING OF INSENSIBILITY LESSON

My traditional schooling taught me all about disconnection and fragmentation and I, in turn, taught my students to be insensible of connections between people, between subjects, and within oneself. At the Free School, I learned a different way of being—how to be my whole self to the students, to see the children as whole people, and to connect and cooperate with others (teachers and students alike).

In my years of traditional teaching, I always felt as if I could not be my self in front of my students. Yes, I did feel that some parts of my personality could come out, such as my natural enthusiasm, humor, organization, and so on, but only those aspects that would support my teaching. For example, it was okay to evidence my sense of humor if it helped students learn content or made the classroom atmosphere positive. My enthusiasm was fine to bring into the classroom because it would raise motivation and classroom energy. But other parts of who I am had to stay hidden for they would have been unproductive to the transmission of the curriculum. For example, my occasional silliness had to remain bottled up, for it might give my students the impression that I was not "professional" and thus did not deserve respect. Or my easily hurt feelings had to be hidden and I needed to develop a thick skin against occasional student criticisms and hurtfulness so as to appear "in charge" and strong at all times. I had to hold back my desire to be physically affectionate with the children as well as resist their attempts to be physically affectionate with me, for fear that normal human touching of an arm, or a hug, would be misconstrued as inappropriate and thus open to liability.

All this changed at the Free School—I felt that I could show my whole self to the children since an entirely different dynamic existed between teachers and students there. Because teachers at the Free School do not hold the power and authority over students' access to privileges and dignity as they do in traditional schools, the students can thus relate to the teachers on a more equitable, and real, level. They do not have to pretend to be someone else in order to curry favor and teachers do not have to hide parts of themselves to maintain an aura of efficiency, productivity, and authority. Teachers and students at the Free School relate as equal human beings, a fact that is most simply illustrated by how the teachers and students are all on a first-name basis. True, the adults do have some level of authority over the students, but it is a "natural authority," one described by John Holt as deriving "from the fact that we are bigger, have been in the world longer and seen more of it, and have more words, more skill, more knowledge, and more experience. To the extent that our authority is natural, true, and authentic, we cannot abdicate it (even if we wanted to)."[1] This authority is not unreasonable; it is not an authority that is closed to challenges, and the students, I believe, unconsciously recognize this. When I was around the Free School students I never felt a barrier of artificiality between us, a barrier caused by false or incontestable authority. Instead I felt a realness, a relating of individual to individual that is difficult to put into words. Essentially, I felt I could be myself, organized and neat, silly, interested in reading, sensitive to harsh words, physically affectionate, and so on. I felt that it was okay for me to air my grievances, to cry (and thus to show what would be considered a "weakness" in a traditional school environment), and to be angry; I felt that nothing horrendous would happen if I let two six-year-old girls give me a hand massage or if I danced around with them in a silly manner; I felt that I could tell a child that I did not want to be around him or her for a while because the child had been mean to me the last time we worked together and didn't need to fear that I would get in trouble with administration or the child's parents; I felt that I could tell kids I was disappointed in their not living up to an agreement without thinking that I was permanently damaging their psyches; I felt like I could tease and be familiar with students and let them tease me back and not "lose control of the class." I felt that by being able to be my whole self with the Free School students I was developing authentic relationships with them, relationships that were satisfying in and of themselves, but also relationships that would ultimately aid the students in their meaning-making, growth process. For meaning making is, essentially, the process of making connections, and if a person feels disconnected from those with whom he or she spends a large amount of time (e.g., teachers), then meaning making will not occur as readily or in a manner that is healthy.

In addition to being able to be whole with the students at the Free School, I also felt that within this educational environment I could truly see the whole child. In traditional schools, I believe, teachers are somewhat prevented from viewing children as whole people. Part of this is due to the power dynamic that induces children to misrepresent who they truly are. But another aspect results from the existence of the standardized, mandated curriculum and the subsequent existence of the traditional "banking" concept of education. The teacher, in such conceptions of education, is placed in a role in which she is expected to view the students as objects, receptacles to be filled, and thus not as real, living subjects, subjects with values, knowledge, and experiences that are valid and valuable. The curriculum, issues of accountability, and information and skills transmission become the focus in traditional schools at the expense of ignoring the child. The child is an object to be fitted to this hard and given knowledge, rather than someone to be understood and valued. Lastly, the factory model of schooling prevents the teacher from truly knowing the whole child. Even the most humanistic teacher who wants desperately to see the whole child and individualize instruction for that child cannot do so because of numbers. I believe that it is unreasonable to expect a single teacher to truly come to know all her students when she has constant contact with groups, not individuals. Stories abound of high school teachers who teach one hundred to one hundred and fifty students a day, of middle school teachers who have sixty to ninety students a day, and of elementary school teachers with self-contained classes that range in average size of twenty to thirty and sometimes more. These ratios of adult to children are not conducive to getting to know the whole child in any depth.

The scene is completely different at the Albany Free School. With teacher-to-student ratios of approximately 1:4, with a lack of a standardized, mandated curriculum and thus an abandonment of the "banking" concept of education, and with a more symmetrical power dynamic between teachers and students, a teacher at the Free School can truly come to know the students as whole people.

It took me a while to realize that the Free School allowed me the time to really get to know the students. During my traditional school teaching I always felt rushed: rushed to cover my lesson plan before class ended, rushed to get feedback to all my students in a timely manner, and rushed to go around the classroom to see how each child was progressing. The number of students I had coupled with a massively broad curriculum that had to be taught in the one hundred and eighty-day school year left me constantly feeling as if I could never get anything done or spend any substantive time thinking about the individual students. When I came to the Free School, I knew I was going to have contact with significantly fewer students and not be responsible for teaching a standardized curriculum, but I still carried with me the habits learned over many years in traditional schools. Because there is seemingly so little time in traditional schools, I became habituated to not delving deeper into problems that arose, such as a student's being defiant. Instead, I developed, out of necessity, knee-jerk reactions. The student did not do what I asked? Ask again. Still refusing? Initiate disciplinary step progression. There was no time to try to reason with the child or probe into why a child was acting in a particular way. If the teacher took the time to do so, she would be slowing down the rest of the class's progression through the curriculum. With these experiences in mind, and these habits ingrained in me, I was slow to realize that at the Free School I could actually take the time to listen to the kids and empathize with their situations. For example, a number of students regularly exhibited rather defiant behavior and seemed to thrive on power struggles. If these students were in my traditional class-room, they would often have been "in trouble" for not doing what I asked or for being disruptive. My first reaction to dealing with these defiant students was to come at them with power and authority and with the expecta-tion that they would do as I say because I am the teacher. To my surprise, these Free School students did not easily acquiesce to my authority and I was at a loss as to how to proceed. There was no in-school suspension or principal I could send them to, there was no after-school detention, and there were really no privileges I could take away from them. What was I to do? Was this something worthy of calling a council meeting? I looked to see what other teachers did with these students and found that they were stopping and taking the time to delve into the reasons for the children's behavior. By talking to the children themselves, the children's parents, and other teachers, the teachers were able to ferret out the roots of the problem and thus could then deal with those roots rather than just the symptoms. I noted in my journal my feelings about observing what the veteran teachers were doing.

September 24:   City hike time. While getting ready to go, Missy got the first graders to clean up a mess that was in the Reading Room. Sarah pitched a fit about it, thinking she was going to be left be-hind. She was whining a lot and crocodile tears going on, etc. That works my nerves so much, and I have no sympathy for it. In the van on the way to the hike, she started in again because Missy made her take off the wings she was wearing on her back and which were causing her to lean forward in her seat. Again that just works my nerves and I was all for taking her back to school (or threatening to do so if she didn't stop crying). What makes me so harsh? Was it only because Sarah's whining/crying/wailing was getting on my nerves, or is it something else? Later, on the walk, I overheard Missy and Dave talking about Sarah in very sympathetic terms, trying to figure out why she behaved in the way she did. *They* are better teachers than I, because they actually cared to probe the root causes of things/behavior rather than have this whole consequence mentality that I do. I really need to work on that; it was certainly *never* something that I worked on in my traditional school teaching—it was always about stop the symptoms, never probe into the root causes and/or try to cure the disease.

September 26: I then saw Blair downstairs, and knowing she, too, was on jobs crew (lunch cleanup duty) I asked her why wasn't she upstairs? She said she didn't want to do it, and I said she needed to. She refused two or three times my fairly calm requests for her to go upstairs. I then asked, did she want me to call a council meeting over something like this, knowing that she would be made to do it. She said yes to call a council meeting, which I did. I probably should have asked another teacher before calling it, but oh well now. So when Missy got down there and I explained what it was about, she sort of got this irritated/exasperated expression on her face, and said that this was not something that we should call a council meeting over, and that we couldn't get the kids who were doing jobs because it was more important for jobs to get done (which I am really wondering about, because if nothing is more important than council meetings, why is cleanup more important?). So, Missy sort of ran an informal meeting, not a formal council meeting, and she said to Blair after Blair said she didn't want to do her jobs, "Do you want to go back up to the kindergarten?" To which Blair said yes. Bridget (Blair's older sister) explained that their mom made Blair do jobs at home when she was being punished and maybe that is why she doesn't like doing jobs. Missy got it out of Blair that she didn't like doing jobs because she didn't know how to do it, and so Missy offered to do them with her. Then Sarah said that Blair had done just a little bit of jobs, but then said, "Let's go downstairs," which indicates to me that it is not so much that Blair doesn't know how to do the jobs, rather, she just didn't want to do them today. Missy said that that was different. She then asked Blair if she wanted to call a council meeting, which she did. What it boiled down to was that maybe Blair hadn't been trained well enough to do the jobs, but was still at fault for not asking for help from anyone, which *was* within her power to do. Reflecting on this whole situation, I can see that this is another case of my not looking more deeply at a problem for the root cause of something *and* it is another case of me not having a sympathetic attitude for the child but rather feeling like it is a power struggle to get her (or him) to do what I (a teacher, damnit!) wants her to do. Again, this is another thing I need to work on. When I get that tightness feeling in my stomach over feeling like I am in a power struggle with a kid, I need to stop, step back, and rethink what I am doing, but that is *so* hard to do, when all my instincts and reactions are telling me to do otherwise.

October 16:   I then wandered into the Science Room and sat reading a book for a while. Around 2:40, Callie, Rebecca, and the other girls came back in from being at the park with Julie [visiting intern teacher from last year]. Callie said something about Rebecca writing "Fuck" on some lightpole near the governor's mansion. At first, I was not really responding to that, and then Elizabeth (who was playing chess with Ajay) said to me, "What do you think of that? Is that okay in your book?" To which I replied that it wasn't, so I started to question the girls a bit more. What finally came out was that it was Callie who had written the word on the lightpole. Elizabeth talked to her some about how that is unacceptable because it gives the Free School a bad name. I said to Callie, let's you and I get some paper towels and go wipe it off, which we did. As I was walking up the street with her, I was sort of at a loss for what to say. I do find what she did unacceptable, but couldn't summon up how to explain that it wasn't good. Finally I just conversationally (not harshly or angrily) said to her, "Have you ever heard the term 'trashy' to describe something or someone?" She said yes, and then I told her that many people would look at someone writing "Fuck" on a lightpole as trashy and did she want people to consider her trashy? She was being very glib in her responses to me and said "yes." (Callie had said to me, "I'm just being a smart ass," so I wasn't feeling that she was being disrespectful to me in her responses; she just clearly didn't want to give me a serious answer.) I told her that if people saw her as trashy they would close doors of opportunity to her and did she want that? I also said that writing on public property wasn't good because it is vandalism and did she want people coming and writing stuff on her house? To all of which she said yes (again being glib). When I got back to the school, I went up to Missy, described to her what happened and my response, and asked how she would have handled it. She said that she, too, would have required Callie to go clean it up, but on the walk there she would have asked what Callie was so angry about, because to Missy writing something like that is an act of anger. Missy said that Callie had been sort of angry acting all day and that I should probe into what the root cause of her action was, not necessarily how it appears.

I began to emulate these teachers' actions in trying to know the whole child, rather than surface behaviors. When I did, I found that power problems fell away, and I got a glimpse of who the child was. For example, I earlier described a situation in which six-year-old Blair was upset with seven-year-old Macon for allegedly stealing her ring. She initially approached me to make him give back the ring. He first refused, saying that the ring was his, which upset Blair a great deal and she was then on the verge of fighting with Macon. I stepped in to delve deeper, and the problem was ultimately resolved happily for all. Had I been in a traditional school I doubt very much if I would have been able to take the time to deal with this altercation. In all likelihood, Blair and Macon would have ended up being defiant of school rules against fighting and I would have had to send them to the principal's office. The issue would not have gotten resolved in the same manner as it did at the Free School, and I would never have obtained any deeper understandings of Blair and Macon.

Being able to overcome the traditional power struggles with the Free School students and thus getting to know the whole child was especially evident with eight-year-old Rebecca and six-year-old Sarah. These two girls were, early on, thorns in my side, for they were constantly defiant. But because my role as a teacher at the Free School was not largely about compelling them to do certain work and behave in certain ways, as it is for traditional teachers, I was able to see other sides to these girls. In November I noted the following in my journal.

> I have noticed that I have gotten to like Sarah and Rebecca a lot more than I used to. I can't say that I like them as much as, say, Ajay and Callie, but I can tolerate and even enjoy them now. Had I been in traditional school with them, I'm not sure if I would have ever gotten to this point. My issues with them have always been power issues (their not doing what I ask them to, etc.), and in a traditional classroom, this is the only level I would have known them on. But being at the Free School, I get to experience them in different ways, can be with them in different ways and thus can get to know them in a wider way.

The Free School, with its low teacher-to-student ratio, its lack of a mandated, standardized curriculum, and its structures for guaranteeing equitable power between teachers and students, is an environment that encourages teachers to get to know children in ways that are virtually impossible in traditional schools. My ingrained lesson of insensibility further withered away with my newfound ability to understand who my students were as fully fleshed out individuals rather than as mere objects occupying seats in my classroom.

I have mentioned in various chapters how the Free School teachers work together in many ways. This was all new to me and it took some time to get used to this heightened level of collegiality. Traditional school teaching is, more often than not, a solitary job. One deals with one's classroom and students on one's own (a habit that often begins before one becomes a teacher, in one's own traditional schooling where the "lone roadrunner" mentality is prominent).[2] Time and the organization of schools work against most teachers watching how others teach. A traditional teacher cannot leave a classroom unattended to observe other teachers and, even when one has a planning period, one is reluctant to use that precious time for observing and interacting with other teachers. Teachers are also conditioned to believe that when another adult is in the room watching them teach, it is for evaluative purposes. This, too, adds to the reluctance to invite others to watch oneself or observe how others teach. Such evaluations can make one either look good or bad vis-à-vis other teachers, and so teachers develop a strong, but underlying and subtle sense of competition (again, a habit of competition that often begins when one is a student in traditional schools). All this conditioning and shaping of who I was did not easily disappear once I entered the doors of the Free School. I was so used to being disconnected from and insensible of others that even while I truly enjoyed having more teacher collegiality, I also, at the same time, struggled with connecting to the other teachers at the Free School.

I loved that at the Free School I could learn how to deal with students in situations by watching other teachers; I got so many good ideas and insights from these observations. But this newfound sense of connection also brought with it some discomfort. I still found myself feeling competitive with the other teachers. On October 3, I wrote about this feeling in my journal.

> Yesterday, when I was teaching Adam how to sew on buttons, Conner came in and was asking about something that only Megan had an answer to. He said he was going up to her to ask, but I reminded him that she was teaching sex ed. right then and did he think it was appropriate to interrupt that for his question. In some ways when I was doing this little interchange, I was sort of showing off to Adam that I was a good teacher/role model. This reminds me of how I was sometimes at my first teaching job, when I would be firm with kids in front of other teachers, sort of showing, "Hey, I am competent, hard but benevolent, etc." In some ways it is me liking to hear myself talk, and liking to appear powerful, obeyed, etc. Is this something that we are trained to be like as teachers? Or is there something in me that seeks others' approval, good opinion? And did that

come from my training in the hidden curriculum, that my worth is only what others think of me?

My feelings of competitiveness also surfaced whenever I succeeded in getting some Free School students to do reading, math, or some other traditionally highly valued academic work. I would experience a sense of smugness over this fact, as if to say to the other teachers—"See, I'm a good teacher." Connection with other teachers was still fraught, for me, with competition.

This issue of wanting to appear competent to the other teachers came to a head in mid-November over apple pies. On October 30, the entire school had gone to a nearby apple orchard to glean unpicked apples from the trees. Traditionally, Free School students used the many apples that were picked to make apple butter or applesauce to sell to raise funds for class trips, and other activities. At the teachers meeting following the gleaning, someone raised the question of who was going to spearhead the use of apples. I enjoy cooking and teaching others to cook, so I tentatively volunteered. I asked about the procedure and was told that although one person heads up the process, students and teachers tend to come and go throughout the day, helping out in fits and starts. That sounded appealing, very communal and so on, and I offered to head things up. The intern teacher Michael also volunteered to be co-head of this project. We soon discovered that we had no up-front money to purchase jars and spices and so devised a plan to raise this seed money. We decided to send out order forms for apple pies (a high, quick-profit item, we believed) that required people to prepay. This would give us money to buy pie supplies and a high profit to then use to purchase materials for applesauce making. On the day for making the pies, Michael took charge of creating the filling (peeling and cutting apples and adding spices) and I took charge of making fifty piecrusts from scratch. Michael set up in the downstairs while I headed to the kitchen. In my journal that evening I wrote the following.

> Today was pie-making day, so immediately after my breakfast duty was over, I went straight into the kitchen to start making piecrusts, I had to make around fifty crusts, and boy did I regret not just buying premade crusts. For the most part I was by myself. Some kids came in to help mix the piecrust dough (Lawrence, Daniel, Allen, Bridget). Allen is very sloppy and I was somewhat critical, which I think made him not want to do the stuff with me. And I think my stress and perfectionism emanate somehow from my pores and maybe makes people not want to work with me. Rolling out the piecrust was a major job and hard to do. For a while Kelby (Hudson Valley intern) was working with me, doing a better job than me, hers were beautifully rolled out. Anita (mother of a preschool student) helped some, too. Kids who helped roll out included Alison and Bridget, Ursula,

and Allen (again, I think I ran him off with my criticality), that was it! No teachers came in to roll any dough or to offer to do so, if they did come into the kitchen. Once all the dough was rolled out, I helped out with cutting apples and mixing up the filling and then filling the crusts and baking. Michael had come upstairs to finish with apple cutting, and Corine came with him. At around 1:45, some of the upstairs kids came in and wanted to help cut apples, which upped the stress level for me 'cause I was nervous about these little preschool kids using knives. And then a lot of upstairs teachers came into the kitchen and were just hanging around and talking, not offering to help, and sort of being in the way as I was taking the hot pies out of the oven and putting them on the counter. Corine was a tremendous help both with the pies and the upstairs kids and I enjoyed (as much as I could enjoy, at least) working with her on that. She also was in the after-school program, so she was able to help all the way to the end (which was 5:15). Conner "helped" a little bit (he's more talk than action), and so did Rebecca. I also felt pressure from having to share the kitchen with Cathryn (the cook), I could tell she wasn't crazy about having to share the space, and I felt pressure that I had to be sure to leave everything spotless. The pies turned out well and tasted good as well as looked good, but that is something I will not be in a hurry to do again. I felt pressure to get it all done in one day because I wanted to go on the trip to Grafton (the school's woodland property) on Friday, which would have been my last chance to go out there, as hunting season starts next week. I also felt pressure to get it done because where would we have put the filling and piecrusts over-night? There was no room in the school fridge for anything. It was frustrating and disappointing. I thought it was going to be a fun time with kids and teachers coming in and out all day, helping out for just a little bit each, but that was not what happened. Out of thirty-four kids, only six helped me, and out of fifteen adults who could have helped, only three did (Michael, Anita, and Kelby). At community circle [a community meeting held on the second Thursday of each month for people to share concerns, hash out issues, etc.] this evening, I said what a frustrating day it was and a disappointing day, too, and that I didn't want any more days like that and was sort of crying as I said it. I was so tired and my muscles ached from working so hard. (Missy had come in after lunch and given me a short back rub, which felt good, but I think I would have preferred an offer of help!) I basically said that not many people helped at all, which is true if you look at the above list. Missy said (again this was at community circle) that I need to draw my limits and express them. Missy was trying to be helpful, but she made me feel worse by making me feel that what happened was entirely my fault.

The next day, I wrote the following.

> At breakfast this morning I was still a bit weepy, feeling angry about the whole pie thing yesterday. Missy sat down at the table where I was eating breakfast with Colleen and said something again like she did last night, that I need to ask for help or set my limits or something like that. I immediately began crying, saying that she is making me feel like it is all my fault. She came over and sat next to me and rubbed my back as she talked (and Colleen tried to console me as well). What she basically said to me was that I needed to have asked for help; she did not know that I was feeling so stressed, I seemed to be enjoying myself, and that she (and others) can't read my mind. I told her that I had expected something different from what Dave had told me about apple stuff, that people would be in and out all day helping out. I told her that I did not expect that I would have to go around and ask for help, that that sort of makes things unpleasant. I said ultimately that it was a fifty–fifty thing, that yes, I should have asked for help, but that also people should have offered without having to be asked, that it is nice to not have to ask for help. She agreed I think. She was also asking where this anger and frustration came from, was there something in my family upbringing that made me be a person who didn't ask for help when I needed it? I have since thought on that, but I don't think it stems from anything in my family, that rather it may stem from my schooling experiences. Elizabeth Dodson Gray wrote in the article, "The Culture of Separated Desks," that schools encourage a "roadrunner" approach to things, that people need to do things alone, that cooperation is not encouraged and is even called cheating, etc.[3] I wonder if my not asking for help is an offshoot of that training I received throughout my education. It certainly meshes with some of my other approaches to education, that I dislike cooperative group activities (to do them or even assign them), I never liked to depend on anyone else for school things (like taking notes for me, maybe that was why I hated missing any classes) because I never felt that they could do as good a job as me, that I prefer being alone/working alone, and so on. Perhaps this is a way that my education has damaged me. I was always successful by myself (and have been rewarded well for being a lone roadrunner) that I feel it almost repugnant to ask for help. I remember thinking, as Missy was talking to me, how uncomfortable I was with her questions; it is evidence of not wanting to face one's problems, but maybe another proof that my education damaged me in that it makes me reluctant to really delve into myself. Who knows?

This experience taught me that I was essentially trained to be competitive, that this competitive nature required that I be disconnected from others in terms of asking for help. I realized that if I wanted to truly connect to others, I would have to break out of my habits of competition and learn how to ask for and seek out the cooperation of others. I know from the positive experiences I had with cooperation and collegiality with the Free School teachers that it is worth it to become connected to others, but the habit of disconnection was not broken overnight. I can honestly say that in my short time remaining at the Free School I worked on breaking this habit. For example, on the day that we made applesauce (about a week after the pie-making) I tried asking for help when the hand crank on the applesauce mill broke. This reduced my stress considerably and I saw the value of connecting to others in this way. I also found that such a request did not make me feel "less than" others and that asking for help is okay to do.

Clearly, my training in the hidden curriculum lesson of insensibility damaged me in many ways. My time at the Free School began to heal me. I am not a fully connected, whole person in my current daily interactions, but I am aware of the incredible value of such connection and strive to constantly increase the connections in my life. In my current teaching I have been making a special effort to present my whole self to the students and calm my tendency to rush, rush, rush to get through the course content. And I have been struggling especially with asking others for help when I need it and trying not to feel so competitive. It has been difficult unlearning the insensibility lesson, but the hardest part, that of naming my problem, is behind me.

UNLEARNING OF CLASS POSITION LESSON

As I detailed in chapter 2, my traditional schooling taught me the lesson of class position, that different people are taught differently according to their social class and that this differential treatment is, somehow, right and proper. At the Free School, I did not find myself treating specific groups of children differently from others. In fact, although I knew that approximately seventy-five percent of Free School students were eligible for free or reduced price lunches (an indicator of the family's low socioeconomic status), I could not readily identify the students who were from a higher or lower social class. In my years of teaching at traditional schools, I rarely had any such trouble.

What was the reason for my inability to identify the social classes of the Free School students? I think a large part of it is because cultural capital is not such a commodity at the Free School as it is in traditional schools. Cultural capital is all about valuing one body of knowledge, or one way of speaking, or relating (the white, middle-class way) over any others. In that the Free School does not overly value this cultural capital, students enter the school on a more equal footing. The Free School's assumptions about learning and knowledge help to create an educational environment in which children are not put into competition or hierarchically ranked with one another, and thus teachers do not view the kids as high track/high ability versus lower track/low ability. The teachers attend to the children as unique individuals and thus they do not, as I did in my traditional school teaching, essentialize the students according to some image of who they are derived solely or partly from their social class. I found nearly all the children of the Free School to be bright and inquisitive and eager to participate in activities that held meaning for them. The students did not seem alienated, as so many traditionally schooled students do, by a value system that negates their experiences or way of knowing—for such a hegemonic value system seems to not exist at the Free School.

In the Free School environment I was not only liberated from my traditional teacher habit of differentiating between students according to their social class, but also found myself questioning my traditional middle-class values. I saw that my ingrained hegemonic beliefs in such things as punishment, hard work always being rewarded, and not getting second chances were, in fact, questionable and damaging to the growth of children. My knee-jerk reactions to certain situations in the school, described in the previous section, were not conducive to allowing children to progress in their knowledge construction and meaning-making process. For example, I tended to be very much in favor of a child being punished for any transgressions (in other words, attending to symptoms) rather than trying to help the child delve deeper to understand the root causes of the inappropriate behavior and thus be able to resolve the core issue. In questioning such middle-class values that I carried with me into the Free School environment, and in understanding that more than one way of knowing, speaking, or relating can be valued, I began the process of unlearning the hidden curriculum lesson of class position. Simply put, grouping kids in my mind by how well they aligned to my traditionally trained vision of what is valued in our society was unnecessary and inappropriate in this environment.

UNLEARNING OF CONSTANT OUTSIDE EVALUATION LESSON

As mentioned earlier in regard to unlearning competition and insensibility, at the Free School I worked on breaking free of my own addiction to others' evaluations of me. But did I also tackle unlearning the practice of constantly evaluating others, students in particular? Yes and no. I still evaluated the students' progress in the sense that I gauged how I could best help them in their meaning making and knowledge construction and I still evaluated them in the sense of trying to know who they were, but these evaluations are quite different from many of the evaluations that traditional teachers do. In other words, my evaluations at the Free School did not have the same effects as the evaluations I did as a traditional school teacher. In traditional schools, the evaluations I did of my students carried much power in terms of controlling the flow of present and future rewards and punishment to the children. Although these evaluations are ostensibly done to help the child, teacher, and parents know the students better, the fact that rewards and punishments get attached creates a situation in which children are defined differently from who they really are. Children who receive frequent positive evaluations often become people who will do whatever it takes (employing moral or immoral means) to ensure that the positive evaluations continue. Thus, children become more focused on the evaluations, on how others define them, and not on their own growth and definition of self. And children who receive frequent negative evaluations often become people who have poor self-images because they have taken on others' definition of who they are rather than creating that definition themselves. Traditional school evaluations are also very exclusionary or narrow in that they primarily measure progress in the transmission of the standardized curriculum, a curriculum that values only certain ways of knowing and learning (read: behaving), and certain bodies of knowledge. If students do not do well in these traditionally valued ways of learning, then negative assumptions or evaluations are attached to the child. When children perform poorly in traditional schools, traditional educators typically do not seek to find out if students have other ways of knowing and learning; they simply continue to hold those children up to the same standards and practices. I want to make clear here that this is not a case of "evil" teachers refusing to see children for who they are but instead one of a system—the traditional system of schooling—that, because of its assumptions about the purpose of education and about knowledge and learning, creates a situation wherein teachers often cannot, even if they want to, value (and thus attach positive evaluations to) other ways of knowing and learning.

At the Free School, evaluations have few to no attendant punishments or rewards. And since this is the case, students do not need to define themselves by how others define them. They can instead focus on finding out who they are, identifying their interests and concerns and so on, rather than trying to conform themselves to narrow definitions of what it means to be a "good" or "successful" person.

Teachers at the Free School are liberated from having to constantly hold the students up to these narrow definitions. They can instead really look to see who the students are and go from there in helping them in their personal growth and meaning making. They thus do not wield extraordinary power over the students, a power that strains and makes somewhat artificial the relationships between teachers and students. Teachers at the Free School, because they do not have to constantly evaluate how well a student is absorbing a standardized curriculum, can focus more on process and less (if at all) on end products.

This change in my habits of evaluation caused me some trouble at first. I had to mentally shift gears a number of times. For example, on September 22, I attended a goddess/girls group meeting, which I detailed in an earlier chapter. In my journal entry I commented that this meeting was "a bit new agey for me." I felt on some level that this was just so much "fluff" and so open-ended. I was uncomfortable, thinking, "What's all this accomplishing?" I saw no clear and evident end product and so, in a way, devalued the whole process. I did comment in my journal that the meeting "was a good space for the girls to just talk about stuff/express themselves," but this was a somewhat reluctant concession. I now know that such space is incredibly valuable, but my training in traditional schooling (as both student and teacher) told me that if there is no end product, then there is no value. Later in my time at the Free School, I openly noticed my favoring of product over process. On October 22, I wrote in my journal.

> After the activities meeting, I went into the Art Room with Colleen and Ursula. They said they wanted to help repaint the front of my lollipop headpiece (Halloween costume). While we were doing it I was noticing that is was messier than I would have done it/liked it, but Ursula commented a couple of times about how much fun this was, that it made me realize what is really important. Who really cares if the costume isn't perfect—isn't it the process that really matters? This is again another example of my school training, that the end product is what is more important. This makes me think of how Missy reacts to the kids' artwork. Me, I don't think much of their stuff, but Missy makes a big deal out of the kids' work, and so maybe what she is seeing is the work and process that went into it and not the end result alone.

My journey into unlearning the lesson of constant outside evaluation and valuing process over product was clearly under way.

Another area of trouble that I experienced as I shifted from traditional teacher evaluations to Free School teacher evaluations was in terms of teacher power. I have previously discussed how I had become accustomed to being a teacher who held authoritarian power over students, a power that derived largely from the fact that I, as a teacher, could control the flow of rewards and punishments to the students depending on my evaluations of them. Because the Free School evaluations did not entail this power, I found myself at a bit of a loss at times, particularly when it came to student behaviors and interest areas. My unlearning of the constant outside evaluation lesson occurred concurrently with my unlearning of the cognitive and behavioral dependence lesson, and since this lesson also involves the issue of teacher power, I will now shift to a discussion of it.

UNLEARNING OF COGNITIVE AND BEHAVIORAL DEPENDENCE LESSON

Children in traditional schools learn early on that they will receive positive evaluations if they behave as the teacher instructs them. This applies not only to doing assigned curriculum work (cognitive dependence) but also to how the children interact with others and comport themselves when working alone (behavioral dependence). The teacher holds a tremendous amount of power over the children's thinking and actions. I learned this lesson well in my time as a student, and when I was a teacher I expected my students to do as I instructed. If my students did not follow my rules and the standardized curriculum that I was teaching, I then withheld whatever privileges I could (movements in the classroom and school, my praise or the praise and high regard of others, classroom rewards, etc.) and I meted out whatever punishments seemed in order (being sent out into the hall, going to the principal's office, attending in-school suspension or detention, not being allowed on field trips, etc.).

As I mentioned earlier, at the Free School I did not have such extreme authority to demand compliance from students. True, as a teacher I could enforce the rules, but if a child did not comply, then it was not I who withheld rewards or gave out punishments, instead it was the council meeting, and even there the focus was not on punishments and rewards, but more on working through and seeking out the root of the problem. So even though I did have some power that goes along with the "natural authority" of being an adult, this power is a far cry from that held by traditional school teachers.

Not only did I learn new ways of interacting with children who did not comply behaviorally, I learned to deal with the fact that I could not compel cognitive dependence either with the threat of punishments or the promise of rewards. I knew going in to the Free School that no learning was compulsory and so did not expect to "push" curriculum on anyone. Even though I realized this at one level of my consciousness, at another level I could not easily get past the fact that I was accustomed to communicating to students that certain knowledge or interests are more valuable than others. Thus, early on, I frequently offered activity ideas or lessons in math and reading and fretted over not seeing the kids taking part in these traditionally highly valued subjects. My journal entries reflect these worries.

> *September 17:* While out at the girls' [Rebecca, Delia, and Miranda] treehouse I asked them if they like to read, and they all seemed to say yes, and I asked then when do they read, at home or at school? And they said at home. This no reading at school is really something that worries me, but most of the kids (except the first graders) seem to know how to read, at least to some level.

> *September 19:* Ajay had a deck of Magic cards, but he doesn't know how to play the real way, so he was sort of making things up. But his rules didn't make any sense to me, and today I wasn't really up to going along with his imagination, and so suggested that we play war instead with a real deck of cards. This seemed to make him

mad and he stormed off in a huff. Blair and I played war and were soon joined by Ursula. It was a good way of teaching which has higher value. I was sad that Ajay stormed off, maybe I should have just gone along with his way of playing, or encouraged Blair to help him make up the game rules, etc. I don't know, I guess I was tired and wanted to play a real game that would help teach stuff. Maybe this is a sign of my training to value "real" academic over imagination and creativity. I need to be careful of this.

October 21: We listened to *Hatchet* this afternoon. I knitted for almost the whole time, although I did mention to Lawrence that seeing the words (following along in the book) and hearing them said at the same time helps to improve reading and did he want to follow along in the book? He said no pretty strongly. This made me worry somewhat because I sort of felt, well, how is this reading class if he is just listening? Whenever I paused my knitting, I would look up in the book where we were and follow along a ways, hoping that my example would inspire Lawrence to do the same. At one point, he did sort of look over at the book with me, but that did not last very long. Why couldn't I just relax about this? Do I somehow feel that just listening was not good enough in and of itself?

October 22: While working on the costume, Ursala asked if after we were done we could go to the museum, which I agreed to. When we were all cleaned up, I went walking around and asked if other kids wanted to go, too. On reflection I almost wish that I had just kept it to Ursula and Colleen (and maybe Ajay) as they are all on the same reading level, etc. and maybe we could have intensively focused on one or two exhibits. When we got to the museum, we looked a bit at the gems and minerals and then went into the Kids Discovery Zone. Most of the kids went straight for the computers and started to play the educational games on them, which is okay, I suppose (why do I even say that like I devalue that sort of activity and that the only worthwhile activity is looking at the exhibits?)

And my journal entries reflect my excessive satisfaction when I got students to take part in the traditionally valued activities or subjects.

October 21: I have been meaning to write about how I am feeling about having some set classes to teach (like algebra, reading, etc.) In some ways I feel good and almost smug that I got kids to do something regular. In other ways I feel good that the kids have wanted to commit to doing something more "academic." Why do I feel both of these ways? For both maybe because I am still caught up in the old culture of schooling and teaching, a culture that says that academics is *the* most important thing and that if you can get kids interested in doing the academics, then that must mean you're a good teacher.

In a way, I think I was still trying to demand cognitive dependence by communicating my value system to the students through the activities I offered and took part in. Luckily for the students, the overall structure of the school, with its emphasis on students creating their own unique curricula, dampened the effect of my conscious and unconscious pushing of a certain agenda. By the time I left in late November, I had realized that my valuing of certain knowledge and interests was inappropriate, for I had repeatedly seen evidence that children learned, progressed, and grew without necessarily working in the traditionally valued "academic" subjects. And so by Thanksgiving I felt a significant reduction in my concerns about and my attempts to push the traditionally valued disciplines and skills, such as reading and math. I relaxed a great deal and attempted to pull in these subjects and skills whenever they seemed appropriate *within* the students' interests rather than as ends in themselves. Thus, I was breaking myself of the habit of trying to train the kids to be dependent on teachers to tell them what to think about and be interested in.

Unlearning the hidden curriculum lessons removed many of the discomforts I had felt as a traditional school teacher. Because of the different structures, practices, and curricula present at the Free School, I no longer experienced apprehension around unequal power dynamics, trying to compel or motivate children to do things they did not want to, making kids behave, seeing kids playact or not being themselves to garner rewards or avoid punishments, around lack of autonomy due to a standardized curriculum, around grading, ranking, and tracking, and around isolation. I felt a tremendous sense of relief during my time at the Albany Free School—not just from my previous discomforts, but also from the idea that the difficulties I faced as a traditional school teacher were solely my fault. By being in a totally different school setting, one that embraced and embodied a vision for education that was so far removed from the traditional, I saw that a systemic approach, not a "tweaking" of individual factors within the system, is what is needed to solve educational difficulties in our society. Where did that realization leave me? Was I to stay in a school whose vision gave me comfort and ease or was there a role for me to play back in traditional schools?

CHAPTER NINE

REFORM OR REVOLUTION—
IS THERE HOPE FOR CHANGE
IN TRADITIONAL SCHOOLS?

What was I to do now that I had seen and come to highly value an alternative educational vision in practice? Should I and other people interested in achieving the ends of progressive education try to slowly and gradually alter the present school system (thereby working within the system of public education) or should I and other people set up counter-institutions that quickly and fully implement the sought-for structural changes and assumptions (thereby working outside the system of public education)? In what direction should I put my energies as a teacher?

INTERNAL REFORM IS THE MORE EFFECTIVE APPROACH

There are particular progressive educators, people generally identified as critical pedagogues or social democrats, who, according to Ron Miller, in his book *Free Schools, Free People*, believe that the struggle to bring about a better world (the struggle against hegemony) needs to occur inside the "cultural arena" of public schools. Social democrats and critical pedagogues believe that it is the struggle that matters more than anything and that to abandon this struggle by leaving the public schools and working for change from the outside contributes to the breakdown of democratic community life. These educators believe that work to change schools from within by means of gradual reforms would help students to learn what it means to be a member of a participatory democracy where dialogue and debate are essential elements of citizenship. To leave the public education system and attempt revolutionary change outside of it would, according to critical pedagogues, deny students the opportunity of learning these skills of dialogue and debate.[1]

Critical pedagogues are also wary of abandoning public education completely because they feel that to do so would be to ignore social and economic realities. Jonathan Kozol in his 1972 book, *Free Schools*, argued that if we set up revolutionary counterinstitutions that negate everything about traditional public schools, then many students, particularly poor and minority students, would suffer by the minimization of their life opportunities. He wrote that, "It is in my opinion both unwise and perhaps destructive [to poor and minority students] to attempt to close our eyes to the existence of such matters [as the system of credentialing]."[2] He further wrote that "acting as if the system of credentials, once ignored, will fall to pieces . . . is insanity."[3] Instead of negating everything about traditional public schools, Kozol recommended helping these students learn to work within the system, while at the same time pointing out how corrupt it is. He felt that the students would, through this process, ultimately end up in positions of power from which they could elicit change. In Kozol's and other critical pedagogues' minds, one could bring about change gradually while also attending to the here-and-now needs of students to have lives in which social and economic opportunities are plentiful (or, at the least, not overly stunted). Michael Apple and James Beane expressed this point eloquently in their book, *Democratic Schools*, when they wrote

> Democratic educators live with the constant tension of seeking a more significant education for young people while still attending to the knowledge and skills expected by powerful educational forces whose interests are anything but democratic. . . . We cannot ignore dominant knowledge. Having it does open some doors. . . . Our task is to reconstruct dominant knowledge and employ it to help, not hinder, those who are least privileged in this society.[4]

Other progressive educators, however, contend that these arguments are flawed, and that gradual internal reform is not and, really, cannot be the means to quickly and most effectively achieve the end goals of progressive education. I turn now to an examination of the effectiveness of a revolutionary approach.

EXTERNAL REVOLUTION IS THE MORE EFFECTIVE APPROACH

To the critical pedagogues' first argument that when people create counterinstitutions outside the public education system they deny children the opportunity to develop skills of dialogue and debate, we need only look at the example of the Albany Free School (as detailed in chapters 5 through 8) to know that a school can be set up in which children learn these vital skills of what it means to be a citizen in a participatory democracy. To the larger issue of closing off the public debate and dialogue on education by some progressive educators who create counterinstitutions and abandon the public education system, the response is as follows: first, their creation of such institutions actually keeps the dialogue going, just on a different level; second, it is not the people in these counterinstitutions who are unwilling to take part in debate, but the public education system itself is the one that cuts off dialogue by its very nature.

Progressive educators involved in schools that actively embody the alternative vision of education strongly disagree that their creation (or proposed creations) of counter-educational institutions eliminates dialogue about the purposes and approaches of public education. They believe that even though they are not working for redefinitions *within* the public education sphere, they are still striving for change, just in a different way. They feel that what they are doing is providing an alternative conception of what education can be, that seeking change also means living change, and by living change they are thus beacons of hope for a society that has lost its way in the educational realm.[5] The Free School teachers Dave, Chris, and Bhawin each gave evidence of this belief in their interviews when they spoke about whether the Albany Free School has an impact on the wider, traditional educational system.

> *Dave:*   I think it depends, but I know at least for our case, there are principals and school administrators out there in the Albany area that recognize that they have . . . say they have a student in their school that's getting in trouble or not succeeding. They recognize students that are maybe a good fit for us and will call us, so maybe, you know, in an overarching way, you know, they believe that traditional schooling is the best, but they also recognize it doesn't fit everybody, and, and they'll send certain kids to us . . . so, I mean, I think that's, that's making a change, that's someone working in the education field saying, "Hey, we don't have all the answers, that there are other ways of doing things and there are some kids we don't, we're not doing the best for them, and here's this place, the Free School, that's going to do this kid right."

> *Chris:*   Yeah, I think so [think that the Free School impacts traditional education]. I don't know how much, I certainly wouldn't want to exaggerate. I don't think we have a huge influence. . . . But maybe an occasional teacher, you know, that we've influenced and maybe they've made a difference in their classroom or, you know, something like that.

> *Bhawin:*   I feel like if you have a school like this, then it's going to have an impact, you know, you say, "You know what? I'm choosing to do everything completely opposite from the public schools" and

say that "that's not right and I feel like this is the way it should be done." . . . I feel like the things that go on here have an effect because we're not sitting in this little bubble and especially in a school like this. . . . I think that a school like this, we're right in the heart of things and you get to be, you get to have a direct influence on many things. . . . One constant about this place is that no matter what, you know, we're going to be here and we're going to be doing our thing and we're not going to wait for someone to say, you know, "It's okay," we're not going wait for someone to say, "Oh, go do your own thing." No, I'm going to be out there, I feel like you can fight for something . . . it's like, you can choose to kind of fight it and fight it and fight or you can choose to say, "You know what? Fuck it, I'm just going to do what I want to do, and you know where to find me, you come find me and you come challenge me, you know, if you have a problem with the way the Free School works, come over here, see what it's like, and either, you know, if you want to challenge it, you can challenge it, you know" . . . and I also feel that it's not our responsibility to have to fight, fight, fight until you break something down, I feel like our responsibility is to live change, you know, I can't, I have no problem with living change and fighting for change as well, but doing them simultaneously. . . . By living change you're fighting for it, you know, by saying, "Look, you know what? I'm against public school and not only am I against them, I'm going to keep yelling at them and fighting, and whatever. I'm going to start a school that's completely different, that it is the way I want my kids to be."

In addition to offering an alternative vision of what education can look like, progressive educators involved in counterinstitutions are also creating spaces where children can learn a different conception of what it means to be a productive, good, healthy person and these children then become adults who engage in redefining (or dialoguing about) what a good society is.[6] I asked the Free School teachers whom I interviewed if they felt that their school had such an impact and they responded as follows.

Dave: I see people that leave here that are beautiful people that have good relationships, and, you know, when they become parents are great parents and they have healthy family lives. To me, that's the heart of social change, is people that do that. . . . They're getting something here that they're not going to get at very many other places.

Bhawin: I think, again, it goes back to teaching kids sort of like the true, the set values of democracy and the set values of being, uh, a responsible person, because we teach those things and then kids leave here and then they live that.

Chris: I think it is possible for schools, smaller schools, independent schools that, like ours, are willing to see the importance of setting up a different paradigm and then sticking to it. . . . These schools can influence children to, you know, develop in a way that, if there were enough of those kids, shoot, then the society would change, we would have a different society.

Missy: I believe in intention, and intention is a big one and I think that my small, positive thinking, for me in being here, I can't, I don't want to underestimate its power, you know? . . . I think it has an effect on anybody, everyone. If I lead a life that I honor and I can feel, like . . . for me and for others it can't not spread. It's contagious, it's a contagious thing, and I love the whole notion of it. It keeps me here.

Progressive educators in counterinstitutions like the Albany Free School are thus keeping dialogue open by presenting a side of an argument through their very existence and through the impact their existence has on their students. Whether public education chooses to engage in this dialogue is another story. Progressive educators involved in schools like these believe that it is not they who are absenting themselves from the public debate on education; rather, it is the traditional education system itself that is denying even the possibility of such a debate or dialogue taking place.

These educators believe that the hidden curriculum lessons of traditional public schooling prevent true dialogue from ever occurring. People who go through the traditional educational system tend not to know how to slow down and delve into critical depth on issues. As Ira Shor put it, "The mind is conditioned to operate at a perceptual speed which repels careful scrutiny."[7] The hidden curriculum lessons also "armor" people to fear any new or different philosophy, and consequently tend to stick with the known, flawed though it may be. Thus, the habits of mind necessary to engage in true dialogue are conditioned out of people by the hidden curriculum lessons of traditional schools. Progressive educators who start counterinstitutions, like the Free School, believe that these hidden curriculum lessons are quite intentional, for the lessons support the status quo political, economic, and social systems. Powerful interests benefit from the perpetuation of these systems and thus try to quell any real debate or dialogue on the purposes and structures of public education.[8] And in quelling this debate, the status quo powers silence minority interests. This, in and of itself, is incredibly anti-democratic. In an ideal democracy, it is true that minority interests do not "get their way," but they should "get their say" in a respectful environment.

The power of status quo political, economic, and social systems denies the minority its voice and in so doing prevents any true and meaningful discussions of different educational philosophies and approaches.

The silencing of the minority is evident in the fact that traditional public schools tend not to engage to any significant degree with the progressive counterinstitutions that exist in their midst. For example, while the Albany Free School teachers felt that individual traditional school teachers or principals looked at them and saw an example of a school that could be effective in certain circumstances (e.g., working with a troubled child, as described earlier), they also felt that these people in traditional schools still were not fundamentally questioning the purposes and approaches of education, and thus were not deeply engaging the Free School in dialogue. In my interview with Bhawin, he stated that the Free School tries to involve itself in the public schools (especially in light of the fact that nearly all the Free School students attend public schools in ninth grade), but that the public schools do not try too much to involve themselves in the Free School. Bhawin stated that the "Albany public school system has never invited us to do a presentation about what we do." And Chris noted that "the Free School has existed in Albany for thirty-four years and we haven't caused the public schools, the local public school system to change in any significant way that I'm aware of [laughing]. You know, they still do the same old crap."

I suggest, and of course this can't be proven, that the traditional school teachers and principals who did interact in small ways with the Free School simply saw the free school as a handy dumping ground for kids who refused to conform to traditional school structures. Such a view has nothing much to do with dialogue or debate, but more with convenience and disposing of problems. If the public schools were truly engaged with the Free School's ideas, and if they truly believed that the Free School philosophy was something to seriously consider for a certain population of children, then I believe that they would attempt to work a bit more closely with the Free School staff rather than just on the rare occasion when they called them up to discuss or send over a troubled child. The onus should be on both parties, the minority and majority, to engage in dialogue. And while the Albany Free School (the minority) has attempted to initiate such a conversation, the public school system (the majority) has only looked at the Free School as something to be used, but not seriously considered. The Albany example surely is not an anomaly, for one can look to many other parts of our society and see that minority voices are, at best, tolerated and, at worst, dismissed out of hand. So, to the critical pedagogues' argument that some progressive educators, by creating counterinstitutions, are absenting themselves from public dialogue, I believe that the latter are right in saying that it is not they who have abandoned the dialogue, but rather the traditional school systems, and the wider political, social, and economic systems that traditional schools support, who have expressed an unwillingness to interact in any meaningful way.

In addition to arguing that internal reform is better than external revolution because it keeps open a dialogue, the critical pedagogues also argue that reform, more than revolution, ensures that certain populations will not be left behind. Critical pedagogues believe that gradual reform is more likely to provide poor and minority students with better social and economic opportunities than revolutionary counterinstitutions. Progressive educators working in counterinstitutions believe that this reasoning is faulty, and that attempting to tweak (gradually reform) the traditional school systems (systems with built-in survival mechanisms that make it difficult for fundamental change to occur, as discussed earlier) in such a way as to encourage poor and minority students to work within the systems in the hopes of getting into a position of power sometime in the future, is, to some degree, morally bankrupt.[9] Progressive educators working in counterinstitutions believe that their schools, because they run counter to the status quo educational systems, cannot possibly do as much damage to poor and minority students as the traditional system already has. In fact, the social advantages children get from attending such schools as the Albany Free School (advantages that include being valued for who they are, learning to give voice to their needs and interests, caring for others, etc.) go much further in repairing the damage and violence done to them in the wider society than any gradual reforms ever could.

It seems as if these two groups of progressive educators are at an impasse over the issue of reform versus revolution, but it is not as cut-and-dried as that. Critical pedagogues, while generally arguing for the importance of the struggle and dialogue within status quo systems, recognize that the traditional schooling system, with its alienating and antidemocratic structures, is a difficult environment in which to bring about change or reform. Several critical pedagogues have cautioned that before true critical pedagogy can take place in schools teachers must be fully aware of these alienating and antidemocratic tendencies of school structures and approaches, and careful to not attempt to teach emancipatory content in a nonliberatory way.[10] Critical pedagogues thus understand that some things about traditional schools must be radically altered before the ends of progressive education can possibly be attained. So, while critical pedagogues seem to largely argue for reform within the public school system, they also concurrently argue for revolutionary reform—their difference from the progressive educators who have set up counterinstitutions is mainly that they seek these revolutionary changes from *within* the traditional education system rather than from without. But can these changes really happen within the system? Ira Shor, in his book, *When Students Have Power*, described his attempts to build a democratic public sphere in his traditional community college class, but also questioned if "such a sphere [was] democratic if it was required."[11] Paulo Freire wrote, in *The Pedagogy of the Oppressed*, about how educators, in order to truly take part in "problem posing" education, must get rid of teacher–student contradictions so that real dialogical relations can occur, and he further argued that the starting point for any curriculum is the present, concrete situation, which must reflect the aspirations of the people. Can teachers within the traditional school environment overcome these elements of compulsion, mandated curriculums, and teacher hierarchy over students—elements fundamental to what traditional public education is all about? If they cannot, then is reform truly possible *within* the traditional school system?

This is a question on which I constantly go back and forth. Some days I am more optimistic and believe that if people are aware that there is a range of choices in educational vision, then they will move gradually, but consistently, toward the more progressive options. Other days I am more pessimistic and worry that the traditional system will never even allow for the realization, let alone a discussion, of choices and thus traditional education should be abandoned as hopelessly nonprogressive and that those interested in progressive educational visions have no choice but to create counterinstitutions. Where I stand each day depends on how tired I am. On the days when my talk of progressive educational ideas is met with rejection or bastardization, I tend to believe more in abandoning traditional education. These days usually are in the majority, unfortunately. Does this mean that I have "jumped ship" from traditional education and am now working in a school that embodies a more progressive vision of education? Surprisingly, or perhaps not, no; I am, in fact, now part of a teacher education program at a state university in Virginia mainly teaching foundations of education courses. Part of the reason for this life choice is practical and the other ideological optimism.

On the practical side is the fact that most of the progressive educational counterinstitutions I have encountered in my research have been places in which existence for the teachers is often hand-to-mouth (unless one has an independent source of income). Teacher salaries are low and benefits are, at best, minimal. I have thought often about whether I could live with an income under the poverty line when I have other opportunities open to me and have found that I simply cannot. Part of this decision comes from family responsibilities, another part from growing up in a traditional family and having gone through a traditional education. Although I *did* unlearn much of my traditional education during my time at the Albany Free School, I have just not been able to find the courage needed to reject almost everything from my past and venture into such an unknown.

The ideological optimism part of my decision to remain in traditional education occurs on the few days when I recognize that my ideas and questions about traditional education are raising new ideas and questions in others. Such days sometime happen when I visit a group of people to talk about educational alternatives or when I raise tricky questions about traditional education in my college courses with my mostly traditionally educated students, questions that cause them to pause and wonder, "What if?" On these days I rejoice and believe that there is hope for change in traditional education. It is then that I believe critical pedagogues are right, that it is the joint struggle to overcome obstacles that will ultimately lead people to embrace and act on new paradigms. On these days I am filled with a fervor to stand by traditional education, not give it up for lost, and serve within it to advocate for progressive ideals and the means by which those ideals could be achieved.

I have begun to realize that there need not be an either–or question of reform or revolution for progressive educators. Both can exist to transform our educational system; change can be fought for on all levels and to many different degrees. One can work for change, one can live change *and* work for change at the same time, one can work within the system, one can work outside the system, one can work for one main goal, or one can work for multiple end goals at the same time—all are valid and useful approaches in the quest for a better world and a better educational system. These efforts can lead us down the path to building a society that, in the words of David Purpel, is committed in word and deed to "the development of a life of justice, freedom, and equality which can be built and sustained through love and compassion, utilizing human potential unlocked by the free and rigorous pursuit of truth."[12]

NOTES

CHAPTER TWO

1. Henry Giroux, "Developing Educational Programs and Overcoming the Hidden Curriculum," *Clearing House* 52, no. 4 (1978): 148.

2. Elizabeth Vallance, "Hiding the Hidden Curriculum," in *The Institution of Education*, 4th ed., ed. H. Svi Shapiro, Susan Harden, and Anna Pennell (Boston: Pearson Custom Publishing, 2003), 85.

3. Philip Jackson, "The Daily Grind," in *The Institution of Education*, 4th ed., ed. H. Svi Shapiro, Susan Harden, and Anna Pennell (Boston: Pearson Custom Publishing, 2003), 14.

4. Ivan Illich, *Deschooling Society* (New York: Harper and Row, 1971).

5. John Taylor Gatto, *Dumbing Us Down: The Hidden Curriculum of Compulsory Schooling* (Gabriola Island, BC: New Society Publishers, 1992).

6. Sarah J. McCarthy, "Why Johnny Can't Disobey," in *The Institution of Education*, 4th ed., ed. H. Svi Shapiro, Susan Harden, and Anna Pennell (Boston: Pearson Custom Publishing, 2003).

7. Jean Anyon, "Social Class and the Hidden Curriculum of Work," in *The Institution of Education*, 4th ed., ed. H. Svi Shapiro, Susan Harden, and Anna Pennell (Boston: Pearson Custom Publishing, 2003).

8. Gatto, *Dumbing Us Down: The Hidden Curriculum of Compulsory Schooling*, 6.

9. JoMills Braddock, Willis Hawley, Tari Hunt, Jeannie Oakes, Robert Slavin, and Anne Wheelock, "Ollie Taylor's Story," in *The Institution of Education*, 4th ed., ed. H. Svi Shapiro, Susan Harden, and Anna Pennell (Boston: Pearson Custom Publishing, 2003).

10. Jackson, "The Daily Grind."

11. Gatto, *Dumbing Us Down: The Hidden Curriculum of Compulsory Schooling*, 8.

12. Elizabeth Dodson Gray, "The Culture of Separated Desks," in *The Institution of Education*, 4th ed., ed. H. Svi Shapiro, Susan Harden, and Anna Pennell (Boston: Pearson Custom Publishing, 2003).

13. Anyon, "Social Class and the Hidden Curriculum of Work."

14. Ruby Payne, "Presentation, Staff Development Workshop" (Montgomey County Schools, NC, 2001).

15. David Purpel, *The Moral and Spiritual Crisis in Education* (New York: Bergin and Garvey, 1989), 71.

16. Ibid.

17. Ibid., 71–72.

18. Nel Noddings, *The Challenge to Care in Schools: An Alternative Approach to Education* (New York: Teachers College Press, 1992), 10.

172   NOTES TO CHAPTER THREE

CHAPTER THREE

1. Zvi Lamm, "The Status of Knowledge in the Radical Concept of Education," in *Curriculum and the Cultural Revolution*, ed. David Purpel and Maurice Belanger (Berkeley: McCutchan, 1972), 154.
2. Ibid.
3. Ibid.
4. Ibid.
5. Ibid.
6. Noel Gough, "From Epistemology to Ecopolitics: Renewing a Paradigm for Curriculum," *Journal of Curriculum Studies* 21, no. 3 (1989).
7. Sylvia Ashton-Warner, *Teacher* (New York: Simon and Schuster, 1963), George Dennison, *The Lives of Children: The Story of the First Street School* (New York: Random House, 1969), John Dewey, *Democracy and Education: An Introduction to the Philosophy of Education* (New York: Macmillan, 1916), Aaron Falbel, "Learning? Yes, of Course. Education? No Thanks," in *Deschooling Our Lives*, ed. Matt Hern (Gabriola Island, BC: New Society Publishers, 1996), Henry Giroux, *Teachers as Intellectuals: Toward a Critical Pedagogy of Learning* (Westport, CT: Bergin and Garvey, 1988), Paul Goodman, *The Community of Scholars* (New York: Vintage Books, 1962), Paul Goodman, *Compulsory Miseducation* (New York: Vintage Books, 1964), Maxine Greene, *The Dialectic of Freedom*. (New York: Teachers College Press, 1988), bell hooks, *Teaching to Transgress* (New York: Routledge, 1994), Illich, *Deschooling Society*, David Andrew Jacobsen, *Philosophy in Classroom Teaching* (Columbus: Merrill Publishers, 1999), George Leonard, *Education and Ecstasy* (New York: Delacorte Press, 1968), Chris Mercogliano, *Making It Up as We Go Along: The Story of the Albany Free School* (Portsmouth, NH: Heinemann, 1998), Ron Miller, *Free Schools, Free People: Education and Democracy after the 1960s* (Albany: SUNY Press, 2002), A. S. and Albert Lamb Neill, *Summerhill School: A New View of Childhood* (New York: St. Martin's Press, 1992), Carl Rogers, *Freedom to Learn* (Columbus: Charles E. Merrill, 1969), Ira Shor, *Critical Teaching and Everyday Life* (Boston: South End Press, 1980), Ira Shor, *Freire for the Classroom: A Sourcebook for Liberatory Teaching* (Portsmouth, NH: Boynton/Cook Publishers, 1987), Ira Shor, *When Students Have Power: Negotiating Authority in a Critical Pedagogy* (Chicago: University of Chicago Press, 1996), Valerie Polakow Suransky, *The Erosion of Childhood* (Chicago: University of Chicago Press, 1982).
8. Gough, "From Epistemology to Ecopolitics: Renewing a Paradigm for Curriculum."
9. Dennison, *The Lives of Children: The Story of the First Street School*, Dewey, *Democracy and Education: An Introduction to the Philosophy of Education*, Falbel, "Learning? Yes, of Course. Education? No Thanks," Paulo Freire, *The Pedagogy of the Oppressed* (New York: Herder and Herder, 1970), Goodman, *The Community of Scholars*, Goodman, *Compulsory Miseducation*, Illich, *Deschooling Society*, Jacobsen, *Philosophy in Classroom Teaching*, Mercogliano, *Making It Up as We Go Along: The Story of the Albany Free School*, Rogers, *Freedom to Learn*, Shor, *Freire for the Classroom: A Sourcebook for Liberatory Teaching*, Shor, *When Students Have Power: Negotiating Authority in a Critical Pedagogy*.
10. Ashton-Warner, *Teacher*, Dennison, *The Lives of Children: The Story of the First Street School*, Dewey, *Democracy and Education: An Introduction to the Philosophy of Education*, Falbel, "Learning? Yes, of Course. Education? No Thanks," Giroux,

Teachers as Intellectuals: Toward a Critical Pedagogy of Learning, Goodman, *The Community of Scholars*, Goodman, *Compulsory Miseducation*, Greene, *The Dialectic of Freedom*, hooks, *Teaching to Transgress*, Illich, *Deschooling Society*, Jacobsen, *Philosophy in Classroom Teaching*, Leonard, *Education and Ecstasy*, Mercogliano, *Making It Up as We Go Along: The Story of the Albany Free School*, Miller, *Free Schools, Free People: Education and Democracy after the 1960s*, Neill, *Summerhill School: A New View of Childhood*, Rogers, *Freedom to Learn*, Shor, *Critical Teaching and Everyday Life*, Shor, *Freire for the Classroom: A Sourcebook for Liberatory Teaching*, Shor, *When Students Have Power: Negotiating Authority in a Critical Pedagogy*, Suransky, *The Erosion of Childhood*.

11. Dennison, *The Lives of Children: The Story of the First Street School*, Dewey, *Democracy and Education: An Introduction to the Philosophy of Education*, Freire, *The Pedagogy of the Oppressed*, Erich Fromm, in *Summerhill: For and Against*, ed. Harold Hart (New York: Hart Publishing Co., 1970), Giroux, *Teachers as Intellectuals: Toward a Critical Pedagogy of Learning*, Goodman, *Compulsory Miseducation*, Greene, *The Dialectic of Freedom*, Ray Hemmings, *Fifty Years of Freedom: A Study of the Development of the Ideas of A. S. Neill* (London: George Allen and Unwin, 1972), John Holt, *Freedom and Beyond* (New York: E.P. Dutton, 1972), John Holt, *Learning All the Time* (New York: Addison Wesley, 1989), hooks, *Teaching to Transgress*, Illich, *Deschooling Society*, Leonard, *Education and Ecstasy*, Mercogliano, *Making It Up as We Go Along: The Story of the Albany Free School*, Miller, *Free Schools, Free People: Education and Democracy after the 1960s*, A. S Neill, *Freedom, Not License!* (New York: Hart Publishing Co., 1966), Neill, *Summerhill School: A New View of Childhood*, Rogers, *Freedom to Learn*, Shor, *Critical Teaching and Everyday Life*, Shor, *Freire for the Classroom: A Sourcebook for Liberatory Teaching*, Shor, *When Students Have Power: Negotiating Authority in a Critical Pedagogy*.

12. C. A Bowers, *Elements of a Post Liberal Theory of Education* (New York: Teachers College Press, 1987), Ruth S Charney, *Teaching Children to Care* (Greenfield, MA: Northeast Foundation for Children, 2002), Dennison, *The Lives of Children: The Story of the First Street School*, Dewey, *Democracy and Education: An Introduction to the Philosophy of Education*, Freire, *The Pedagogy of the Oppressed*, Giroux, *Teachers as Intellectuals: Toward a Critical Pedagogy of Learning*, Goodman, *The Community of Scholars*, Goodman, *Compulsory Miseducation*, Hemmings, *Fifty Years of Freedom: A Study of the Development of the Ideas of A. S. Neill*, Holt, *Freedom and Beyond*, Holt, *Learning All the Time*, hooks, *Teaching to Transgress*, Illich, *Deschooling Society*, Lamm, "The Status of Knowledge in the Radical Concept of Education," Leonard, *Education and Ecstasy*, Mercogliano, *Making It Up as We Go Along: The Story of the Albany Free School*, Miller, *Free Schools, Free People: Education and Democracy after the 1960s*, Neill, *Freedom, Not License!* Neill, *Summerhill School: A New View of Childhood*, Rogers, *Freedom to Learn*, Shor, *Critical Teaching and Everyday Life*, Shor, *Freire for the Classroom: A Sourcebook for Liberatory Teaching*, Shor, *When Students Have Power: Negotiating Authority in a Critical Pedagogy*, Nina Wallerstein, "Problem-Posing Education: Freire's Method for Transformation," in *Freire for the Classroom: A Sourcebook for Liberatory Teaching*, ed. Ira Shor (Portsmouth, NH: Boynton/Cook Publishers, 1987).

13. Ashton-Warner, *Teacher*, Bruno Bettelheim, in *Summerhill: For and Against*, ed. Harold Hart (New York: Hart Publishing Co., 1970), Dennison, *The Lives of Children: The Story of the First Street School*, Dewey, *Democracy and Education: An Introduction to the Philosophy of Education*, Freire, *The Pedagogy of the Oppressed*, Fromm, Gatto, *Dumbing Us Down: The Hidden Curriculum of Compulsory Schooling*, Goodman,

Compulsory Miseducation, Greene, *The Dialectic of Freedom*, Hemmings, *Fifty Years of Freedom: A Study of the Development of the Ideas of A. S. Neill*, Holt, *Freedom and Beyond*, Holt, *Learning All the Time*, Lois Holzman, *Schools for Growth* (Mahwah, NJ: Lawrence Erlbaum, 1997), Meghan Hughes, and Jim Carrico, "Windsor House," in *Deschooling Our Lives*, ed. Matt Hern (Gabriola Island, BC: New Society Publishers, 1996), Illich, *Deschooling Society*, Lamm, "The Status of Knowledge in the Radical Concept of Education," Leonard, *Education and Ecstasy*, Mercogliano, *Making It Up as We Go Along: The Story of the Albany Free School*, Miller, *Free Schools, Free People: Education and Democracy after the 1960s*, Neill, *Freedom, Not License!* Neill, *Summerhill School: A New View of Childhood*, Rogers, *Freedom to Learn*, Mimsy Sadofsky, "A School for Today," in *Deschooling Our Lives*, ed. Matt Hern (Gabriola Island, BC: New Society Publishers, 1996), Shor, *Critical Teaching and Everyday Life*, Shor, *Freire for the Classroom: A Sourcebook for Liberatory Teaching*.

14. Dewey, *Democracy and Education: An Introduction to the Philosophy of Education*, Freire, *The Pedagogy of the Oppressed*, Giroux, *Teachers as Intellectuals: Toward a Critical Pedagogy of Learning*, Goodman, *The Community of Scholars*, Goodman, *Compulsory Miseducation*, Holt, *Freedom and Beyond*, Illich, *Deschooling Society*, Leonard, *Education and Ecstasy*, Mercogliano, *Making It Up as We Go Along: The Story of the Albany Free School*, Miller, *Free Schools, Free People: Education and Democracy after the 1960s*, Rogers, *Freedom to Learn*, Shor, *Critical Teaching and Everyday Life*.

15. Freire, *The Pedagogy of the Oppressed*, 80.

16. Gough, "From Epistemology to Ecopolitics: Renewing a Paradigm for Curriculum."

17. Charney, *Teaching Children to Care*, John Taylor Gatto, *A Different Kind of Teacher* (Berkeley: Berkeley Hills Books, 2001), Goodman, *Compulsory Miseducation*, Greene, *The Dialectic of Freedom*, 120, Holt, *Freedom and Beyond*, Noddings, *The Challenge to Care in Schools: An Alternative Approach to Education*, Rogers, *Freedom to Learn*, Shor, *When Students Have Power: Negotiating Authority in a Critical Pedagogy*.

18. Ashton-Warner, *Teacher*, 12.

19. Ibid., 30.

20. Mercogliano, *Making It Up as We Go Along: The Story of the Albany Free School*.

21. Freire, *The Pedagogy of the Oppressed*, 72.

22. Ashton-Warner, *Teacher*, Dennison, *The Lives of Children: The Story of the First Street School*, Dewey, *Democracy and Education: An Introduction to the Philosophy of Education*, Freire, *The Pedagogy of the Oppressed*, Goodman, *The Community of Scholars*, Goodman, *Compulsory Miseducation*, Hemmings, *Fifty Years of Freedom: A Study of the Development of the Ideas of A. S. Neill*, Holt, *Learning All the Time*, Illich, *Deschooling Society*, Leonard, *Education and Ecstasy*, Mercogliano, *Making It Up as We Go Along: The Story of the Albany Free School*, Miller, *Free Schools, Free People: Education and Democracy after the 1960s*, Rogers, *Freedom to Learn*, Shor, *Critical Teaching and Everyday Life*, Shor, *Freire for the Classroom: A Sourcebook for Liberatory Teaching*, Shor, *When Students Have Power: Negotiating Authority in a Critical Pedagogy*, Suransky, *The Erosion of Childhood*.

23. Gough, "From Epistemology to Ecopolitics: Renewing a Paradigm for Curriculum."

24. Goodman, *Compulsory Miseducation*, Holzman, *Schools for Growth*, hooks, *Teaching to Transgress*, Jonathan Kozol, *Free Schools* (Boston: Houghton Mifflin, 1972), Miller, *Free Schools, Free People: Education and Democracy after the 1960s*.

25. Dennison, *The Lives of Children: The Story of the First Street School*, Dewey, *Democracy and Education: An Introduction to the Philosophy of Education*, Falbel, "Learning? Yes, of Course. Education? No Thanks," Freire, *The Pedagogy of the Oppressed*, Goodman, *The Community of Scholars*, Goodman, *Compulsory Miseducation*, Illich, *Deschooling Society*, Jacobsen, *Philosophy in Classroom Teaching*, Mercogliano, *Making It Up as We Go Along: The Story of the Albany Free School*, Rogers, *Freedom to Learn*, Shor, *When Students Have Power: Negotiating Authority in a Critical Pedagogy*.

26. Bowers, *Elements of a Post Liberal Theory of Education*, Dennison, *The Lives of Children: The Story of the First Street School*, Dewey, *Democracy and Education: An Introduction to the Philosophy of Education*, Freire, *The Pedagogy of the Oppressed*, Fromm, Henry Giroux, *Stealing Innocence* (New York: St. Martin's Press, 2000), Giroux, *Teachers as Intellectuals: Toward a Critical Pedagogy of Learning*, Goodman, *The Community of Scholars*, Goodman, *Compulsory Miseducation*, Greene, *The Dialectic of Freedom*, Hemmings, *Fifty Years of Freedom: A Study of the Development of the Ideas of A. S. Neill*, Holt, *Freedom and Beyond*, Holzman, *Schools for Growth*, hooks, *Teaching to Transgress*, Kozol, *Free Schools*, Leonard, *Education and Ecstasy*, Mercogliano, *Making It Up as We Go Along: The Story of the Albany Free School*, Miller, *Free Schools, Free People: Education and Democracy after the 1960s*, Ashley Montagu, in *Summerhill: For and Against*, ed. Harold Hart (New York: Hart Publishing Co., 1970), Neill, *Freedom, Not License!* A.S Neill, *"Neill! Neill! Orange Peel!"* (New York: Hart Publishing Co., 1972), Neill, *Summerhill School: A New View of Childhood*, Rogers, *Freedom to Learn*, Shor, *Critical Teaching and Everyday Life*, Shor, *Freire for the Classroom: A Sourcebook for Liberatory Teaching*, Shor, *When Students Have Power: Negotiating Authority in a Critical Pedagogy*.

CHAPTER FOUR

1. Mercogliano, *Making It Up as We Go Along: The Story of the Albany Free School*, 5.

2. Ibid., 7.

3. Ibid., 9.

4. Giroux, *Teachers as Intellectuals: Toward a Critical Pedagogy of Learning*.

5. Mercogliano, *Making It Up as We Go Along: The Story of the Albany Free School*.

6. Ibid., 6.

7. Ibid., 19.

8. Kristan Morrison, "What Else Besides Grading? Looking for Alternatives in All the Right Places," *Paths of Learning* Spring, no. 16 (2003): 32.

9. Ibid.

10. Corrine Glesne, *Becoming Qualitative Researchers* (New York: Longman, 1999).

CHAPTER FIVE

1. Chris Mercogliano, e-mail to author, February 6, 2004.

2. Chris Mercogliano, *Teaching the Restless: One School's Remarkable No-Ritalin Approach to Helping Children Learn and Succeed* (Boston: Beacon Press, 2003), 11.

CHAPTER SIX

1. Neill, *Freedom, Not License!*
2. In the fall of 2006, the school opened up a high school program, the Harriet Tubman Free School.
3. Sherry Shapiro, "Re-Membering the Body in Critical Pedagogy," in *The Institution of Education*, 4th ed., ed. H. Svi Shapiro, Susan Harden, and Anna Pennell (Boston: Pearson Custom Publishing, 2003).
4. Ibid.
5. Freire, *The Pedagogy of the Oppressed*, 74.
6. Michael Apple and James Beane, *Democratic Schools* (Alexandria, VA: Association for Supervision and Curriculum Development, 1995), Giroux, *Teachers as Intellectuals: Toward a Critical Pedagogy of Learning*, Maxine Greene, "And It Still Is News," in *After Deschooling, What?*, ed. Ivan Illich (New York: Harper and Row, 1973), Greene, *The Dialectic of Freedom*, Jane Roland Martin, *The Schoolhome: Rethinking Schools for Changing Families* (Cambridge: Harvard University Press, 1992), Miller, *Free Schools, Free People: Education and Democracy after the 1960s*, Noddings, *The Challenge to Care in Schools: An Alternative Approach to Education*, David Orr, *Ecological Literacy: Education and the Transition to a Postmodern World* (Albany: SUNY Press, 1992), Shor, *Critical Teaching and Everyday Life*, Shor, *Freire for the Classroom: A Sourcebook for Liberatory Teaching*, Shor, *When Students Have Power: Negotiating Authority in a Critical Pedagogy*.
7. Giroux, *Teachers as Intellectuals: Toward a Critical Pedagogy of Learning*, Greene, *The Dialectic of Freedom*, Martin, *The Schoolhome: Rethinking Schools for Changing Families*, Orr, *Ecological Literacy: Education and the Transition to a Postmodern World*.
8. Jill Freidberg, "International News and Communication—Mexico," *Education Revolution*, no. 37 (2003): 25.

CHAPTER EIGHT

1. Holt, *Freedom and Beyond*, 59.
2. Gray, "The Culture of Separated Desks."
3. Ibid.

CHAPTER NINE

1. Miller, *Free Schools, Free People: Education and Democracy after the 1960s*.
2. Kozol, *Free Schools*, 38.
3. Ibid., 40.
4. Apple, *Democratic Schools*, 17.
5. Hemmings, *Fifty Years of Freedom: A Study of the Development of the Ideas of A. S. Neill*, Leonard, *Education and Ecstasy*, Miller, *Free Schools, Free People: Education and Democracy after the 1960s*.
6. Hemmings, *Fifty Years of Freedom: A Study of the Development of the Ideas of A. S. Neill*, Miller, *Free Schools, Free People: Education and Democracy after the 1960s*.
7. Shor, *Critical Teaching and Everyday Life*, 63.

8. Gatto, *Dumbing Us Down: The Hidden Curriculum of Compulsory Schooling,* Ronald Gross, "After Deschooling, Free Learning," in *After Deschooling, What?,* ed. Ivan Illich (New York: Harper and Row, 1973), Miller, *Free Schools, Free People: Education and Democracy after the 1960s.*

9. Holt, *Learning All the Time,* Illich, *Deschooling Society,* Shor, *Freire for the Classroom: A Sourcebook for Liberatory Teaching.*

10. Freire, *The Pedagogy of the Oppressed,* Shor, *Freire for the Classroom: A Sourcebook for Liberatory Teaching.*

11. Shor, *When Students Have Power: Negotiating Authority in a Critical Pedagogy,* 111.

12. Purpel, *The Moral and Spiritual Crisis in Education,* 72.

BIBLIOGRAPHY

Anyon, Jean. "Social Class and the Hidden Curriculum of Work." In *The Institution of Education*, 4th ed., edited by H. Svi Shapiro, Susan Harden, and Anna Pennell, 127–139. Boston: Pearson Custom Publishing, 2003. Originally published in *Journal of Education* 162, no. 1 (1980): 67–92.

Apple, Michael, and James Beane. *Democratic Schools*. Alexandria, VA: Association for Supervision and Curriculum Development, 1995.

Ashton-Warner, Sylvia. *Teacher*. New York: Simon and Schuster, 1963.

Bettelheim, Bruno. In *Summerhill: For and Against*, edited by Harold Hart, 98–118. New York: Hart Publishing Co., 1970.

Bowers, C. A. *Elements of a Post Liberal Theory of Education*. New York: Teachers College Press, 1987.

Braddock, JoMills II, Willis Hawley, Tari Hunt, Jeannie Oakes, Robert Slavin, and Anne Wheelock. "Ollie Taylor's Story." In *The Institution of Education*, edited by H. Svi Shapiro, Susan Harden, and Anna Pennell, 121–126. Boston: Pearson Custom Publishing, 2003. Originally published in *Realizing Our Nation's Diversity as an Opportunity: Alternatives to Sorting America's Children*, edited by Alma Clayton-Pederson and Robert Saffold, Jr., 9–12, 1993, ERIC, ED 369845.

Charney, Ruth S. *Teaching Children to Care*. Greenfield, MA: Northeast Foundation for Children, 2002.

Dennison, George. *The Lives of Children: The Story of the First Street School*. New York: Random House, 1969.

Dewey, John. *Democracy and Education: An Introduction to the Philosophy of Education*. New York: Macmillan, 1916.

Falbel, Aaron. "Learning? Yes, of Course. Education? No Thanks." In *Deschooling Our Lives*, edited by Matt Hern, 64–68. Gabriola Island, BC: New Society Publishers, 1996.

Freidberg, Jill. "International News and Communication—Mexico." *Education Revolution*, no. 37 (2003): 25.

Freire, Paulo. *The Pedagogy of the Oppressed*. New York: Herder and Herder, 1970.

Fromm, Erich. In *Summerhill: For and Against*, edited by Harold Hart, 250–263. New York: Hart Publishing Co. 1970.

Gatto, John Taylor. *A Different Kind of Teacher*. Berkeley: Berkeley Hills Books, 2001.

———. *Dumbing Us Down: The Hidden Curriculum of Compulsory Schooling*. Gabriola Island, BC: New Society Publishers, 1992.

Giroux, Henry. "Developing Educational Programs and Overcoming the Hidden Curriculum." *Clearing House* 52, no. 4 (1978): 148–151.

———. *Stealing Innocence*. New York: St. Martin's Press, 2000.

————. *Teachers as Intellectuals: Toward a Critical Pedagogy of Learning.* Westport, CT: Bergin and Garvey, 1988.

Glesne, Corrine. *Becoming Qualitative Researchers.* New York: Longman, 1999.

Goodman, Paul. *The Community of Scholars.* New York: Vintage Books, 1962.

————. *Compulsory Miseducation.* New York: Vintage Books, 1964.

Gough, Noel. "From Epistemology to Ecopolitics: Renewing a Paradigm for Curriculum." *Journal of Curriculum Studies* 21, no. 3 (1989): 225–241.

Gray, Elizabeth Dodson. "The Culture of Separated Desks." In *The Institution of Education*, 4th ed., edited by H. Svi Shapiro, Susan Harden, and Anna Pennell, 233–240. Boston: Pearson Custom Publishing, 2003. Originally published in *Educating the Majority: Women Challenge Tradition in Higher Education*, edited by Carol Pearson, Donna L. Shavlik, and Judith G. Touchton. New York: MacMillan, 1989.

Greene, Maxine. "And It Still Is News." In *After Deschooling, What?*, edited by Ivan Illich, 129–136. New York: Harper and Row, 1973.

————. *The Dialectic of Freedom.* New York: Teachers College Press, 1988.

Gross, Ronald. "After Deschooling, Free Learning." In *After Deschooling, What?*, edited by Ivan Illich, 148–160. New York: Harper and Row, 1973.

Hemmings, Ray. *Fifty Years of Freedom: A Study of the Development of the Ideas of A. S. Neill.* London: George Allen and Unwin, 1972.

Holt, John. *Freedom and Beyond.* New York: E. P. Dutton, 1972.

————. *Learning All the Time.* New York: Addison Wesley, 1989.

Holzman, Lois. *Schools for Growth.* Mahwah, NJ: Lawrence Erlbaum, 1997.

hooks, bell. *Teaching to Transgress.* New York: Routledge, 1994.

Hughes, Meghan, and Jim Carrico. "Windsor House." In *Deschooling Our Lives*, edited by Matt Hern, 134–139. Gabriola Island, BC: New Society Publishers, 1996.

Illich, Ivan. *Deschooling Society.* New York: Harper and Row, 1971.

Jackson, Philip "The Daily Grind." In *The Institution of Education*, 4th ed., edited by H. Svi Shapiro, Susan Harden, and Anna Pennell, 9–26. Boston: Pearson Custom Publishing, 2003. Originally published in *Life in Classrooms*. New York: Teachers College Press, 1968.

Jacobsen, David Andrew. *Philosophy in Classroom Teaching.* Columbus: Merrill Publishers, 1999.

Kozol, Jonathan. *Free Schools.* Boston: Houghton Mifflin, 1972.

Lamm, Zvi. "The Status of Knowledge in the Radical Concept of Education." In *Curriculum and the Cultural Revolution*, edited by David Purpel and Maurice Belanger, 149–168. Berkeley: McCutchan, 1972.

Leonard, George. *Education and Ecstasy.* New York: Delacorte, 1968.

Martin, Jane Roland. *The Schoolhome: Rethinking Schools for Changing Families.* Cambridge: Harvard University Press, 1992.

McCarthy, Sarah J. "Why Johnny Can't Disobey." In *The Institution of Education*, 4th ed., edited by H. Svi Shapiro, Susan Harden, and Anna Pennell, 35–41. Boston: Pearson Custom Publishing, 2003. Originally published in *The Humanist* 39 (1979): 30–34.

Mercogliano, Chris. *Making It Up as We Go Along: The Story of the Albany Free School.* Portsmouth, NH: Heinemann, 1998.

————. *Teaching the Restless: One School's Remarkable No-Ritalin Approach to Helping Children Learn and Succeed.* Boston: Beacon Press, 2003.

Miller, Ron. *Free Schools, Free People: Education and Democracy after the 1960s*. Albany: SUNY Press, 2002.

Montagu, Ashley. In *Summerhill: For and Against*, edited by Harold Hart, 48–63. New York: Hart Publishing Co., 1970.

Morrison, Kristan. "What Else Besides Grading? Looking for Alternatives in All the Right Places." *Paths of Learning* Spring, no. 16 (2003): 22–28.

Neill, A. S. *Freedom, Not License!* New York: Hart Publishing Co., 1966.

———. *"Neill! Neill! Orange Peel!"* New York: Hart Publishing Co., 1972.

Neill, A. S., and Albert Lamb, ed. *Summerhill School: A New View of Childhood*. New York: St. Martin's Press, 1992.

Noddings, Nel. *The Challenge to Care in Schools: An Alternative Approach to Education*. New York: Teachers College Press, 1992.

Orr, David. *Ecological Literacy: Education and the Transition to a Postmodern World*. Albany: SUNY Press, 1992.

Payne, Ruby. "Presentation, Staff Development Workshop." Montgomey County Schools, NC, 2001.

Purpel, David. *The Moral and Spiritual Crisis in Education*. New York: Bergin and Garvey, 1989.

Rogers, Carl. *Freedom to Learn*. Columbus: Charles E. Merrill, 1969.

Sadofsky, Mimsy. "A School for Today." In *Deschooling Our Lives*, edited by Matt Hern, 120–125. Gabriola Island, BC: New Society Publishers, 1996.

Shapiro, Sherry. "Re-Membering the Body in Critical Pedagogy." In *The Institution of Education*, 4th ed., edited by H. Svi Shapiro, Susan Harden, and Anna Pennell, 333–351. Boston: Pearson Custom Publishing, 2003. Originally published in *Education and Society* 12, no. 1 (1994): 61–79.

Shor, Ira. *Critical Teaching and Everyday Life*. Boston: South End Press, 1980.

———. *Freire for the Classroom: A Sourcebook for Liberatory Teaching*. Portsmouth, NH: Boynton/Cook Publishers, 1987.

———. *When Students Have Power: Negotiating Authority in a Critical Pedagogy*. Chicago: University of Chicago Press, 1996.

Suransky, Valerie Polakow. *The Erosion of Childhood*. Chicago: University of Chicago Press, 1982.

Vallance, Elizabeth. "Hiding the Hidden Curriculum." In *The Institution of Education*, 4th ed., edited by H. Svi Shapiro, Susan Harden, and Anna Pennell, 85–98. Boston: Pearson Custom Publishing, 2003. Originally published in *Curriculum Theory Network* 4, no. 1 (1974): 5–21.

Wallerstein, Nina. "Problem-Posing Education: Freire's Method for Transformation." In *Freire for the Classroom: A Sourcebook for Liberatory Teaching*, edited by Ira Shor, 34–46. Portsmouth, NH: Boynton/Cook Publishers, 1987.

INDEX